UNVEILINGGLORY

IN ALL AREAS OF LIFE
TO ALL PEOPLES OF THE WORLD

I Heard Good News Today 2:
BIGLIFE

By: Charissa Roberson

Published by Mission Minded Publishers in the United States for UnveilinGLORY and Big Life Ministries. Copyright © 2015. The illustrations inside were designed by Bob Sjogren and created by Markus Benyamin Diredja.

Special thanks goes out to the following for all of their hard work in making this book become a reality:

John Heerema and the Big Life Ministry Team
Jason Gerlach (Who overviewed the project for Big Life)
Susie O'Berski (Who gathered the best stories for Jason)
Mary Ellen Roberson (Charissa's mom for editing, guidance and encouragement)
Debby Sjogren (Editing)
Wendy Hale (Editing)
Martha Hollowel (Editing)
Victoria Bard (Detail Czar!)
Stacie Bard (Content Advisor)
Stephani Jenkins (Content Advisor)
Karen Warchuist (Content Advisor)
Markus Benyamin Diredja (Artwork)
Carolyn Lantz (Proofing)

Bob and Debby after talking with Charissa about the book at her home.

And a tremendous thanks goes out to all of our supporters who keep Debby and myself in full-time Christian work so we can produce life-changing materials like these. Thanks for faithfully giving year after year! We wouldn't be here without you. (You are going to meet the men and women found in these pages and they are going to thank you for your faithfulness. Won't that be a glorious day!)

Bob Sjogren

All of the stories on the following pages
are true stories
and the majority have happened since the year 2004.

It all began with
one man reading one book.

As of the writing of this book (December of 2014),
Big Life Ministries has seen over
180,000 former Muslims, Buddhists and Hindus
come into a relationship with Jesus Christ
and have planted over 1,400 house churches.

We pray that this will give you a great vision
for what God can do through you
in a 10 year period!

FOREWORD

UNVE
AT L

*Discover
God's Hidden
Message from
Genesis to
Revelation*

God's
Bottom
Line

Discover Your Global Role
In His Global Plan

Bob Sjogren

BOB SJOGREN

How This Book Got Started!

In 2012, I got an e-mail from a man I had never met before. These were the words I read:

In 1999, my wife Kathy and I were excited about life. We had a 2 year old daughter and a son on the way. Business was great, we were involved in a fantastic church, and our life in Naples Fl. seemed—perfect. Then one day a woman at our church asked me if Kathy and I would be on the Missions Committee. I told her she had the wrong people and Kathy and I shared a laugh about the thought.

However, she kindly asked us to pray about it and asked us to read your book, <u>Unveiled At Last</u> (now retitled, <u>God's Bottom Line</u>). A few weeks went by, then one Friday night about 11:00 I remembered the book. I told Kathy as we were getting ready for bed that I was going to stay up for a few minutes to start reading the book, just in case I ran into this woman at church. I wanted to be able to tell her truthfully that I had begun reading it so she wouldn't bother me again.

That night the Lord used your book to radically change my life. The facts about the 10/40 Window broke my heart for the first time. I imagined how it must break God's heart that so many people were dying without knowing HIM and none of us really cared. The thought of someone in that area dying every second without ever hearing HIS name overwhelmed me.

At one point in the book, you asked a very simple question that tore me up. You asked: Are you living a little life in your own little world, or are you willing to lead a big life, a life with a big kingdom impact? I suddenly remembered Kathy and I playing with our daughter two weeks earlier talking about our "perfect life."

I realized that our life was really—perfectly shallow. It was all about us. Even though we were serving in our local church we had become very comfortable having very little kingdom impact. I woke Kathy up at 3:00 AM and told her she needed to read the book, NOW!

The Lord used your book to impact her life as well. The next morning we were lying on our living room floor crying out to the Lord to forgive us for our shallow life. This was the same place we had thought we were enjoying the "perfect life" two weeks earlier. The Lord convicted us to sell our business and begin a church-planting ministry in the Middle East and South Asia.

Big Life has seen God start nearly 6,000 churches through our indigenous church-planters and nearly 90,000 former Muslims, Hindus, and Buddhists have come running to a new life in Jesus.... We now work in India, Nepal, Bangladesh, Cambodia, Bhutan, Pakistan, as well as several new limited, or no access areas. We serve an awesome God!

John Heerema

When I read this I was stunned. After a private time of worshiping and thanking the Lord, I called John and set up a time to go down and meet with him and his team in Florida. (I was soon to be there speaking at a Perspective's class.) While there, I heard story after story of what God was doing in these countries. I told John, "We need to put these in writing." He agreed.

During that same time, one of my personal supporters was telling me about how her home-schooled daughter was writing for a local newspaper—at the age of 13! Knowing she was a gifted writer, I asked her (and her mother) if she would be interested in taking prayer letters from Big Life missionaries and putting them into story form. Both eagerly agreed.

As a result, Charissa Roberson—at the ripe old age of 14—has written the stories you are about to read. They were written specifically for this book!

On the next two pages I've also included a "Flow Chart" of how John's ministry spread. He has primarily only led a few people to the Lord, but he has empowered them to go out and reach others. Page VII starts with John's ministry in India. Page VIII starts with John's ministry touching Afghanistan and Pakistan. This graphically shows how one life can touch so many other lives. (And note, John's initial e-mail to me was in 2012. Now, three years later, look at how many more people they've brought into the kingdom. Their ministry is exploding!)

In 2 Timothy 2:2 we are told:

> And the things you have heard me say in the presence of many witnesses entrust to reliable people who will also be qualified to teach others.

There are four "generations" in Paul's admonishment to us:

PAUL ⟶ TIMOTHY ⟶ RELIABLE PEOPLE ⟶ OTHERS

This is something we all should be doing. It is a command in Scripture. We should be pouring our lives into others who should be training others, who in turn, train others. I pray that as your children read these stories and see how one life impacted so many others, they'll catch a vision for doing something similar in their lives. May we all follow this example given to us.

Though these stories were written for children, my faith was challenged as I read them. I hope your faith grows through these are much as mine has.

Wanting to help others see the awe-inspiring glory of our Father,

Bob Sjogren
President, UnveilinGLORY

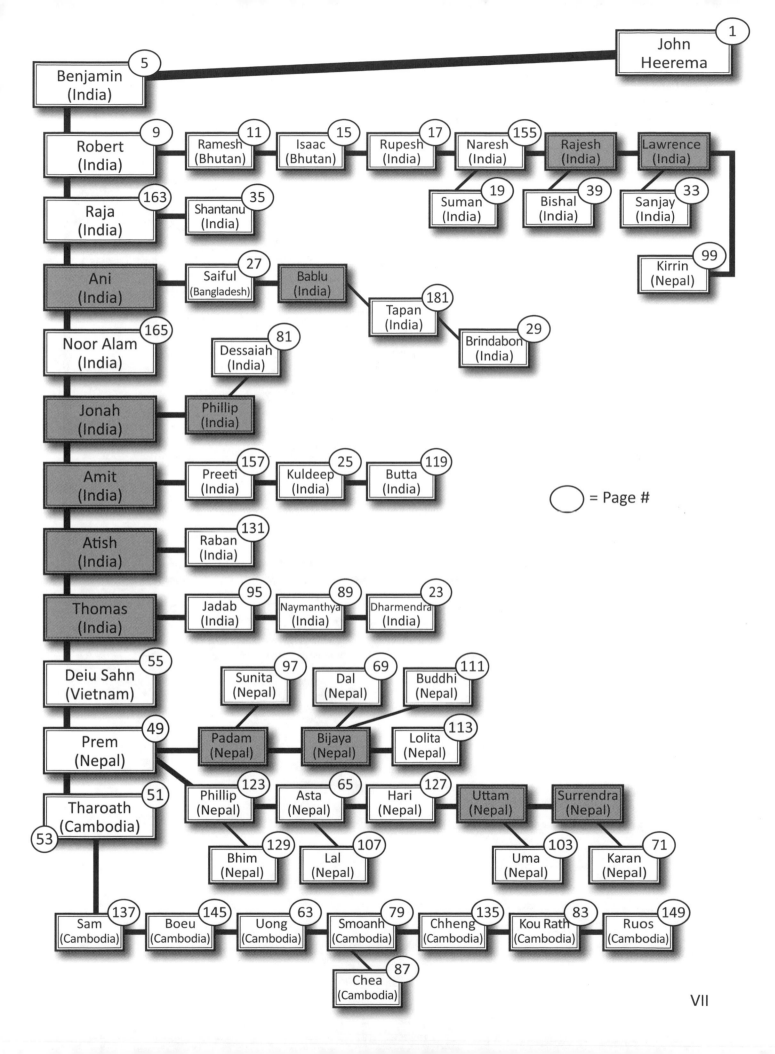

= Page #

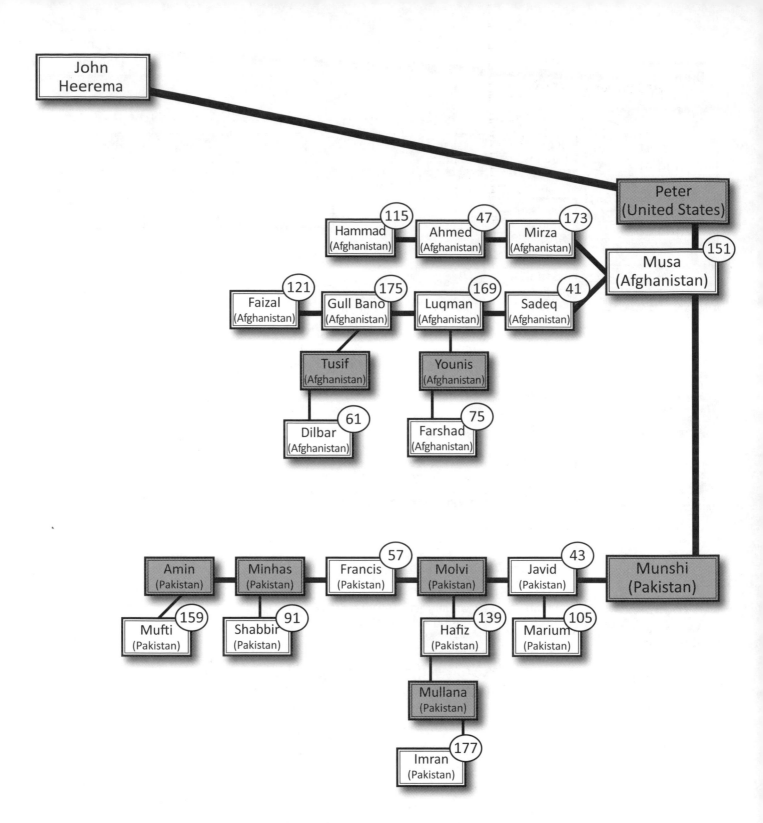

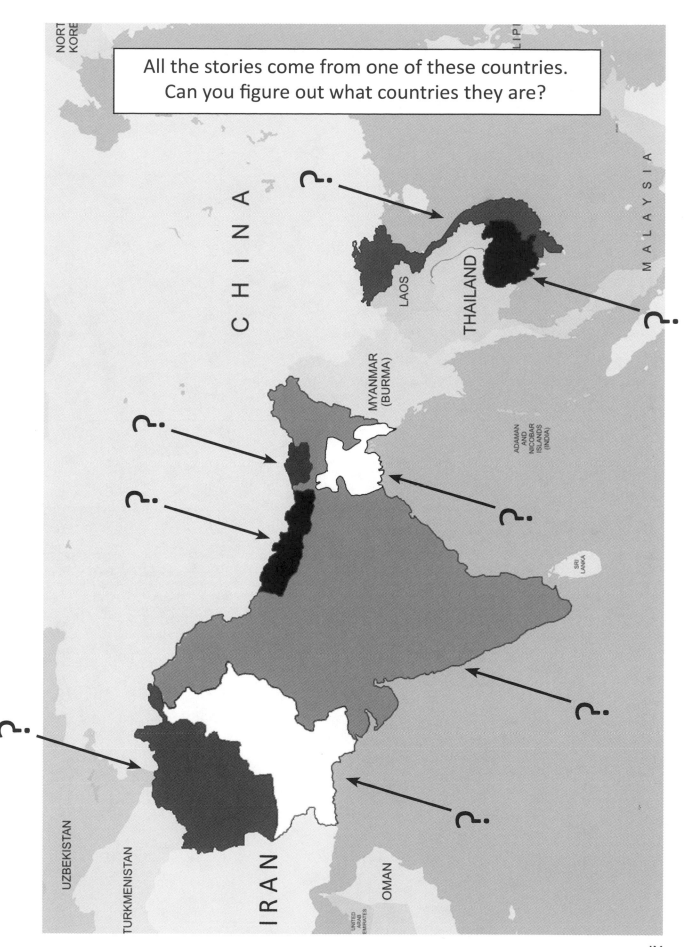

All the stories come from one of these countries.
Can you figure out what countries they are?

Table of Contents

The Imam

They were everywhere—watching him when he left the hotel, following him wherever he went, monitoring his phone calls. As a foreigner in this land, his actions were under constant examination. Home seemed so far away.

His name was John Heerema, and he was on a mission trip to Iran. Because Christians were not welcome there, John had agreed to train Iranian young men how to play baseball. While playing and hanging out with the Iranian teenagers, John had been able to share about Jesus multiple times. The kids were curious and eager. They asked John lots of questions. Here in Iran, people were desperate for the truth.

But they were scared—and lonely. And they felt trapped by their culture.

Now John knew exactly how they felt. He stood by the window of his hotel room, looking down at the busy street. He felt edgy and wary, especially after what had happened today. He had been sitting with the baseball team, relaxing after a hot game, when two dark-clothed men had approached. One was clearly an important man, dressed in long, flowing robes. The other was his translator. They came and asked to speak with John. With the baseball team gathered around him, the man, through his translator, began to question John. Straight out the man asked, "Are you a Muslim?"

John felt his mouth go dry. Suddenly his heartbeat was racing. "No," he said. He remembered what he had been taught before coming here. Never deny Christ. John took a deep breath. "I am a Christian."

The man talked with John for a long time. The baseball kids listened, fascinated, as John explained his faith. At last, the man rose to leave. John's hands were clammy with sweat, and he watched the robed figure anxiously. What would happen now? Would he be reported?

The man didn't say a word. He nodded to John and the baseball team, and then he left.

Even now, back at the hotel, John felt slightly shaky remembering the interview. He had witnessed to the entire baseball team and an important Muslim figure. They had all heard the message of Jesus.

His mind raced back to the present as the phone rang and startled him.

John turned away from the window and picked it up. "Hello?" The voice that responded was chillingly familiar. It was the translator. "I have a message from the Imam," he said. The Imam? John felt his hands begin to tremble as he realized that the man with whom he had shared his faith was an Islamic leader.

"He would like you to meet with him at the park down the street—tonight, at midnight." The line clicked and went silent.

John slowly lowered the phone from his ear. An Islamic leader wanted to meet with him in the middle of the night. *Why? He's going to kill me*, John thought in panic. *It will be dark, and there will be no witnesses.* John wrenched his mind away from those thoughts and tried to calm himself. *No. If the Imam wanted to kill him, he could have just sent someone to the hotel. Maybe there was another reason for the meeting.*

But what?

A few minutes before midnight, John put on his jacket and slipped his Bible into his pocket, praying for the Lord to work His will that night. Relief hit him when he realized that most Iranians were still up at midnight. At least there would be witnesses.

The translator was silent and impassive, waiting for him at the entrance to the park. When John drew near, the translator turned into the park and gestured for him to follow. No words were spoken. John cast a glance backwards, reluctant to leave the brightly lit street with its throngs of late-night passersby. Then, breathing a quick prayer, he hurried after the translator.

The translator led John to a secluded corner where the Imam sat quietly on a small bench. John looked around. The place was deserted, dimly-lit, hidden. The perfect place to carry out an unseen assassination: quick, no trouble, no witnesses. The Imam looked up as John approached, and motioned for him to sit.

John took a few shaky steps toward the Imam, conscious of the man's eyes boring into him. He sat down on the bench.

The translator walked forward, stood behind them, and looked up and down the path making sure they were alone. John felt the air thicken around him, making it hard to breathe. This was it. The translator gave a sharp nod to the Imam, and the Imam turned towards John.

John fought an insane urge to close his eyes.

"I would like to talk with you," the Imam said softly. John looked up. He sounded shy, almost nervous as the translator mimicked his tone.

"I want to know more about your relationship with Jesus Christ."

John stared at the Imam. He was looking at John intently, his hands folded in his lap calmly, his eyes hungry. This was no trap. The Imam wanted to know about Jesus.

Please, Lord, give me the words to speak to this man, John prayed. "What would you like to know?" he asked the Imam.

They talked for long time. The Imam asked deep and difficult questions, and John answered every one. The knowledge John shared seemed to fill the Imam with awe. He leaned forward in his eagerness to know more.

"I always know that Jesus is with me," John explained. "He is in control of my life, and I live every day to serve him."

"When do you pray to him?" the Imam asked.

"I pray to him all the time. I prayed as I walked here. I prayed as I taught the young men baseball. I can talk to God anytime." John was feeling more and more confident.

"How do you..." The translator paused as the Imam made a small gesture in the air, as if unable to locate the right words, "achieve this kind of relationship with God? What must you do?"

"There is nothing you can do to earn it. You must simply believe that Jesus Christ died for your sins, and accept him as your Lord and Savior. His grace is a free gift."

The Imam looked up and held John's gaze. There were tears glimmering in his eyes. "I want to have the kind of relationship you have. I want Jesus to be my Savior."

John could feel a presence stirring inside him, all around him, taking his breath away. God was moving mightily in this place. "I would be glad to pray with you," John said.

The two bowed their heads together, and the Imam accepted Jesus as his Savior. When they finally stood up from the bench, the Imam drew a string of prayer beads from within his robes. With a radiant smile, he pressed them into John's hands and said, "I do not need these any longer. I can pray to Jesus at any time. He lives in me!"

As John walked away through the park, alone with the night, he could barely contain the emotions welling up within him. What a difference a few hours could bring! He had gone from fear as he left the relative safety of the hotel, to relief as he saw the activity and lights around the park, to a growing anxiety as the translator led him deeper into the park. There fear had gripped him again as he contemplated what the Imam wanted from him. Even now, John was still in a whirl of confusion and exhilaration at what had happened next. As the Imam began to speak, John had swung yet again from terror to immense relief, to astonishment at the Imam's request to know about Jesus, and then to firm determination to clearly share the Gospel. At the end of the conversation, as the Imam gave his life to Christ and offered John his prayer beads, John felt nothing but complete joy and amazement.

He served an awesome God.

John returned home to the States a short while later. There he received several emails from the newly saved Imam, asking for deeper details about the Christian faith. His wife, Kathy, was also amazed by the story of the Imam's radical conversion. In addition to his continued correspondence with the Imam, John received an email from the Iranian Olympic Committee, asking John to return to Iran to train baseball players for an international tournament to be held in their country. John was overjoyed. God was doing unbelievable things! Now he had a chance to return to Iran and share Jesus with even more people. It was a perfect opportunity.

But in one single day, everything changed. It was September 11th, 2001. Four jets were hijacked and purposely crashed. Three hit their targets at the Twin Towers and the Pentagon, and thousands of lives were lost. As a result of the event, the Iranian Olympic Committee told

John that there would be no tournament. And John was no longer welcome in Iran.

John didn't understand. Why, after everything was going so well, had it all fallen apart? Why had God allowed this to happen? What did he want John to do if he could no longer set foot in Iran? John rubbed his hands over his face, fighting the discouragement and doubt that was threatening to crush him. He had thought that God wanted him to be involved in overseas missions; he had been sure of it. And for a moment he thought he had seen God's plan for him unfolding in Iran.

But it now felt like he was running into a brick wall. He could see no path forward.

Frustrated in India

John was desperate to spread the gospel on a global scale. With the Iranian door closed to him, he now begged God to open another. *Please show me your way, Lord,* John prayed. *Use me to reach the nations.*

A short while later, John received an email from the Indian Olympic Committee. They wanted him to come to their country and train baseball players for a team just like he had done in Iran. John wasn't interested in the opportunity. There were already lots of Christians and missionaries in India. It wasn't a closed country like Iran. This wasn't the challenge he had been wanting.

He responded to the email, and declined their offer. But they wrote back, begging him to reconsider. After another refusal, and yet another plea, John began to waver. It seemed like God was trying to get his attention. *But India?* John sighed, tapping his keyboard. *What could it hurt? If I go, I will be able to confirm whether or not God really wants me there.* John finally wrote back to the Olympic Committee and told them that he would come to India for nine days.

The trip did nothing to lift John's spirits. He trained the baseball players, but that was it. He wasn't given any chances to spend time with them or share his faith. Television companies followed him everywhere so that he could barely get a moment alone. He found himself thinking of Iran and the amazing experiences he had had there. What could there possibly be for him here in India? He just wanted to go home.

Finally the last night of his trip arrived. John dragged himself through one last news conference on Saturday night, unenthusiastically answering all the reporters' questions. At last the news crews began to drift away and John hoped that he would finally have some peace.

"I have one more question, Coach Heerema," a voice piped up.

John looked at the reporter, stifling a sigh. "Yes?"

"Are you a Christian?"

"Uh, yes, I am," he replied, slightly taken aback.

"So am I," the reporter said eagerly. "Would you like to come to my church tomorrow?"

John nodded to the reporter, smiling. "I would love that."

The next morning the reporter took him to the church. It was not one of the clean, tall, well-structured buildings he had seen in the city. This church was a musty brick building, with a dirt floor and dim lighting. John was the only white man there. The rest of the building was packed with the poor of India. They were covered with dirt and grime and dressed in rags for clothing. They talked excitedly to him in a different language, trying to shake his hand with their filthy fingers. John felt disgusted and uncomfortable. What was he doing here? As soon as the service was over, he would get out of this dark hole.

As the worship began, John stood with his eyes raised to the ceiling, attempting to block out the ugly sights around him. Then a movement caught his eye. A man was coming down the center aisle, his eyes fixed on a rough wooden cross erected at the front of the building. But this man, he was crawling along the dirt floor. His fingers dug into the earth to drag his body forward inch by inch, with agonizing slowness. John looked down, and his stomach turned in horror. The man had no legs. Yet he didn't ask for help or take his eyes off the cross for one moment. John's throat constricted. His heart was suddenly heavy with shame.

More people came down the aisle—children draped in ragged clothes, a woman covered with open, oozing sores. Two men limped on crippled limbs, and another, led by a young child, walked forward with white, unseeing eyes. John felt sick. He wanted to turn his eyes away—but he couldn't. These people were the lowest of the low, the untouchables. They lived their lives every day in terrible poverty. And yet as John watched, they praised God with smiles of pure joy. They raised their voices, young and old, man and woman, in worship to their Savior. They didn't look like people without hope. They had Jesus, and that was all they needed.

One song caught his attention—even though it was in Bengali. *That's "Because He Lives, I Can Face Tomorrow"* John thought to himself. Was God speaking to him?

John could barely see anything through the tears filling his eyes. He clenched his fists, his nails digging into his palms, as he felt the Holy Spirit speaking directly to his heart. *These people don't need things, John. They need me.* He covered his mouth with a hand as sobs began to shake his shoulders. *I'm sorry,* he prayed. *I've been so focused on myself that I've failed to see what you want me to see. I've been seeking what I want, not what Your will is. You don't want me in Iran, You want me here. These people in India need You. Please, show me what you want me to do.* John squeezed his eyes shut, tears spilling down his cheeks.

"It's okay, mister."

John looked down.

A small Indian boy was smiling up at him, his big, round brown eyes gazing into John's. The child's tattered shirt slipped off one shoulder and his skin was coated with dirt, but he looked peaceful and content. He reached out and touched John on the arm. "He lives," the boy whispered, his joyful smile growing wider.

John carried the memory of those people with him when he returned home. They may have been poor in body, but they possessed the greatest wealth of all—Jesus.

He made three more trips to India, working with the baseball team, but he was never given any freedom to share his faith. What did God want? It was on the fourth trip that John met a man named Benjamin. He was a strong believer in Jesus Christ and had been assigned to be John's liason. He and John quickly formed a close friendship. They spent many hours talking about Christianity in India. Most of the churches were Western, with hardly any Indian attendees. The people of India had few churches of their own.

John wanted to change that. The beginnings of a plan were forming in his mind, and now he presented his idea to Benjamin. "I want to begin planting churches in India, so that the people can embrace Christianity as part of their own culture."

Benjamin's eyes sparked with excitement. "Yes, but it is not just the cities that need churches. Most of the people are in the villages. We must reach them too."

The next time John returned to India, it was not as a baseball coach. He was done coaching. He traveled with Benjamin to visit several villages in the country. Another man, an interpreter, came along with them. His name was Ani. He had started his own fellowship in another village, which he took John to see. Ben specifically recruited him to help give John a vision for the villages.

John watched as the village leader led the service. "Ani," he asked, confused. "If you started this fellowship, why are you not the pastor here?"

Ani smiled broadly. "If I am the pastor, I must stay here, where the fellowship is. Instead

I teach this man to lead the people here. Once a month I come back to check all is okay and encourage them. Then I go and start another fellowship for Jesus, somewhere new."

John was deeply inspired by Ani's ministry. Ani could disciple growing fellowships while continuing to plant new ones. It was a fantastic strategy for impacting the villages.

"Ani," John asked casually. "How many villages are in this one area?"

Ani grinned. "Sixteen hundred." Benjamin smiled. His strategy was working!

John's eyes widened, and for a moment he couldn't speak. As Ani laughed at him, John realized just how much work there was to be done for the Lord here in India. Benjamin had been right. The villages needed to be reached, and they were open and ready for the Gospel. What if there was a ministry that could empower and equip Indians to reach their own people?

Before John flew back to the states, he was able to talk with Benjamin one last time. "I have an idea for a new ministry," John began hesitantly. "We could train Indians to plant churches in their own villages. Then they could disciple others to reach more villages. It would keep spreading—to villages all across India, maybe even across Asia."

Benjamin nodded. "That is a wonderful idea. But why do you seem anxious?"

"Well," John swallowed. "I know this is a lot to ask, but, would you be willing to partner with me in this ministry?"

Benjamin began to smile. "John, of course I will work with you. And by God's will, we will plant many churches."

When John returned home, he shared his excitement with Jim Powers and Pat Stuart. They all agreed to name the ministry, "Big Life."

"
Are you living a little life in your own little world, or are you willing to lead a *big life,* a life with a big kingdom impact? "

Bob Sjogren
God's Bottom Line (pg. 88)

Did
You
Know...

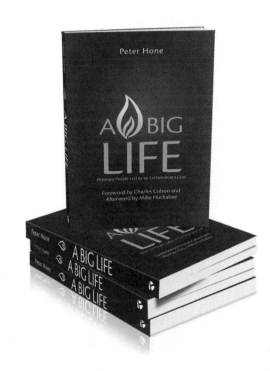

A Big Life tells the story of how thousands of believers, from suburban America to the jungles of the subcontinent of India, Pakistan, and beyond, were brought together in a phenomenal work of God.

Get a **free copy** by emailing:

info@blm.org

The Empty Hole

Robert was angry. He was always angry.

Robert had grown up rebelling against the strict Buddhist traditions of his family. He didn't understand why they worshipped their ancestors. It didn't make any sense to him. Though he didn't need Buddhism, Robert knew that something was missing in his life. He was constantly troubled with a fierce anger always ready to flare up. He tried to forget the emptiness he felt by drinking and using drugs. He was only thirteen years old.

His parents wanted a good life for their son. "We'll send you away to school," they told him. They hoped that allowing Robert to escape the poor influences of his home town would help him quit his dangerous habits.

But the new city didn't change anything. Robert drank more, and more often. He hung around with bad people. Robert could sense an empty hole inside of him where something wasn't right.

His life was a mess. He was angry and drunk and confused.

His aunt was a Christian. "Pray to Jesus," she said kindly. "He can help you." Robert wasn't interested.

Then, just a short while later, Robert's father became ill. It was a sickness of the mind. "Father?" Robert said hesitantly, kneeling beside his father's chair. "Father, I'm back…:"

His father stared blankly.

"Father? Can you hear me?" Robert asked, panicked. His father didn't respond. He continued to gaze at the air, seeing nothing, hearing nothing.

Robert leaned back, stunned. His father had no idea he was even there. Tears stung Robert's eyes. He clenched his fists, bending over and resting his forehead on his father's knee. He didn't move.

"Robert…" His mother came up behind him and touched his shoulder. Robert jerked his head up, not looking at her. He looked at his father's expressionless face. "You've tried everything?" he asked.

His mother nodded slowly. "Doctors, medicines, prayers…even witchcraft."

"And nothing helps." Robert nodded, digging his fingernails into his palms.

"Your aunt wants us to bring him to her Christian gathering. What do you think?"

Robert stood up. "Do whatever you like," he said shortly, and strode away. That night he opened a new bottle of liquor.

His family was forced to place Robert's father in an institution. He was unable to work and provide for his family, and they had no idea what they were going to do without his income.

"Please," Robert's aunt insisted. "Let us pray over him." At last they took Robert's father to the Christian gathering, where they prayed many fervent prayers over him.

From that moment on, Robert's father began to recover. After a month he was totally healed and started work again. The doctors who had seen him were amazed. They couldn't understand how he had recovered. But Robert's family knew it was the power of Jesus Christ. They believed in Him and were saved.

Except for Robert. Why should this Jesus be any different from the many gods his family had worshiped in his youth? Yes, he had seen the miracle. The amazing power had come from

Jesus, Robert believed that. But Jesus must simply be a deity of healing, nothing more.

Robert went back to his wild lifestyle, drinking more alcohol than before and using more drugs. The empty hole inside of him was even greater. Eventually he became sick. The substance abuse had caused it. Robert knew this, but he couldn't stop doing it. It made the pain worse—but he couldn't stop. Now gravely ill, lying in a bed in the hospital, Robert could tell he was dying. His face was wet with tears flowing from the brutal pain racking his body. "Jesus," Robert whispered. "Jesus...forgive my sins. Get me out of the mess I have made of my life. Help me find the right path. Please...I will give my life to you and follow you forever." He clenched his teeth against the agony crying, "Please, help me!"

A week passed. If you had been standing outside the hospital on the morning afterwards, you would have seen a young man, healthy and full of life, striding through the doors with a brilliant smile to the world. This man's name would be Robert. But he is not the same person who entered through those doors with a body full of poison and a heart full of anger. This Robert is a believer in Jesus Christ, and his heart now belongs to Him.

Robert immediately wanted to learn more about Jesus. A pastor taught and discipled him, and Robert read the Bible eagerly, almost hungrily. Robert told his story of salvation to the people in his home town. From those who responded to his words, Robert was able to begin three small house churches. Robert soon discovered that he had a talent and a passion for teaching. He became well-known for his Christian instruction, and received a job at a discipleship school. Over the next eight years, Robert taught over 2,000 students from the school.

Robert put all his energies into his young students. He shared his life story with them, hoping that they could learn from his mistakes and not make them in their own lives. But he also wanted them to know that anyone can be changed by the power of God's love—even someone like him.

But somehow, as exciting as the work was, Robert still didn't feel fulfilled. There was a nagging thought in his mind that he wasn't doing all that God had called him to do. He remembered a man he had met a while before, a Big Life church planter named Benjamin.

"We are called to reach the villages with the gospel and plant churches there," Benjamin had said. Robert remembered listening, captivated. For days afterwards he could think of nothing else. And now Robert found himself thinking about Benjamin and the villages again. Constantly they surfaced in his mind, even during the busiest of days at the school. Finally, Robert accepted that God was trying to tell him something. He believed that God was calling him to the villages.

Robert resigned from his position at the school. He had no other income, and food soon became scarce for him. Somehow he managed, once having nothing to eat except peanuts. The school offered him his job back. But Robert refused. He knew that God had told him to join Benjamin and Big Life in their work. His wife agreed—that was all he needed to know.

Robert sought Benjamin out, and told him what he wanted to do. Benjamin was thrilled to have Robert join their team. Robert became the head of operations over an area including Northeast India, Nepal, Bhutan, and Sikkim. Now he continues to train and disciple, and with others they have started 1,375 Christian fellowships in his region of influence.

Robert is far from the lost, troubled young man that he was before. He has peace in his heart. He no longer feels that empty hole inside him. It has been filled, with the only piece that would fit—Jesus.

Crushed Dreams Brought Back to Life

Ramesh had big dreams. Although he was still young, he often lay awake at night and imagined what his life would be like when he grew up. He would be well-educated, with a career of his own, and lots and lots of money. One day, he would take up the responsibility of providing for his parents. It was their custom for the oldest son to take care of his parents when they could no longer take care of themselves, and Ramesh was an only child. With his earnings, he would be able to live well and give his parents anything they wanted.

When Ramesh was old enough to begin school, he did so eagerly, determined to make a way for himself in the world. But at nine years old, his plans came to an abrupt halt.

Ramesh was attacked by an evil spirit. It was in the middle of his studies one day. Suddenly, Ramesh felt his body seize up. He crashed to the floor, convulsing violently, his eyes rolling in his head. He couldn't speak; he could barely breathe. He couldn't control anything, and his body was not his own. A horror filled his mind until he wanted to scream in panic, but no sound came from his mouth. Then instantly it was over. Ramesh lay limply on the floor, his chest heaving. Cold sweat drenched his clothes. He stared at the ceiling as his parents rushed towards him, shouting in fright and calling his name. His heartbeat was racing and it *wouldn't slow down.*

Over time, the seizures became frequent and vicious. As was the custom, Ramesh's parents offered up prayers and sacrifices to the Hindu gods, but with little hope. No god had ever answered their prayers, no matter how many rituals they performed. And Ramesh made no change.

The doctors thought it was epilepsy. The seizures seemed to be symptoms of the disease, but Ramesh knew that it was something different. The doctors couldn't understand. They hadn't felt that evil, total, mind-numbing terror. It made his skin crawl. In those moments Ramesh had no say in what his body did, and even his conscious thought seemed distant.

It destroyed Ramesh. He couldn't continue his studies; his dreams of a better life for himself and his family were crushed. His parents tried everything to heal him, knowing that Ramesh was their only security in old age—and their only child. But Ramesh gradually became weaker and weaker. The brutality of the attacks left him sobbing and trembling, and when he came to himself, he would just lie silently in his bed. Hot tears seeped from his eyes, soaking into his pillow. Ramesh didn't bother to wipe them away. He was letting everyone down. He was a burden.

The spirit was killing Ramesh, slowly, yes, but inevitably. Ramesh's health was now beyond recovery. He had trouble opening his eyes; his skin was pale and clammy. His parents stood over his bed, watching him. Their hands were clasped, their eyes red with sleeplessness and weeping. There was nothing more they could do.

"Hello!" the woman said cheerily. "I thought I would stop by to visit your family today."

Ramesh's parents stood in the doorway, looking oddly at this lady who had just knocked on their front door. They weren't quite sure how to react to her bubbly greeting.

"I'm Hastun," she said, extending her hand.

Still hesitant, Ramesh's parents shook hands with her.

Hastun was a Christian, and a kind, tender-hearted person. She noted the dark circles around Ramesh's parents' eyes, and the tired lines on their faces. "Do you need prayer?" she asked gently.

They didn't answer immediately, but Hastun saw the desperate glance they cast each other. Frowning, Hastun peered inside the house. She gasped. Lying on the bed inside was Ramesh, deathly white, his limbs twitching.

"Is he, your son?" Hastun asked.

Ramesh's parents nodded. Tears filled his mother's eyes.

Hastun raised herself up to her full height and squared her shoulders. "We must pray for him."

Ramesh's parents, weak and exhausted, let Hastun sit them down beside Ramesh's bed. Then Hastun held Ramesh's cold hands and prayed. Ramesh woke up as Hastun began to speak. Blearily, he peered at this woman who was speaking with such passion, her eyes pressed closed, her hands holding tightly to his. At last she said, "Amen," and opened her eyes to look at Ramesh.

He met her gaze, fascinated by the strength and warmth in her eyes. Something in that prayer—it awakened a spark of life in Ramesh's heart. Maybe there was still hope.

Hastun didn't leave the house until she had talked with Ramesh and shared the entire Gospel story. His parents sat in silence, listening. She spoke about Jesus and his powerful love. She told Ramesh how Jesus had healed many people, just like him, and how he had died for the sins of the whole world. "To receive eternal life, all you must do is accept Him as your Savior," she said firmly.

When Hastun, with a last heartening smile, finally said good-bye, a peace had entered the house. Ramesh's parent's faces had relaxed, and a faint light shone in their eyes. As for Ramesh, he felt alive for the first time in what had now been years. It was the name of "Jesus" still echoing in his ears; it was the stories of the miracles; it was the message of hope and joy brought by their unexpected visitor. Ramesh knew, he *knew*, deep down, that something was about to happen.

Ramesh, who had been gradually fading away, began to steadily get better. His parents started to smile again, and Ramesh started to get up out of bed. The evil presence that had clung to him was receding a little more every day. He could walk about now with new strength in his limbs. Happiness surged through him with each step. *He was getting better.* He was going to be well.

It was Jesus. The woman had prayed to Jesus, and Jesus had healed Ramesh. When he was well enough, Ramesh began attending a Christian fellowship near his home. Soon afterwards, Ramesh accepted Jesus as his Savior as did his parents. Ramesh felt the last shade of darkness vanish completely and warmth like a tidal wave of love cover over him. He was free at last.

Ramesh threw himself back into his studies, but now his passion was to learn more about Jesus. He still dreamed, but his dreams were now to serve the Lord.

Ramesh studied the Bible diligently, and eventually met Robert with Big Life Ministries. Robert trained Ramesh in the ways of the Lord. Today, Ramesh is now planting churches in his home country and raising a family of his own to love and serve the Lord.

Works Prepared in Advance

Isaac was born into a strong Christian family. Before, it had not been so. His parents had been devout Hindus. But after Isaac's older sister's miraculous healing, the whole family had become followers of Jesus.

Isaac's mother asked God constantly for a son, and in time, she gave birth to Isaac. Filled with joy, she dedicated the little boy to the Lord's service.

Yet Isaac was a frail, sickly child. He was constantly ill, and never able to fully recover. At the age of five, Isaac's health took a severe turn for the worse. As his family gathered around him, weeping and praying, little Isaac passed away.

Fellow believers came to comfort Isaac's family for their loss. Their good friends embraced them and cried with them over Isaac's tiny body. Pastor Dawa was there, too. He stood silently watching as the family prepared Isaac for burial.

"Wait," he said softly. Everyone became quiet and looked towards him. Pastor Dawa motioned for Isaac's family to cease their preparations. "Come, gather together. Let us pray."

The group of Christians linked hands, bowed their heads, and prayed. They prayed earnestly for Isaac and for his family. Then everyone there felt a mighty presence stir the room sending charges of power through the air like electricity. They gripped each other's hands more tightly knowing at that moment that something amazing was about to happen—something that could only be from God.

And something did happen—Isaac took a breath.

The group broke apart in shock and excitement; dozens of voices were instantly talking at once. With a cry of joy, Isaac's mother rushed to her son and gathered him in her arms. Everyone crowded around the small boy. Isaac sat up and hugged his family, smiling peacefully, and people began to laugh through their tears. Their nerves still seemed to tingle with the knowledge of Jesus's power working right in their midst that day.

As for Isaac's mother, she thanked God again for her son—this time for returning him to her. She rededicated Isaac to Him.

The years passed, and Isaac thought less and less of Jesus and grew up into a strong, stubborn young man. Though dedicated to God, he determined to live on his own. He turned away from the teachings of his family and of Jesus.

His mother was heartbroken. She had dedicated Isaac to Jesus twice hoping that he would grow into a man of God. But despite the miracle that Jesus had done in his life, Isaac refused to acknowledge Him as Lord.

Isaac thought he was doing pretty well without God.

As for Isaac's mother, she thanked God again for her son—this time for returning him to her. She turned to Ephesians chapter 2 and read verse 10. "For we are God's handiwork, created in Christ Jesus to do good works, which God prepared in advance for us to do."

Isaac's mother rededicated her son to God, praying that he would grow to fulfill the works God had prepared for him.

Contrary to his mother's prayers, Isaac thought he was doing pretty well without God. "I'm free," he thought. "I can do whatever I want, with no Christian rules to stop me." However, Isaac's mother never stopped praying for him. She begged God to somehow bring Isaac back to Himself.

Had Isaac heard her prayers, he would have laughed. He was in control of his own life. No one and nothing could stop him.

But oh, how wrong he was.

A short time later, Isaac fell sick again. It was a terrible illness, and Isaac knew that he was dying. He was terrified. He thought that there was no one who could save him this time, for he had abandoned God.

Isaac's mother, however, knew better. She saw this sickness as God answering her prayers. She gathered the Christians together, and they prayed over Isaac—just as they had when he was five years old. Isaac lay on his bed, listening to their prayers, and felt tears seeping from his eyes. God's hand touched him once again, and Isaac was healed.

It was then that Isaac truly understood the power of God's love. He recognized the miracle that had been done in his life. Completely shaken and humbled, he asked Jesus to be his Lord. Isaac vowed to serve Him for the rest of his life.

Isaac began studying the Bible in earnest. He learned much about his Savior and about His commands for his disciples. Later, in answer to God's calling, Isaac started working with young people. He taught them about Jesus and told them how they could live for God's glory. As Isaac spent time with the youth and got to know them, he was overwhelmed with the desire that every one of them should become a child of God. Isaac realized that he was starting to see mankind through God's eyes. Each morning he prayed that God would make his vision even clearer and fill his heart with love and compassion for the lost.

Then Isaac became involved with Big Life Ministries. He began working with Pastor Karma. Through Big Life, God taught Isaac some powerful lessons and showed him how God was actively working in people's lives.

Isaac received training from Big Life to plant churches in the villages of his country. Isaac was extremely excited. He told his mother all about the plans to begin churches and about what God was doing in his life. She listened happily, smiling to herself. God was using her son just as she had prayed he would—doing the works God had prepared in advance for him to do for His glory.

From being raised from the dead to being saved from death's grip a second time, God has now used Isaac to plant eight churches with memberships equaling 166 members altogether.

The Overdose

Rupesh sat cross-legged on the hard floor. It was evening. Outside the lighted windows, the sky was swiftly darkening to navy blue. The rest of the orphans were clustered around him. They listened to a lady giving a Christian devotional, as she did every night. She talked about Jesus and read a passage from the Bible. Then someone came out with an instrument or two and sang a few praise songs. Every morning, every evening. Rupesh had heard it all a hundred times.

He couldn't remember a life outside the orphanage. As far as he knew, he had never had a family. Instead the orphanage workers cared for him feeding him, giving him shelter, and trying to raise him into a godly young man. They meant well. But they couldn't personally love one child out of so many. Rupesh doubted they even noticed how his attention wandered during the worship services. Some of the children—a good number of them—loved the daily messages and songs. Many were planning to grow up and serve Jesus. But Rupesh had never felt any desire to follow Jesus. It wasn't that he disliked the devotionals, or the Christian work-ers, but Christianity just wasn't for him. Rupesh didn't think he needed a Savior.

The orphans sang the final song in a ragged but enthusiastic chorus. Rupesh struggled against a yawn. It was getting late.

At last, aching with tiredness, Rupesh crawled into his bed and burrowed beneath the cov-ers. The other orphans settled into their beds, exchanging a few, quick good-nights. Soon the only noise was their gentle, steady breathing and the occasional squeak of a bedframe. Rupesh lay awake for a little while longer. He listened to the sleeping room and watched the pale moonlight seeping in through the window. At times like this, when sleep was yet to claim him, his thoughts began to stir. He didn't like what he felt. Loneliness...fear...even anger. Rupesh closed his eyes, matching his breathing with the other orphans. Sleep would be welcome to-night. A heavy drowsiness stole over him, and Rupesh felt himself drifting away into slumber. It was at that moment, the last second of consciousness before he completely fell asleep, that he realized how very alone he was.

As Rupesh grew up, the loneliness stayed with him. He tried to hide it, as if that would distance him from it. But though he appeared to the world as a wild, fun-loving, street-wise young man, he was really just a troubled teenager searching for happiness and love. In his quest for joy, Rupesh began drinking alcohol and trying drugs. It made him feel powerful. Rupesh felt a heady sense of exhilaration by leaving the teachings of the Christian orphanage. He was his own man now.

"No, Rupesh," some of his old friends pleaded with him. "This will not make you happy. Jesus will give you true joy!"

Rupesh believed that he was free of the godly principles with which he had grown up. But when his friends confronted him, he still felt guilty. That made him angry. "Don't tell me about Jesus!" he shouted at them. "I know how to live my life!" He became bitter against Christians. They had always tried to tell him what to do all his life. They wouldn't do so any longer. He did have happiness—at least he thought he did.

But he was betrayed by what little happiness he had. The thing he had come to rely upon so heavily turned on him and dealt him a mortal blow. Rupesh lay alone on his bed—helpless—

an overdose of drugs surging through his body. *You're going to die*, a voice whispered in his head. *I'm dying, I'm dying.* The realization hit him hard. He fixed his eyes on the ceiling, trembling violently. His limbs felt heavy and every part of him longed to fall asleep. But it was not slumber that beckoned so enticingly. Not this time. Rupesh knew that if he closed his eyes, he would never open them again.

He clung to consciousness, tears blurring his tired, blood-shot eyes. It was his only hope. Stay awake...stay alive. But eventually he would become too weak. He would slip away, and there would be no one to pull him back. The thought terrified him.

Maybe he was hallucinating, but in a single moment, everything grew still and silent. Rupesh felt a presence of power pressing in all around him—a power he had never felt before. Maybe it was only the effects of the drug. No. Somehow Rupesh knew this was something different.

Then an image was rising from the bed. It was himself, a white shade, emerging from his body. He stiffened in fright as the form slowly drifted upwards. Was he dying? What was happening? The shape stopped, hovering in the air, and then gently began to descend. Rupesh watched in entranced terror as the figure merged with his own body again. Something had just happened to him. It was as if someone was calling to him. *"Yes, that was it. Someone is calling to me,"* Rupesh realized.

Rupesh's lips felt heavy as he began to form words. He could barely think clearly enough to connect his sentences together; he just knew that he must pray. The call had to be from Jesus. He was the only One who could save him. How many times had he been told? And yet he had rejected the truth.

"J-Jesus," Rupesh stammered thickly. "Please, heal me. Save me, Jesus...." He felt tears constricting his throat. For what seemed like hours he prayed, weeping in shame and fear and awe. Jesus was the only One. Rupesh had been so blind.

Suddenly, he gave a great gasp. New breath filled his lungs. Rupesh blinked away the water in his eyes, as his shaking hand wiped his face. It was then that he realized that his head felt clearer and his body lighter. He was still dizzy, but his senses were returning to him. He could think straight again. Within a few minutes, Rupesh knew that the drug had left his body.

Rupesh slid from his bed and fell to his knees. Jesus had heard his cries, and He had answered with a miracle. Jesus had shown mercy to him, a person who had rejected Him so many times and had refused to accept His love. Rupesh sobbed brokenly, aghast at his own sin. "You are the Savior," Rupesh whispered. "You died to save me. I accept your sacrifice! I need you to forgive my sins and make me clean. You are my Lord, and I will serve you forever."

Rupesh held true to his vow. Through the power of the Holy Spirit, he left behind his addictions and lived a new life. He then met Robert who heard about his conversion and discipled Rupesh. Through Robert's training, Rupesh eagerly shares his faith to those who have never heard. He now travels from place to place sharing the Gospel and teaching young people like himself that Jesus is their only hope.

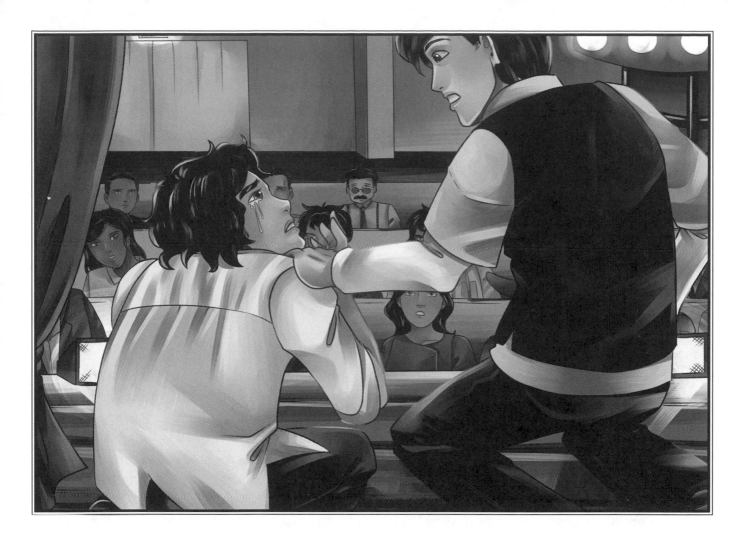

Crying on Stage

What did it feel like to have someone who loved you? To have a father and a mother who kissed you goodnight and took care of you and comforted you? Suman dreamed of it often. He longed for love so much that his heart ached.

His birth mother had never been around. Did she die? Did she just leave? There were too many questions no one answered. Though he had once had his father, one morning Suman woke up and his father was gone too. A short while later, Suman received the news that his father had died. Suman was in shock. Both of his parents had deserted him. Had he been worth anything to them? To anyone?

Now Suman lived alone with his stepmother. She didn't care what happened to him, and never spent any time with him. No one cared. Suman hurt so much, deep down inside, like someone had stabbed a knife into his heart and left it there. No one had loved him enough to stay. They had all forsaken him.

Suman sat outside, his knees drawn up to his chest, peering at the world from beneath his black, wispy locks of hair. The people were walking by, chatting happily, exchanging news and gossip. Suman listened to their laughter as if he could feed off their joy. It helped, a little, to see smiling faces.

One day a lady walked by gazing around her. Suman watched her curiously. She seemed to be looking for something. Her keen gaze suddenly turned towards Suman, and a beautiful smile lighted her face. Suman stared back at her drinking in the sight of that radiant smile turned towards him. He basked in it like it was sunlight.

The lady began walking towards him. Suman clutched his knees a little tighter, feeling slightly wary. The lady stopped a little ways away from him and crouched down to his height. "Hello," she said gently. "What is your name?"

"Suman," he said. His voice felt rough and faint, as though he hadn't used it in days.

"I'm putting on a play soon, Suman. A Christian drama. But I need someone to fill a part for me. I was just looking for a young boy who would fit the role. And then I saw you." Her eyes were sparkling. "You are just as I imagined the character," she said. "I wonder, would you be interested in being in a play?"

Suman looked at her, eyes wide. "Me?"

She smiled. "Yes."

Suman twisted his fingers together. He couldn't stop a smile tugging at his mouth. "I, I think it would be—nice."

The time Suman spent with the cast and crew of the play was like nothing he had ever experienced. Everyone was kind and helpful, and they all wanted to get to know Suman. They joked and played with him, and they listened attentively whenever he spoke. Then there was the time spent working on the play itself. Suman played a young boy who had nobody to take care of him, and felt alone, scared, and unhappy—just like Suman himself. He was playing the perfect role. And though there were sad parts in the play, the final message was one of hope, salvation, and love. Suman felt his heart being deeply affected by the story. During the rehearsals, the Christians around Suman shared about Jesus, God's Son, who came to earth to save sinners from death. Suman took in their words, confused, but fascinated. Could there really be Someone who loved everyone, no matter how small or insignificant they were?

When the day of the performance came, the drama played out smoothly. On his cue, like he had done so many times in rehearsals, Suman walked out onto the stage. But this time, it felt so big—so empty. Loneliness surged up within him again, that familiar urge to curl up out of sight. He turned to the audience, his heart weighing heavy in his chest. "I'm all alone," he said softly. "No one is here for me. " He bit his lip, tears burning his eyes. "I don't know what to do." The audience watched silently, hanging on his words.

Suman swallowed and looked upwards. "Is there Someone who cares?" he called out. "Anyone? Please, please…" Suman sank to his knees, sobs shaking his chest. He rocked back and forth, and suddenly the tears were real tears, and it was his heart breaking. The audience had faded away—it was just him, alone. This was no longer a play. Suman squeezed his eyes shut. There was no one here for him. There never had been. Could there possibly be Someone who would love him for who he was?

He felt a hand touch his shoulder. Suman jerked his head up, almost forgetting that this was another actor, not a real stranger. "What is wrong, my friend?" the actor asked concernedly.

Suman wiped his tears. "I-I have no one to care for me," he stammered. "I am all alone."

The actor knelt down and took Suman's hands. "We are never alone. None of us. There is a God who loves us, and He will always take care of us."

Suman gazed up at him. "Really?"

The actor smiled. "Really. He sent His Son, Jesus, to die for our sins. If we believe in Him and ask Him to be our Savior, He will rescue us from all evil. He will always be there for us. He will never leave us all alone."

New tears slid down Suman's cheeks, but he smiled through them. "Jesus loves me?"

"Jesus loves you more than you can ever imagine."

Suman was crying long after the curtain fell. The cast and crew huddled around him, comforting him and praying over him. At last Suman raised his head, his eyes shining. "I want to ask Jesus to be my Savior," he said. The Christians knelt beside Suman as he prayed to Jesus to save him from his sins so he could glorify God.

The play was finished, and the stage was being torn down; the actors and crew members were beginning to go their separate ways. Suman watched it all, smiling in perfect happiness. He could feel a change inside him. The wounds in his heart were being soothed away by beautiful, indescribable love. It moved through him like a living force, calming his mind, strengthening his heart and giving him peace. Suman knew he would never be alone again. Jesus had loved Suman enough to give His life in Suman's place, and one day, Suman would meet Him face to face. That day would be the start of a forever by His side.

Bad times came after Suman's salvation. His Hindu community shunned him, and he was forced to leave his house and his village. Everyone rejected him including his step-mother. At one point it would have broken Suman's heart, but that was before he knew Jesus. Nothing could dampen the hope he had now.

Suman moved to another village, where he met a Christian pastor named Naresh. Naresh became a mentor to the young man, training him in God's Word and teaching him how to walk with his Lord. Soon Suman was helping Naresh in his ministry.

Today they now travel from village to village sharing the Gospel with those who are lost and alone.

Did You Know...

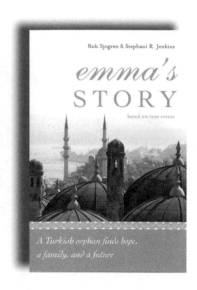

In 2005, Bob Sjogren teamed up with another homeschooled student to write *Emma's Story*?

It is a true story of a four-year-old Turkish girl whose family died in the 1999 earthquake. After four days in the rubble, she was discovered by an American rescue dog and then sent to a mentally handicapped institution to die. Bob's friends visited there and ended up adopting her. Emma now lives in Arizona.

The story of how it happened will blow you away! It's a great family read and is written in the context of an angelic battle!

Find out more about the book at: UnveilinGLORY's bookstore: www.UnveilinGLORY.com/ bookstore

A Failed Test

Dharmendra stopped going to church. He had been brought up in a Christian household, and now he felt like it was stifling him. He wanted to have fun with his friends. Their wild, carefree lifestyle lured him irresistibly. He had been hanging out with them more and more often and spending less time at church and with his parents. Now he had quit attending church altogether.

"Dharmendra," his mother pleaded with him, "you will ruin your life. These friends will get you into trouble!"

He ignored her. As time went on, he began to fall into many bad habits. He partied with his friends and became involved in unwholesome activities, and his structured life started to fall apart. He barely studied and his grades plummeted. When he was younger he had done well in school and had been devoted to his studies, his family, and his church. He had been proud of his respectable image. Now he hardly remembered when he had last prayed to Jesus. He neglected everything that had once been so important to him.

Is this the freedom you were looking for? The question kept nagging at him. *You have become trapped by bad choices and harmful habits. Can you truly call that liberty?* Dharmendra squeezed his eyes shut as if he could drive the doubts away by doing so. He didn't know anything for certain anymore.

But one thing was sure—his final examination was very soon. All of the kids around him were studying intensely, knowing how important this test was. Dharmendra knew that he should be doing the same. The thought of the test nagged at him, but he didn't ever sit down to study. His friends invited him out. He went. He arrived home late and slept later, barely making it to school. There everyone was talking about the upcoming examination. Dharmendra remembered again that he wasn't prepared. It was a matter of days until the test.

Dharmendra groaned and rolled over in his bed. The sun was filtering brilliantly through his window rousing him into wakefulness. He sat up, yawning hugely. Then realization hit him like a heavy weight in the stomach. The examination was today. He snatched at his textbooks and papers, hurriedly trying to skim through the pages. There was so much he needed to know; he couldn't possibly learn it all now. But it was alright. He had always done well on tests. He would pass; he'd always passed.

At school the atmosphere was tense. Everyone was quiet while doing some last minute studying or simply mentally preparing themselves for the important examination. Dharmendra didn't know what to do with himself. He lounged outside the test room feeling alternately confident and stricken with panic. For a moment he allowed himself to imagine what would happen if he failed. He would be one of the kids who was careless, irresponsible, and foolish. Dharmendra clenched his hands together. They were cold and sweaty.

The test began a few minutes later. Dharmendra filled out the questions the best he could, but as he progressed his heart sank lower and lower. He didn't know nearly enough. He hadn't done well on his schoolwork for months now, and he hadn't taken the time to learn the material. Maybe, maybe he could scrape by and pass. Definitely not with a good grade, but maybe….

When Dharmendra got his test back, his hands were shaking. He turned the paper over and found the grade. Dharmendra stared, his heart thudding. He had failed. He would not graduate. Dharmendra stood alone as the rest of his school friends laughed in relief, clutching their test papers. They had all passed. They had *all* passed, and he hadn't. Guilt and shame crept over him, strangling him as he held that paper in his hand. It was his fault. His parents had encouraged him, helped him, and warned him. His teachers had taught him. He had thrown it all aside. Now he suffered the consequences that his parents had said would come. They were right.

Dharmendra entered his home and handed the paper to his parents silently. They glanced at the grade. They didn't seem surprised, only solemn.

"You realize that this is a result of your lack of responsibility," his father said firmly.

Dharmendra nodded, looking at the floor. It blurred through the water in his eyes. "I—I'm—sorry," he whispered. Tears slipped from his lashes. "I failed—everything." His voice began to grow more determined. He lifted his head and stared at his parents. "I know. And I'm sorry."

But it didn't change anything. He hadn't completed his grade. His friends were going to move on and he was going to be left behind. Dharmendra was deeply depressed. He stopped hanging out with his friends. Their revelry didn't satisfy him anymore. He needed something more, but he didn't know what it was.

It had been many days—long, hard and lonely days—when Dharmendra met a man who would change everything. He was a pastor of another local church. He spoke with Dharmendra often, and helped the young man through his feelings of failure and disappointment.

"Yes, you have made some grave mistakes," he said. "But you recognize that, don't you?" Dharmendra nodded.

"We are all sinners, and deserve death. But God sent his Son, Jesus, to save us. He loves us even while we do wrong things. He offers us freedom from our sins and eternal life." The pastor smiled at Dharmendra. "He loves you. He wants you, Dharmendra. Will you surrender your life to him?"

Dharmendra thought often on his conversations with the pastor. He picked up his Bible and began reading it again. Every day his situation became clearer. He was a helpless, lost sinner. He needed a Savior. He had been brought up in a Christian family, but he had never truly realized until now the depth of his wrong-doing—or the scope of Jesus' love. The Gospel had never seemed more beautiful until he understood what it really meant. Jesus had died for a failure like him, and He promised to set him free. That was the freedom Dharmendra was seeking: freedom from sin and new life in Christ.

Dharmendra confessed his sins to Jesus and asked Him to save his soul. From that moment on, he had the promise of eternal life and the presence of a God who loved him more than he could ever imagine. He began attending church regularly again. He read his Bible, learning more about Jesus and how to walk closer to Him. His parents supported him every step of the way.

Being left behind, Dharmedra retook his last year of school. In 2004 he retook his final examination again and passed with a higher grade than he could ever have hoped for. Dharmendra was filled with joy, and he thanked Jesus constantly for his grace. Dharmendra began working to serve the Lord in his area. He served in a children's ministry for some years, and then later partnered with Big Life, to plant churches and teach others about Jesus Christ. Through the power of God, Dharmendra's ministry is reaching many.

The Boy with no Voice

Kuldeep didn't know what it meant to say hello or good-bye. He had never said, "I love you," not even to his parents. He had never said anything.

He was born without a voice. His family didn't know what his words would even sound like if he had been able to speak them. They went to many doctors hoping that there would be a cure.

"Maybe," the doctors said, frowning, "in a few years he'll be able to make sounds. But we don't know if he'll be able to form actual words."

Kuldeep's parents didn't lose hope. They were Hindus, and they did everything within their religion to try to heal Kuldeep. They took the little boy on pilgrimages. They made sacrifices and performed rituals. They even tried witchdoctors. But Kuldeep remained silent.

"How is your son?" his co-worker asked.

Kuldeep's father sighed heavily. "There is no change. He remains without a voice."

His co-worked looked down. "I'm sorry to hear that," he said quietly.

Kuldeep's father nodded, his throat closing up. The tears came without him realizing. His co-worker's voice held such kindness and compassion. It released some deep sorrow in his heart that he hadn't known he was carrying. "Thank you," he whispered.

His co-worker placed a hand on his shoulder. "You know, there is Someone who performed many great miracles—even healing the mute."

Kuldeep's father wiped his eyes. "Who?"

"Jesus," his co-worker said simply.

"And does he—still perform these miracles?" Kuldeep's father asked.

His co-worker smiled. "I believe He does, with all my heart."

When Kuldeep's father returned home that night, he was brimming with eagerness. He didn't know why this hope should be any different from all the others—the ceremonies that had been futile, the sacrifices that had been without result. But there was something about Jesus that his co-worker had said. It was worth a try. He sat down in front of Kuldeep, taking his hands. "We're going to go to a Christian fellowship, Kuldeep," he whispered. "They're going to pray for you to be healed. Do you think it will work?"

Kuldeep didn't say anything, but he smiled staring at his father with his big, deep eyes.

The fellowship met a few days later. Kuldeep's father took him to the church, where his co-worker met him outside. "They are delighted to pray for your son," he said excitedly. "Everyone's waiting inside."

The three of them made their way into the church. The pastor and the crowd of Christians welcomed them inside, greeting the newcomers happily. Kuldeep and his father sat in the congregation as the Christians sang worship songs, prayed, and listened to the pastor's message. They had a time of prayer over Kuldeep, where the pastor led them in a plea for Jesus to give the boy a voice.

Kuldeep enjoyed the songs. He swayed in time to the music with a delightful expression on his face. His father watched him, smiling. When the service was over, the pastor asked Kuldeep's father to attend again. "We will continue to pray for your son," he said.

Kuldeep's father did return the next week. It was a wonderful time of peace and joy for both him and Kuldeep. They listened to the music and heard the teachings about God and Jesus and the Holy Spirit. And the Christians prayed over Kuldeep. The boy watched them curiously. His father bowed his head along with the others as they asked Jesus for healing.

The third week they came once again. Kuldeep sat, moving gently to the music. His father sat beside him, starting to sing a few lines of the song. The pastor came and knelt beside them. He began to pray. "Dear Lord Jesus," he said softly, calmly, "We ask that you give this child, Kuldeep, a voice to praise and glorify you. Please heal him. Let him speak in Your Name."

Kuldeep's father had closed his eyes letting the prayer and the music soothe him. Suddenly, he stiffened, his eyes snapping open. There was a small, quiet voice, singing the praise song. A voice he had never heard before...a voice coming from right beside him. He twisted around and saw his son looking up at him smiling. It had only been a few words. But his son...his beloved, precious, voiceless son, had sung. Kuldeep's father threw back his head, laughing in pure joy. He leapt to his feet. He could barely breathe with happiness, and his eyes were blurry with tears. "My son!" he shouted, smiling until he couldn't smile any bigger. "My son spoke!" He turned to the people beside him, grasping their hands and repeating the unbelievable truth. "He spoke, my son spoke!"

Kuldeep watched him happily. The pastor knelt on the floor beside him, smiling as well, and breathing a grateful prayer to God.

From that day, Kuldeep could speak without any trouble—as if he had never been silent. His family saw the power of Jesus in their little son, and before the week had gone by they had all accepted Jesus as their Savior. Kuldeep, too, when he had grown into a young teenager, asked Jesus to forgive his sins and be his personal Lord.

"Never forget, Kuldeep," his father told him. "Never forget that Jesus gave you your voice. Use it for him!"

It wasn't long after when Kuldeep's father had a sudden heart attack. He went into a coma. Kuldeep sat by his father's bed clutching his hand. There were tears in his eyes. "Please get better, father," he said in a low voice. "I love you."

The doctors shook their heads gravely. "It will take a long time for him to recover. A very long time." But Kuldeep's family had already heard the doctors pronounce one hopeless case—and instead they had experienced a miracle. They knew that Jesus had the power to heal. Together, the family knelt around Kuldeep's father and prayed.

"Please Jesus," Kuldeep prayed, "Heal my father like you healed me. Let him wake up. I know you can do it. I believe you will."

Three days of fasting and constant prayer passed. And then, Kuldeep's father opened his eyes. The doctors were shocked. There was no tangible explanation for this sudden, complete healing. Kuldeep flung his arms around his father's neck. "Jesus did a miracle again," he cried. "He gave you back to us."

His father smiled, holding his son close to him. "Nothing is impossible for our Lord, Kuldeep. Nothing!"

Kuldeep's walk with Jesus was greatly strengthened by his father's healing. He decided to fully devote his life to serving God. When he was sixteen, he went to Bible college, and later became a translator at several medical camps. During this time, Kuldeep was introduced to an organization called Big Life. He felt a passion and a calling for their ministry, and soon he began working with them as a church planter. Kuldeep, the boy with no voice, now preaches the Gospel to the villages around his home proclaiming the praises of his Savior.

Isa The Savior

Reading the Quran was one of the most important parts of Saiful's life. Every day he would read a portion of the Quran and reflect on its meaning. In addition to this, he prayed five times a day and kept all the religious holidays. All his family members were strict Muslims. They encouraged Saiful to read the Quran devotedly.

One day, Saiful came across a strange verse. It stated that Isa (Jesus) was equal with the word of Allah. The verse said that Isa was the Savior. Saiful read the verse over and over forgetting about the rest of the section. What an odd thought. Why was Jesus considered "the Savior"? What did that mean?

Saiful pondered this concept constantly over the following days. He talked with his friend about it. "What does this verse mean?" he asked.

His friend read through the verse, and a puzzled frown creased his features. "I'm not sure," he said slowly. "Maybe you should ask Ani."

"Who is Ani?" asked Saiful.

"He's an Indian Christian who has come to our town. He would know about Jesus."

Saiful was anxious enough to know the meaning of the verse that he decided to go speak with Ani. Ani was happy to assist. He not only answered Saiful's questions about Jesus; he told him the whole Gospel story.

"Jesus came to earth to die for mankind's sins," Ani explained. "To be saved by Him, you must accept His sacrifice."

Saiful listened, a little confused. This teaching was completely different from what his Muslim family practiced. "But, what else must you do?" he asked.

Ani smiled. "Nothing—only believe. Jesus does the rest."

Saiful was amazed. Only believe. It was simple, precious.

He had to know more. Saiful began attending a Christian church. There he listened to messages about Jesus and songs about His love. Saiful felt his heart being pulled, irresistibly, towards Jesus—the Savior. He realized what terrible things he had done. He realized he was lost without Jesus. He believed. And that was all. Saiful's vision blurred as his eyes filled with tears; perfect peace and joy entered his soul. He knew that Jesus had saved him, just as He had promised.

Saiful was baptized, proclaiming his faith in Jesus. It was a time of rejoicing.

But his family, the ones who had raised him and grown up with him, did not share his joy. They refused to see him. Even his wife rejected him. Finding out he had become a believer, she gathered other Muslims around her and screamed, "Get out. Get out of this house. Get out of this village. Get out of our lives. You are dead to us now."

Saiful was confused and deeply hurt. All his life he had been surrounded by people who cared for him and wanted him to succeed. Now they were all gone. All his neighbors and the other villagers were angry with him. He was all alone.

But I am here, a voice reminded him. *You will never be alone. Trust in me, and I will support you.*

Saiful did trust in God. He continued to proclaim Jesus' name and share the gospel in his Bangladeshi village, even throughout the persecution. Saiful began to fully realize the joy of Christ. It was not happiness, based on circumstances. It was a constant, ever-present hope—the promise that God, and His love, would always be there. Saiful vowed that he would not forsake Jesus, and would serve Him in his life until the day it ended.

Over time, the bitterness and hostility from Saiful's friends lessened. God had brought him through the time of trouble and into a time of great fruitfulness. As his faith strengthened, he not only won others to the Lord, but he trained them to travel with him. Saiful started a team of church planters, and they began to journey to other villages throughout Bangladesh. Together, they have planted 192 churches with over 1,500 people attending those churches.

Saiful has never been happier. He and his team know that there are people eager to listen and ready to respond. And even though bad times may come, though their heart may not feel happy, there will still be joy—one that never fades—because they know they are never alone.

The Perfect Rest

Everyone had problems. Brindabon knew that. But should he always feel so burdened and weighed down? Shouldn't there be some happiness in life?

Some people turned to alcohol to forget their troubles. Some people simply tried to ignore it. But Brindabon had devoted himself to religion. He worshipped idols. He believed that his prayers and sacrifices would bring him fulfillment and would take care of the issues in his life. But instead he felt increasingly depressed and restless. He faced each morning with hopelessness. He had done everything for his gods, but they brought him no peace.

Brindabon sat outside his house, watching the village. He felt exhausted with it all. It was just another day dragging by without life or zeal.

"Brindabon!"

Brindabon turned his head slowly. His friend was walking up the street, waving cheerily at him. Brindabon frowned. He knew he was supposed to know him, but he had forgotten his name. What was his name and why was he so happy?

His friend walked up to where Brindabon was sitting. Now he could see that his friend was holding a bunch of small booklets in his hand. Curious (but not wanting to show it), Brindabon squinted at the pamphlets, trying to make out the cover.

"How are you?" his friend asked.

Brindabon looked up. "Alright. I suppose," hoping he didn't have to address him by name.

His friend smiled again. *Why did he keep doing that?* "Only alright, my friend? That is too bad. Here," he took one of the booklets in his hand and offered it to Brindabon, "maybe this will cheer you up."

Brindabon took the booklet, holding it with uncertainty. His friend nodded to him and went on his way walking energetically down the road. Brindabon watched him go. Then he looked back down at the booklet. Shrugging, he leaned back, flipped it over, and began to read.

It was in the very first phrase. *"I will give you rest."* Brindabon's eyes locked on the words. He felt as though someone had spoken those words just to him—whispering them in the back of his mind.

"I will give you rest," Brindabon read in a whisper. For years he had been searching for peace in his heart, but had found none. He had come to the conclusion that the world was a place of misery and hopelessness, and that there was no solution to the despair he felt. But was this little booklet now giving him the answer?

Who was the "I"? Who had spoken those words? Who is this person who knows exactly what I need to hear? Brindabon thought. How could anyone know his heart like this? He had never spoken of the inner emptiness he felt. The idol worship was supposed to be enough. But it never was.

Brindabon read the promise one more time: "I will give you rest." Seized with a sudden passion, Brindabon sprang up and dashed out into the street. He had to find the friend who had given him the booklet. He had to know who it was who could give him rest.

Brindabon searched everywhere. He walked every street twice over, knocked at every house, asking for the man with the booklets. Oh, how he wished he had known his name. But he was nowhere to be found. Brindabon was in torment. He needed to know! He had just been given the first clue to finding peace, and now the trail had gone cold. His no-named friend seemed to have disappeared. Brindabon poked his head into another empty alley. With a grunt of frustration he bent his head and marched down the street turning sharply around a corner.

He slammed into a man coming the other way. Startled and disoriented, Brindabon staggered backwards. "I'm sorry," he mumbled, regaining his balance. Brindabon started to continue on his way.

"Where are you off to in such a hurry?" the man asked. His voice was unfamiliar, but it sounded so lively that Brindabon checked to be sure that it wasn't his cheerful, elusive friend. The stranger smiled at Brindabon. He had deep eyes, and his face was worn. He wore the look of someone who has seen much pain. But there was a determined spark in his eye and a set to his jaw. This was a man with a purpose.

Brindabon studied the man curiously. This was the second time today that he had seen such confidence and optimism in a person. Maybe this stranger had another clue. "I am looking for a friend," Brindabon said. "He gave me this…" Brindabon pulled out the booklet and handed it to the man. "I want to know what it means. But I can't find him."

The man studied the booklet for a moment. When he raised his head, his smile had grown even wider. "I am Tapan," he said, shaking Brindabon's hand. "And it seems we were meant to meet. For I know exactly what this booklet is talking about."

Tapan told Brindabon that the person who offered rest, hope, and life was Jesus. "Jesus is God's Son," he explained. "He is the Savior." He explained that anyone who trusted in Jesus and asked for forgiveness from their sins would be saved and have eternal life.

Brindabon listened eagerly. From the moment that Tapan had begun speaking, Brindabon had sensed that there was something different about this man and this message. It held power and truth that Brindabon had never encountered before. At last Tapan had answered all Brindabon's questions except one.

"Why, why are you so happy?" Brindabon asked hesitantly. "Isn't the world full of trouble?"

Tapan paused, and Brindabon saw sadness pass over his face—yet the sparkle in his eye somehow remained. "Yes, my friend. The world is full of pain and darkness." He gazed steadily at Brindabon. "But Jesus has overcome the world. And with Him as my Lord, I always have hope and joy, no matter what happens."

Brindabon was silent. He could not speak; tears were filling his eyes. Tapan leaned closer and put a hand on Brindabon's shoulder. "Would you like to come to my fellowship tomorrow?" He asked gently.

Brindabon nodded. It was all he could do.

At the fellowship there were many believers. As Brindabon stood in the midst of them, he saw ordinary people just like him with lives just like his. He also saw the radiant joy on their faces and the adoration in their voices as they sang praise to God. There was truly something different about their God. It was Jesus. It was the Savior. It was the one who promised rest. Overcome by awe, Brindabon sank to his knees. Right there he bowed his head and prayed to Jesus for the first time, asking Him to forgive his sins and save his soul.

When Brindabon opened his eyes, everything had changed. He stood up amid the crowd of Christians, his face wet with tears but his eyes shining with joy. He opened his arms to heaven and praised Jesus's name. He had found the answer. Peace was flooding his heart until it overflowed. Jesus was everything, and nothing else mattered.

Brindabon was baptized and began serving Jesus in answer to His call to plant churches. He felt joy every day as he woke up to begin the Lord's work. And when he lay down at the end of each day, he had perfect peace—and *perfect rest*.

You're Finished

Sanjay grew up in a good Hindu family. He was taught about the many gods and learned to worship them from a young age. His family even took him to the great Ambhotiva Temple, dedicated to the god Shiva. When young Sanjay saw the large statue of Shiva, his heart swelled with awe. Sanjay wanted to serve Shiva. At that moment, he vowed to live in goodness to prove his devotion.

But as time went on, Sanjay fell in with a group of boys who introduced him to drinking. Sanjay became addicted to alcohol and started stealing to pay for it. His actions brought dishonor to his parents, who pleaded with him to stop, but Sanjay could not. The good opportunities for his life started to fall away. He couldn't keep a job, and his friends abandoned him. For when he was drunk, his pleasant personality turned dark, and he would have violent outbursts of anger.

At last Sanjay realized his addiction was ruining his life. Somehow, he had to quit drinking. But where could he find the power to stop?

Desperate for relief, Sanjay decided to make a pilgrimage to Shiva's temple. He started on the five mile trek, over rugged, rocky terrain. He went barefoot, and though his feet were cut and bruised by the rocks, he knew that every painful mark would serve as a sign of his devotion. At last he stumbled into the temple, falling to his knees before Shiva's statue. Tears stung his eyes. He felt hope for the first time in what seemed an age. Maybe his troubles were finally over.

Things did seem to improve after Sanjay's pilgrimage. He was even able to get a job at a tea plantation. But after a while, Sanjay's old habits returned. He stole money from a co-worker, and when the manager found out, he fired Sanjay. Sanjay was unable to face his parents. He had already brought shame upon them—how could he return home simply to disgrace them further? Instead Sanjay spent his earnings on whiskey. He soon felt the familiar haziness coming over him making his troubles seem to disappear. As his temper rose, he got involved in a vicious brawl. A man sneered at him, "You're finished, Sanjay."

The next thing Sanjay knew, he was trying to open his eyes. His head throbbed painfully, and his mouth was dry. As Sanjay looked around him, he saw unfamiliar land—the mountains close behind and a cliff at his right. How had he come here? Then his memory gradually returned, and Sanjay dropped his head into his hands. He had been drinking again. The guilt and the shame filled him until he felt like he was made of darkness. Sanjay sobbed until no more tears would come. At last he raised his head, and his eyes fell on the cliff lying just a few steps away. He got to his feet and walked to the edge.

Sanjay gazed down at the long drop, but he wasn't afraid. The man had been right—he was finished. Sanjay felt almost peaceful as he realized that it would all soon be over. He closed his eyes and let himself fall.

Sanjay awoke. His head was aching more painfully than he could have imagined, and his whole body felt brutally sore. He was lying on his back on a bed staring up at a white ceiling.

"How are you feeling?" a voice asked.

Sanjay managed to whisper a reply. "My head hurts."

The doctor, who had spoken, came and stood over Sanjay's bed. "You have severe head injuries, and bruises all over your body, but no broken bones. It's a miracle you survived—you fell 160 feet. But now, rest."

Sanjay slept.

When he opened his eyes again, a man had come to see him. He was friendly and very kind. He told Sanjay that everyone was saying he had been saved by a miracle.

Sanjay suddenly felt hope. "Was it Shiva who saved me?"

"No, Sanjay." The man smiled gently, his voice compassionate. "Jesus saved you."

The name was unfamiliar, but sweet to Sanjay's ears. "Who is Jesus?"

"He is your Savior," the man said. "Would you like to meet him?"

Sanjay hesitated. He had asked for help from Shiva countless times, and the god had never rescued him. This miracle that had saved his life must have come from a different source. "Yes," Sanjay said. "I would."

The man prayed for him, and returned to visit Sanjay many times. One day he brought Sanjay a book –the New Testament.

Sanjay spent his days in the hospital reading the book and praying to Jesus. He asked for help with his addiction. When Sanjay was released from the hospital, his battle to stop drinking continued. But this time, Jesus was with him. Because of His help, Sanjay was able to over-come the addiction, and he knew then that his dependence on alcohol was over for good. He would never go back to drink; he would now turn to his Savior. Sanjay gave his heart and life completely to Jesus.

His relationship with Jesus strengthened and his compassion for others grew as well. He began telling the story of his salvation to his people, and how they too could have freedom. Sanjay still serves Jesus today, planting churches in the mountain villages of his homeland so that more and more people can know the salvation story.

The Evil Spirit

His legs were weak. The dust of the road choked him as he breathed unevenly, stumbling over the rocks and dirt. Every muscle in his body screamed for rest. Somehow he pressed on. He clutched the jug tightly in his hands knowing that if it spilled his whole journey would have been for nothing.

Surely he was almost there by now. But still the faint lump on the horizon didn't appear. He paused, bending over to rest his elbows on his knees. He hung his head and tried to catch his breath. Just a little farther....

How tempting the water in the jug had become. His throat was parched, and his tongue was sticking to his mouth—and the clear, pure water sloshed gently inside the jug. But it was holy water. To drink it would be a grievous wrong. He grasped the jug more securely and continued walking. Soon the long journey would be over. Soon he would have completed his duties.

Shantanu had walked over 70 miles. And each year, Shantanu took the holy water on this long walk to where the idols stood and poured it over them. He was completely devoted. So he should have been greatly blessed. But Shantanu was troubled by pains and evil presences, and no matter how many rituals he performed, he did not receive relief. Maybe this time it would be different.

Shantanu closed his eyes briefly as he saw the fuzzy shape of the idols on the horizon. It would not be long now.

When at last he stood before the Hindu idols, Shantanu carried out the ceremony with the utmost care and reverence. He trickled the holy water over the idols, watching as it glimmered wetly across the stone. He prayed softly for blessing and good fortune. Then the last droplet dripped from the jug. It was finished. He had done his part.

Shantanu returned home 70 more miles carrying the empty jug. Had anything changed? He still felt the piercing pain inside him. His head was still full of those terrible, horrifying images. His heart was still aching with depression. No. Nothing had changed. The evil spirit hadn't fled.

Lying exhausted in his house, his eyes were fixed wide-open—staring, seeing nothing—as pain stabbed through his abdomen. His limbs twitched violently. The air was seeping from his lungs; his chest burned. Darkness pressed behind his eyes, filling his vision, his mind, and his heart until he screamed in utter terror.

Shantanu came to his senses, gasping and shouting hysterically. He flailed his arms desperately as if trying to fight off an invisible enemy. Slowly he realized that the fit had passed. He was still lying on the floor, drenched in sweat, his pulse sounding like a drum in his ears. He covered his face with his hands. Why had the gods not helped him? He had worshipped them faithfully, done everything that was required, and they let him suffer like this? Tears slipped between his fingers. *Why?* Why should he worship gods who brought him such pain and hopelessness?

As the days passed, Shantanu faced constant agony and lingering doubt. What was the answer? How could he be free?

It was at that same time that a Christian named Raja came to Shantanu's village. He spoke about Jesus and his free gift of salvation. When Shantanu saw Raja preaching in the village, he ignored him. Christians were to be hated. They proclaimed falsehoods. But, he had heard of the miraculous healings that had occurred through this—Jesus. There were many stories, many wondrous stories. The prayers of the Christians seemed to be powerful indeed.

No. Shantanu shook his head angrily. He was from a family of priests. He was a devout Hindu, proud of his religion and loyal to his gods. This Christian teaching was foolishness. And yet, Shantanu realized that he couldn't take any pride in his idols. What of his many prayers had ever been answered? He had done everything right—with nothing to show. But then these Christians…. Disgusted with himself, Shantanu forced the thoughts from his mind and turned to head home. Raja's voice seemed to follow him as he left.

Shantanu opened the door of his house and collapsed over the threshold as blinding pain shot through his entire body. He lay with his fingernails digging into the floor, a ragged scream tearing from his throat.

Twilight had fallen. Shantanu staggered from his house, pale and weak. He glanced around the village with panic-stricken eyes, and then broke into a run. His chest was heaving, the evening air icy on his damp skin. He barely knew where he was going. He ran through the streets, asking directions of the passers-by, until at last he stood before a small building. He hesitated briefly, and then pounded on the door.

Raja opened up to him. "Can I help you?"

Shantanu couldn't speak. He gasped, clutching at his chest, sweat dripping down his face. Raja gently guided him inside, looking concerned. A few other Christians were in the house.

They quickly looked up as Shantanu stumbled into the room leaning on Raja's arm.

The Christians gathered around Shantanu leading him to a chair. "Are you alright?" one asked him.

Shantanu took a breath, shaking his head. "I, I need your prayer—" He cried out and clutched the chair arm, a spasm of pain stiffening his body. The Christians laid their hands on him and immediately began to pray. Shantanu closed his eyes, moaning softly through his lips. He felt fear and anger and sorrow building inside him, wanting to explode and overtake him. The Christians prayed intensely asking the power of Jesus to drive out the evil presence from Shantanu.

As they spoke the name of Jesus, Shantanu gave a cry of pure agony and slumped back in his chair. He breathed, quickly at first, and then more slowly. He glanced up at the Christians, awe in his haunted eyes. "I'm free," he whispered. "I'm—free." Sobs shook his shoulders. Raja and the Christians knelt beside him speaking compassionately to him.

After his sobs subsided, they shared the Gospel with him. Shantanu listened. He had felt the power of Jesus move in him. As the Christians told him the message of salvation, Shantanu recognized the truth. Shantanu was freed that night, from the evil spirit inside him, and from the sin in his heart.

Shantanu received a new life. He no longer worshiped idols; instead he searched eagerly after Jesus. He learned as much as he could, reading the Bible, worshipping with other believers, and growing in his faith. Soon he was sharing the way of salvation with other Hindus, who, just like him, needed a Savior.

Did
You
Know...

You can play a vital role in bringing the Gospel to the end of the earth through the power of prayer.

Subscribe to receive weekly prayer requests and praises that Big Life receives from its partners around the world.

To subscribe go to: www.blm.org/prayer

A Gift for his Son

Bishal huddled in the doorway staring out at the living room anxiously. His father wasn't back yet.

Bishal's father went out at night often nowadays. He drank a lot and smoked. Bishal didn't know anymore if it was a good thing when his father came home. He didn't act like himself, and he always stank of alcohol and tobacco.

Bishal slid down to sit on his bedroom floor, leaning his head against the doorframe. He was tired, but he couldn't get to sleep. He had frequent nightmares about evil spirits and monsters. Maybe it was from watching his grandmother perform her rituals. Bishal rubbed his eyes. He was still young, but he knew that his family wasn't alright. Everyone was stressed and weary. Sometimes his father even shouted at his mother when he had too much to drink. When he did, Bishal would hide under his covers trying to block out the noise. The anger in his father's voice made him flinch.

He didn't think his family had much money either. His mother talked about it in a quiet voice when she thought Bishal couldn't hear. Didn't she know that her whispers worried him more than if she told him the truth?

Bishal's legs were starting to go to sleep. He slowly got to his feet feeling cold prickles tingling through his limbs. *Would his father ever come back?* Bishal worried about that more and more these days. His father never seemed happy to be home. Maybe he liked it better in the dark streets and taverns. *What was it like out there when all the good people had gone inside and to bed? Did his father ever get scared by the night?* And then a horrible thought hit him. *Did he even want his father to come back?*

The front door opened. Bishal jumped involuntarily and took a step towards bed. Then he paused and quietly moved toward the door peeking out into the living room. It was his father. He entered the house quietly, almost soberly. He didn't seem to have the same crazed look that he wore when the poison was in his veins. Had he not been out drinking? If so, where had he been? Bishal quietly closed the door and pressed his cheek to the doorframe to listen.

His father stopped on the threshold with his head down. Bishal's mother walked towards him. She had steeled herself for rage, but now she extended her hands compassionately.

His father spoke before she reached him. "I'm sorry—for everything I have done to you."

His mother stopped as if she had been frozen. She stared at his father, and Bishal re-opened the door and peeked to see a watery glint in her eyes. "Madan..."

His father took her hands. "I will stop drinking and smoking, and I will be the man that you need me to be. I'm," his voice trailed off, and he began to cry. Bishal stared, watching each shining tear like it was a precious diamond. His father was crying.

"I'm so, so sorry," his father whispered, "for failing you all this time."

His mother began to sob. She fell into her husband's arms. His father stroked her hair, tenderly, gently. His face was kind. Bishal felt a sudden wetness on his face, and he sniffed, wiping the tears away. He pulled back from the door and crept to his bed. There was a faint hope in his heart, soft and glowing. It warmed him all the way down to his cold toes.

His father didn't go out again. He took up his responsibilities and helped his wife manage the house and the money. He spoke kindly to everyone. Bishal's mother couldn't believe the change that had come over him. "What happened?" she asked him. "That night when you changed."

He smiled at her, and then at Bishal. "I made a very important decision. I decided to trust Jesus as my Savior."

Bishal's mother looked at him, with something like fear in her eyes. "You—are a Christian?"

Bishal's father clasped her hand. "I am a follower of Jesus. And he teaches me to love everyone, to care for my family, to be faithful to my wife and an example to my children." Bishal's mother was silent, but there was a tiny trace of a smile in the corner of her mouth.

Bishal's father began to talk about Jesus a lot. He brought home a Bible, and read from it to the family. They gathered together and listened whenever he opened the book. Bishal felt drawn by some sort of irresistible curiosity. *What had changed his father from the angry, troubled man that he had been into someone with a heart full of love and kindness?* His family had never been so peaceful or so happy. Bishal could even spend time with his father without being afraid. Bishal caught himself smiling contentedly as his father, his voice passionate and eager, read a passage from the Bible. *Who was Jesus?* Bishal wondered. *Someone who could change hearts and lives, Someone who taught to love, and Someone who brought fathers back to their children.*

Bishal's father shared the story of his salvation with the family. He told them how he had realized that he was a sinner and had done terrible things worthy of death. "But," he continued, "Jesus died in my place. He rose again, and defeated death forever. He is the only way to eternal life. He will save us from our wrongdoing if we believe and trust in him." He fell silent for a moment. He gazed into the air, like he was remembering how beautiful that promise had been when he first heard it and still was now. Then he took a breath. "I decided to follow Jesus. He forgave me of all my sins and gave me new life. Now I will live eternally in heaven with him."

He leaned forward. He was looking at Bishal, and then at his wife. "I don't want to spend that eternity without you," he said softly.

Bishal remembered it so well. He remembered what the floor had felt like beneath his knees when he knelt to pray, how his hands had been shaking with emotion, how his voice had faltered as he asked Jesus to save him. He remembered how his heart had instantly begun to beat faster, like it had new life pumped into it. He could still feel the tears on his skin and his father's hand on his shoulder. The love in his soul was never ending, more powerful than anything he had ever felt. The whole family was saved.

Together, Bishal's family began actively doing the Lord's work. Bishal's father became a church-planter with Big Life. After Bishal received training, he also started a ministry as a church planter. Now they both are working to reach more and more people with the Gospel. Bishal always remembered how his father's life had changed his own. He had given his son the greatest gift of all—the knowledge of Jesus. Bishal would never forget it.

The Man on the White Horse

When Sadeq was born, he did not breathe for twenty-two minutes. His family mourned him as though he were dead. But then his chest started to rise and fall, and he began to cry. This was the first time that Jesus saved Sadeq's life.

When Sadeq was three, he was found lying, unconscious, on the floor of his house. He had drunk a bottle of oil. His father carried him to the home of his employer—a Christian. As a Muslim, Sadeq's father believed that while Christians cannot enter heaven, Allah will give them whatever they pray for on earth. So he asked his employer to pray over Sadeq. He did. Sadeq recovered a few days later, and everyone said his healing was a miracle. His father, though immensely grateful for his son's life, refused to believe that Jesus had healed him.

Then when Sadeq was seven, he became very ill. He was taken to the hospital, where he lay in a fever for several weeks. In desperation, Sadeq's father again came to a Christian, a pastor, to beg prayer over his son. While the pastor was praying for Sadeq, the little boy had a dream. He dreamed that a man on a white horse offered him water and lamb's meat, saying that if Sadeq ate and drank, he would be healed and live forever. Sadeq ate and drank, and then the dream faded. As it did, Sadeq's fever broke. He was healed. But still Sadeq's family didn't believe that the healing had come from Jesus. On Sadeq's eighth birthday, they had him begin studying the Quran.

When Sadeq was ten, he and his brother went to fetch firewood. As Sadeq was pushing a big wheelbarrow along the railroad tracks, his brother suddenly shouted that a train was coming. Sadeq tried to move the wheelbarrow off the track, but it was too heavy. He panicked. The train was coming down upon him, and he had no time left to throw himself off the tracks. In the brief spilt-second before the train reached him, Sadeq looked to his right. He saw the man on the white horse standing beside the tracks watching over him. Then the train filled his vision with a deafening roar.

Sadeq awoke by the railroad in his father's arms. His father was crying over him. The entire village heard about the miraculous survival, and Sadeq's father gave praise to Allah.

At age thirteen, Sadeq fell sick once more. He dreamed of the man and his white horse. The man carried Sadeq up to a high mountain, where he showed him the villages lying below. "You will bring healing to all these hearts," the man said, "in the same way that I have healed you, and will do so again."

As Sadeq grew up, he continued to study Islam. He got a job with an employer who was a Christian, and one day Sadeq got into an argument with him. Sadeq asked how Jesus could be the Son of God. In reply, his boss gave him a copy of the New Testament.

"It is not a sin to read it," his boss said.

Sadeq read. When he came to Matthew he read a verse that told people to love their enemies. Sadeq was disturbed. Muslims were taught that it was good to bring trouble to your enemies. Then Sadeq read in Luke, where it stated that Jesus was the Son of God. In a burst of anger, Sadeq threw the New Testament to the ground.

That night, Sadeq had a dream about a man at a gate. When Sadeq walked up to the gate, the man looked at him and shook his head. "I do not know you," he said. "I cannot let you in." Sadeq awoke in the morning, shaken, and told his boss about the dream.

"That is the teaching of Jesus," his boss said.

Sadeq picked up the New Testament again and continued reading. The words began to speak to him in a powerful way, especially John 14:6: "I am the way, the truth and the life." When Sadeq read that, he knew that Jesus was the Son of God. Only Jesus could offer forgiveness. Only Jesus could be the way to heaven. Sadeq gave his heart to Him.

Sadeq began attending prayer meetings with his boss, where he was soon baptized. Afterwards, he returned home to share his salvation with his father. His father wept, for he had known that the miracles in Sadeq's childhood were from Jesus—he had just refused to believe it. But Sadeq's mother overheard them talking. She was very upset, and she threw Sadeq out of the house.

Sadeq left with tears in his eyes. Though he hurt deeply, he did not give up on his family. One day when his parents were away, he came back to his house. He was able to show "The Jesus Film" to his brother and sister and see them come to salvation in Jesus. Sadeq also shared the gospel in his uncle's village. He passed out New Testaments and converted the New Testament into a CD for those who couldn't read, but who still wanted to know about Jesus.

Then Sadeq remembered his dream, when Jesus had shown him the villages and said that Sadeq would bring them healing. Immediately, Sadeq devoted his whole life to serving Jesus and fulfilling His purpose for him.

In time, Sadeq approached Big Life to ask if they would accept him as a church planter. They asked him, "Why do you want to serve Jesus?"

"Because He saved my life," Sadeq replied firmly.

Sadeq now works with Big Life, bringing Jesus's word and love to the Pashtun nation.

The Carpenter

Sergeant Razzaq hated the police station. It was run-down, hot, and stuffy. The windows didn't open, and the doors didn't stay closed. But no one would come to fix up the station. "Useless," Razzaq muttered darkly, as he raised his cup of tea to his lips, "this whole place."

There was a knock at the door. It was the religious teacher of Razzaq's village, the Maulvi, holding something under his arm.

Razzaq put on his best glower as the Maulvi entered the building. Razzaq despised the man.

The Maulvi came straight to the point. He, too, clearly didn't want to speak to Razzaq for longer than was necessary. "Two Christian infidels have been discovered with these." He tossed the items which he had been carrying onto Razzaq's desk.

Razzaq examined them: a New Testament and a DVD labeled "The Jesus Film". Razzq shrugged. "So? It is not a crime to own Christian materials."

The Mualvi's face reddened slightly. "There have been complaints," he said in a forcibly calm voice. "These two Christians have been distributing their materials, and trying to convert others to their faith. I want you to find them and arrest them, immediately."

Razzaq purposely waited before replying, watching the Maulvi's eyebrow beginning to twitch. He loved it when he could make that happen. "I will look into it," he said finally.

"Good," the Maulvi snapped. He turned and swept out of the office. Razzaq slumped into his chair and picked up the tea cup. He would go after these Christians when he had finished his tea—and not a moment sooner.

Javid looked outside his window as he heard a car door slam. An unfamiliar van was parked outside, and a police officer was walking across the yard towards the house.

Calmly, Javid opened the door. "Please, come in," he said.

The officer entered the house and looked keenly at Javid. "You have been accused of trying to convert Muslims to your faith," the officer said gruffly. "Is this true?"

Javid held the officer's gaze, but did not reply.

"And your partner...where is he?"

"I have no partner," Javid said evenly.

But the officer had pushed his way farther into the house, and now he threw open a bedroom door. "You," the officer shouted to the boy who was sitting inside. "Outside, now!"

Javid felt panic grip him. "No, please, he has done nothing—" The policeman growled at him to be quiet and shoved both him and the boy out of the house and into the van. The boy looked up at Javid with terrified eyes as the vehicle rolled away.

Javid's mind was racing. What could he do? He had known that something like this might happen, as he was indeed distributing Christian materials, along with his partner. But that partner was not the boy sitting beside him, like the policeman seemed to think. The boy was Javid's nephew, Nawaz, a recent convert to Christianity—and completely innocent of any crime.

He and his partner had vowed to keep their secrets at all costs, but what was he to do now that Nawaz was involved? Javid did the only thing he could. He began praying, desperately: "Let the boy go free. Please, let him go."

Razzaq wasn't pleased. That boy, he was so young! The Maulvi would not hesitate to sentence him with the same punishment as any other man. And with a crime like this—the verdict could be death.

But if Javid confessed, there was a possibility that Razzaq could let the boy go. The Maulvi was coming to the station in a few days to check on Razzaq's progress. Maybe Razzaq could have the boy gone before he arrived.

Razzaq began to smile. What he wouldn't do to cause the Maulvi some trouble.

Javid and Namaz were placed in a cell in the old police station. There Razzaq asked Javid about his ministry, about what they were doing and where they were doing it. Javid refused to answer.

Razzaq began to beat Javid, over and over, continuing to ask him questions, but Javid said nothing in reply. Only when Razzaq stepped back and let Javid slump to the floor did he speak.

"Please," he said, raising his hand toward Razzaq in pleading. "Please let Namaz go. He has done nothing."

Razzaq left the cell.

He came back again and again, asking Javid more questions. When Javid didn't answer, Razzaq beat him. Javid was covered in blood and bruises, and still he said nothing except to beg for Namaz's release.

Razzaq found himself feeling a grudging respect for Javid. Despite the pain, the man refused to bend. But the Maulvi would be returning any day now. If Javid would just renounce his beliefs.

Razzaq shook his head angrily. "That stubborn, foolish man." But he could see much of

Javid's determined nature in himself. Maybe that was what made him reach his decision at last.

Razzaq came into the cell, just as he had for several days now. Javid braced himself for more questioning, and more blows.

But Razzaq stayed at the doorway. He was silent for a moment, and then he barked. "You! Boy. Get outside—there is a van waiting to take you home."

Javid couldn't believe his ears. He got to his feet and pulled his nephew into an embrace. "Thank God," Javid whispered. "Go home, Namaz. And don't stop praying for me."

With tears in his eyes, Namaz left the cell, looking back at his uncle. Javid nodded firmly to him. Then Razzaq slammed the door.

Razzaq could get nothing out of Javid. When the Mualvi arrived, Javid would be in his hands. Since Razzaq didn't like the Mualvi, he felt a desire, stronger than ever now, to keep Javid away from him. But Javid would not confess, so what could Razzaq do?

"What do you do for a living?" Razzaq asked suddenly. He was sitting in Javid's cell.

Javid looked up at him lopsidedly, one of his eyes swollen shut. "I'm a carpenter."

Razzaq glanced at the cell door, barely hanging on its hinges. A sly gleam entered his eye as he thought of the sticking windows. And of the Maulvi, whom he loathed.

"Tell you what, carpenter," Razzaq said. "If you repair this station, I will let you go."

Javid's one working eye widened. "Sir?"

"Come back tomorrow to start work. If you don't show up you'll land yourself right back in this cell." Razzaq threw open the cell door. "Go."

As Javid slowly exited the cell, Razzaq thought about what he had just done. It would anger the Maulvi, definitely. But Razzaq felt he was doing the right thing by letting Javid go free. Razzaq grinned. And it would be fun to see how much the Maulvi's eyebrow was going to twitch.

Javid's heart was light as he stepped out of the police station. He was free, as was Namaz—and now Javid had several weeks' worth of time to spend with this Razzaq. There would be time, as he worked on the station, to share the salvation story. Razzaq was a stubborn man, Javid could see, but he knew that some time—sometime soon—Razzaq would see the truth.

Books in the Backseat

Ahmed lived in a refugee camp. He was a driver for one of the officers there, taking him to his various destinations. Ahmed's boss was very special to him. He was always kind and greeted Ahmed with a smile whenever he climbed into the passenger seat. When Ahmed's boss attended meetings, he would bring newspapers for Ahmed to read while Ahmed waited for him to return.

Ahmed had finished the last line of print in the latest newspaper when a pile of books, stuffed in the backseat of his boss's car, caught his eye. He read the first cover, and an awful feeling of horror crept into him. They were Christian books, teaching blasphemy. Ahmed sat back in the driver's seat sickened.

When his boss climbed back into the car, Ahmed took a deep breath. "Sir...you need to get rid of your books. They cannot be read." His hands shook a little on the steering wheel. He hated confronting this man he respected so much; he hated what he had found out about him.

"Ahmed..." his boss said, in his calm, kind voice. "These books are not blasphemous. Let me explain." He began to speak about the Quran, its teachings, and how they compared to the words of the New Testament. He spoke about Jesus, and Ahmed became confused. His boss's words made sense to him, and they were very logical, but completely different from what he had learned. Suddenly, Ahmed had to know more.

He opened the book, the New Testament, and began to read. At first he was hesitant, even fearful. But as he read, he became captured by the words of Isa, Jesus. This man was so much more than the simple prophet of whom the Quran spoke. He was powerful, loving...he was God's Son. Ahmed read the book every day in his boss's car.

Meanwhile, Ahmed's marriage was arranged with the daughter of a mighty warrior, whose family had gained much honor in battle. The couple lived in a small room adjoined to Ahmed's family's house. There, Ahmed hid a copy of the New Testament, so it would be close to him at all times.

Living with a Muslim family, his life at home was strikingly different from the days he spent in the car with his Christian boss. Ahmed began waking in the morning with a sense of excitement knowing that he would soon be talking with his boss about Jesus and the New Testament. Ahmed drank in every word he heard. He was starting to recognize Jesus's love in his boss's words and actions.

One day, Ahmed's boss introduced him to a foreign pastor, who was ministering in the refugee camps. They spoke together about Jesus. As they talked, Ahmed realized that he had come to accept Jesus as Lord—as *his* Lord. He knew that he was a sinner, as the New Testament taught, and he believed that Jesus was the only one who could save him. Ahmed broke down, sobbing, as the immense power of Jesus's love swept over him. The pastor prayed with him, and Ahmed was baptized. As he returned home that day, his heart was lighter than he could have ever thought possible. Jesus had saved him. But that meant that...he was now a Christian, not a Muslim. What would happen if his family found out?

But the only thing his family noticed was the pleasant change that had come over Ahmed. He was more patient now, and he spoke lovingly to every member of his family. They didn't know what had happened to him, but Ahmed did. He could feel the Holy Spirit inside him making him more like Jesus.

Then his wife found the book hidden in their room—the New Testament. At first Ahmed didn't understand why his family was waiting for him out front when he returned home after work. Worried, Ahmed climbed out of his car.

His father strode up to him, shaking with rage. "What is this? Have you been reading this?" He shook the New Testament in Ahmed's face. Ahmed's family crowded around him, angry and anxious, shouting questions at him until their collective noise drowned out any words.

"Stop!" Ahmed cried. "Yes, it's true." His family quieted, staring at him with shocked faces. "I am a Christian."

For a moment everything was still. Then his father struck Ahmed to the ground. The rest of his family fell upon Ahmed kicking and beating him. His mother and sister hung back pleading with the men to stop. Ahmed curled in a ball as blows rained down on him from every direction, pain erupting across his body. He couldn't shield himself—his attackers were too many. They were his family, and they were killing him.

Then a sudden peace washed over him and Ahmed's body relaxed. He murmured softly through his bleeding lips, "My Jesus, I'm coming to you." He closed his eyes and was gone.

Ahmed awoke on his bedroom floor, wrapped in a haze of pain. The door was locked trapping him inside. He knew that he would soon be killed for becoming a Christian. Then, slowly, the door creaked open. Ahmed steeled himself for what would come.

But it was his sister, alone, and tears were streaming down her cheeks. She ran to her brother and knelt beside him. "Please," she sobbed. "Go! Now, before they come." He embraced his sister and struggled to his feet, managing to rush painfully through the door and out of the house.

Hours later, Ahmed collapsed at his boss's house in the city. His boss took Ahmed in and treated his wounds. Then, he took him to the home of some Christian friends, who hid Ahmed from the men now searching for him. Ahmed escaped to Afghanistan, where he spent the next seven years away from his family.

Then one day, he met his cousin in the city. After a tearful reunion, he gave Ahmed the news that his family was now living in Afghanistan, all except for his father, who had died in battle. Ahmed went to see his little sister, now grown and married. She wept into his shoulder as he hugged her and thanked her for what she had done for him all those years ago.

Ahmed now knew where his wife was living. Though he longed to see her, he was afraid of how she would respond. But when he visited her house at last, she flung her arms around him with cries of joy. "I'm so sorry," she gasped through her tears. "What happened to you was all my fault." She touched his face and looked deep into his eyes, which were now swimming with tears. "I've missed you so much," she whispered.

Ahmed's wife said that she would come and live with him; Ahmed's brother, sister, and her husband moved in with them as well. Ahmed was dizzy with happiness. God had given his family back to him, and in time, all of them came to salvation in Jesus. Ahmed began working with Big Life Ministries to spread the gospel to his countrymen, and both he and his wife started fellowships of their own ministering to the new believers in Afghanistan.

Kicked Out by his Father

Prem loved to learn. He had an ear for music, and played the guitar well. At school he was a brilliant student, and even on his own he was constantly reading and thinking. He had so many questions about everything in his world.

Prem's family worshiped over thirty different gods. Prem's logical mind could not understand this. He did see the evidence of an all-powerful God at work—but only one, true God. Prem set himself to discover who this God was. He learned about many different religions and talked with dozens of religious leaders but to no avail. He then read every book he could find on belief systems and their gods, but still nothing satisfied his search. Where was the true God whom Prem was looking for?

He arranged a meeting with yet another religious leader, a Christian pastor. Wearily, Prem told the pastor about his search, and asked if he knew anything about the one true God.

The pastor smiled. "I know exactly who you are looking for. His name is Jesus."

Prem looked up, his heartbeat quickening. *Jesus*. Something about that name touched him deep inside his heart. He knew at once that he had come to the end of his search.

The pastor gave him a Bible and Prem began reading. The words of Jesus captivated him. Jesus had come to save the lost and the sinners. "It is not the healthy who need a doctor," Prem read, "but the sick, for I have not come to call the righteous, but sinners." Prem read that line through several times. One of the Hindu gods had said the exact opposite—that he had come to kill all sinners and only save the one who was righteous.

A huge weight lifted from his shoulders. Jesus had come to save sinners like himself, to give them eternal life, and to not destroy them. Jesus was the truth. Jesus was his answer. Prem asked Jesus to save him that day. He wept with joy and relief as he felt the power and love of God sweep over him, and from that moment, his life belonged to Jesus.

"Father! Mother!" Prem burst into the house. "I must tell you something."

His family looked up, confused.

"I have become a Christian," Prem said earnestly.

For a long moment no one said anything. His father's face grew hard, his eyes stony.

Prem felt the smile fading from his face. He should have known. He had left Hinduism for another religion. His family would not be happy for him.

"Prem!" His sister said, shocked. "Christians are low caste!"

His father took a step towards him. His voice was low, threatening. "No Christians are permitted in my house."

Prem stood his ground. He was only seventeen, but he knew the Hindu belief system better than any of his family. "Show me where it is written that Christians are low caste," Prem said.

His father did not answer him. He seized Prem by the arm and dragged him to the door. Prem staggered as his father shoved him forcefully through the doorway. His father's brow was furrowed in anger. "You are not welcome here anymore," he said. He shut the door with a bang. Prem was stunned. For a long moment he stood there looking at the closed door. Then he slowly turned and walked away through the dust, leaving his home behind. From the moment he left, a day did not pass when Prem didn't think of his family or pray for their salvation.

He found a place to live, with Christian friends, and worked at any job he could find. He no longer had his family's income to support his education, but Prem couldn't bear the thought of giving up his schooling. So during the day he worked and earned enough money to attend night school. It was a lonely life.

After four years of praying for his family, Prem's father contacted him for the very first time. He said he wanted Prem to come home. Prem was scared. Why did his father suddenly want to see him? He had forbidden Prem from returning after forcing him out of the house. What would happen to Prem if he went back? Prem asked one of his Christian friends, who was from a high caste, to make the trip with him—he gladly agreed to come along and support Prem.

When they arrived at the house, Prem's father showed them in without a word. The whole family was gathered. Prem's parents sat together. His father glanced at his mother, and then took a deep breath. "We want to ask you about your God," he said.

For a moment, Prem couldn't say anything. He could barely process what he had just heard. Then, his voice shaking, he replied, "What would you like to know?"

His family asked Prem lots of questions. Prem was trembling the whole time, begging God for courage and the ability to answer wisely. Finally, when the talking had died down, Prem pulled out his guitar and began to play. They were simple songs about Jesus's love. Prem's soothing, steady voice and the melodious notes of the guitar filled the air with sweet song. Quietly, Prem's friend walked over to his parents, kneeling beside them. He took their hands, clasped them over each other, and began to pray. Both of Prem's parents started to cry.

As Prem sang and his friend prayed, his father and mother were saved. Prem was overcome with happiness. He had his family back, and he could finally share the joy of knowing Jesus with them.

Prem's thirst for knowledge had not ceased. He wanted to learn as much as he could about Jesus and his Word. He attended Grace Bible Church, where he received a degree in theology. Prem served the Lord in a variety of capacities as an evangelist with the local church, later as a youth pastor, and then as a teacher at the Discipleship Training School in South India. After four years of teaching, Prem came back to his home town and started a church there.

Then Prem met someone named Benjamin Francis. They became fast friends, and soon Benjamin was telling Prem about his vision of reaching the villages for Christ.

"I hope to see a church in every village," Benjamin said earnestly. He told Prem how this was being accomplished through a ministry called Big Life. Prem was amazed. He could tell that God was working in a powerful way through Benjamin and his team.

Sometime later, Benjamin came to see Prem. He brought a man from Big Life in the United States. Together, the two men asked Prem to join Big Life's ministry.

Prem was astonished, and a little nervous. This was a big decision to make. "Should I leave behind my church?" he asked anxiously.

"Maybe God is calling you to be the pastor of hundreds of churches, not just one." Benjamin smiled at him.

Prem realized that this was the path God wanted him to take. He prayed for courage and for the ability to see his life through God's eyes.

Today, Prem still travels from village to village fulfilling that vision.

Our Way of Life has not Changed,
but our Lord Has

Tharoath was a good person. He devoted his life to doing thoughtful and kind works for others. He thought that if he did enough noble deeds he would earn a place in heaven. Every morning, Tharoath would try to think of something nice he could do that day. It did make him happy to help others, but there was always a sense of urgency behind his actions. He never knew when his life might end, and what if he hadn't done enough?

Tharoath's whole family was Buddhist. They believed as Tharoath did. Always they would stop to help someone in need or go out of their way to do a kindness. But Tharoath's mother and sister felt something missing from this daily routine. Their actions felt empty, unfulfilled. What was the true purpose of doing these good things?

They found their answer in Jesus. Suddenly, it all made sense. They were to live their lives as witnesses for Jesus, doing for others as Jesus had done for them. The good deeds were to point others to his saving grace—grace was the *only* thing that could get them to heaven.

Tharoath's mother and sister excitedly went home to share what they had discovered. "Tharoath!" They cried happily. "Jesus has saved us! We have become Christians."

Tharoath couldn't believe it. How could they turn away from the religion they had followed all their lives, forsaking their god and their way of life?

"No," they tried to explain. "Our way of life has not changed. But our Lord has. We will do things just as we did before, but now for His glory, to spread His love."

But Tharoath refused to listen. He was angry. He continued to follow a devout Buddhist lifestyle, trying to save up enough good works...and then he would see his mother or his sister smiling and laughing with someone, pure joy shining in their eyes. They looked so content. Tharoath longed for that happiness in his own life. He was doing everything right, but he felt lonely and lost. Could it be that there was more to it than simply "doing right"? Could it be that this Jesus was the answer?

Angrily, Tharoath shook the thoughts away. No. He would follow Buddhism, and he would not abandon it.

Then one morning Tharoath rose to get out of bed—and immediately fell back on his pillow. His body was weak and trembling; he knew at once that he was terribly ill. Tharoath prayed to Buddha for relief, but none came. The healers could do nothing. Tharoath was scared. What if he didn't make it through the sickness? And what if he couldn't get into heaven?

Who could help him?

As he lay in bed, drifting between death and life, he thought about his sister. His mother. That perfect peace on their faces—who could have given it to them?

Jesus.

Tharoath's eyelids flickered. "Jesus..." he whispered. He sensed the power in that single name as it passed his dry, cracked lips. Jesus had saved his mother and sister. Jesus could save him.

"Please, Jesus, redeem my life," Tharoath prayed, "and I will live it for you."

Jesus answered; Tharoath was healed. Immediately Tharoath understood what his mother and sister had tried to tell him. Jesus *was* the reason. Tharoath realized that good works were not what saved a person, but they were a result of salvation. This love and joy welling up inside him was too great to hold in. It had to be shared.

Tharoath no longer feared death. He knew that his eternity was secure with Jesus. Now all that mattered to him was serving his Lord in any way he could.

A Person of Peace

Big Life missionaries travel to many different countries all over the world, sharing the gospel and starting churches in response to God's calling. At every place the missionaries go, they always search for a "Person of Peace". This is someone from that country, who has been filled with the Holy Spirit and has been called to help Big Life in their ministry. If, during their initial trips to the country, the missionaries are unable to find a Person of Peace, they understand that they are not supposed to begin work in that place at that time. Luke 10:5-6 describes the person they seek: "When you enter a house, first say, 'Peace be to this house.' If someone who promotes peace is there, your peace will rest on them; if not, it will return to you."

Jeff and Forrest, Big Life missionaries, were flying to Bhutan. A missionary in Singapore had contacted Big Life, saying that he felt strongly about beginning work in the neighboring country of Cambodia. The Big Life director of South Asia, Benjamin Francis, prayed about this, and was able to make contact with Doris Chan—of the Methodist Missionary Society in Cambodia—who said she was interested in learning more about Big Life. It looked like a promising start, and now Jeff and Forrest were on their way to meet up with Benjamin in Bhutan. Then they would all continue on to Cambodia.

Doris Chan was happy to meet them—but very surprised. She had no idea that they were coming! The emails about their arrival had somehow been lost. Without any preparation, the best she could do for Jeff, Forrest, and Benjamin was to find them a room at the Missionary Society's Bible school and hire a van that could drive them around the country.

The three missionaries' high spirits became more subdued. If this was how the trip began, what would happen in the days ahead? Was this really the right thing to do? On a wall in the Bible college, they found a map of Cambodia. For a long time, Jeff, Forrest, and Benjamin prayed over the different villages and cities, asking for God's will to be done.

In the next two days, the three got to see a lot of the city. The van driver, Santik, was friendly and eager to help. He told them about the country, and took them to many churches and other Christian gatherings. Jeff and Forrest were excited about these Christians, but they were anxious. Where was the Person of Peace? God had always provided a Person of Peace at every place where Big Life now ministered.

On the second day of driving, the missionaries discovered that Santik was running a church gathering in his home.

"You have a house church?" asked Forrest excitedly.

Santik smiled. "Yes. We meet tonight, if you would like to join us."

All three of the missionaries looked at each other, astonishment and excitement mixed on their faces. Had the Person of Peace been right in front of them all this time?

They attended Santik's house church that evening. It was a wonderful time; the Cambodian Christians were filled with the Holy Spirit as they worshipped and fellowshipped together. Jeff noticed one young man near the back, sitting quietly. He looked to be still in his teens.

When Jeff awoke the next morning, he remembered that today was their last day in Cambodia. Over breakfast, the three missionaries began to talk about Santik.

"Do you think he is the Person of Peace?" asked Jeff.

"No," said Benjamin unexpectedly.

Forrest looked at Benjamin. "How can you be sure? He pastors a church, and he's eager to minister—"

"No," Benjamin said again. "Don't ask me how I know. But it isn't him."

Suddenly a call came to Benjamin's cellphone. He answered—it was Doris Chan. When he hung up, his face looked puzzled. "She just had a phone call from someone who says he met us yesterday. He wants to meet us at the mall in two hours." He paused, looking at his companions. "He said it was urgent."

When they arrived at the mall, Jeff immediately recognized the person waiting for them. It was the quiet young man who had been at back of the church the night before. What could he want to talk to them about so badly?

Benjamin led the young man over to a café table, where they immediately became absorbed in conversation. The discussion seemed so intense that Jeff and Forrest left them together and sat down at a different table. For almost an hour they waited, occasionally glancing at Benjamin and the young man. The Cambodian's countenance was so youthful, that Jeff couldn't shake the feeling of him being only eighteen or nineteen.

At last Benjamin walked up to the table where Jeff and Forrest sat. He was smiling with perfect contentment. "We have found our Person of Peace," he said simply.

Jeff nearly choked on his coffee. "Him? But surely not—he's so young!"

Benjamin shook his head. "He's twenty-eight, married and has a little girl. His name is Taraoth. For many months now God has been calling him to witness to the villages, and last night—when he met us—the call was more powerful than ever before. He is filled with the Holy Spirit. He is our Person of Peace."

As Jeff and Forrest met and spoke with Taraoth, they felt a deep assurance. This was the man whom God had chosen. The four shared a time of prayer, strengthening and encouraging each other. When it was time for Jeff, Forrest, and Benjamin to leave, their hearts were filled with joy. God had answered their prayers, and ministry would begin in Cambodia.

As of today, Taraoth has been used by God to start 175 home churches with 1,300 people in all. Tharoath and his team have even begun to move across the border of their home country and deeper into more areas that need to know about Jesus.

The License

Deiu Sanh was awakened in the pitch-blackness by his wife's moans. She was struck with a fit of seizures, and numbness began to creep over her body. Deiu Sanh rushed his wife, Han, to the Buddhist priests. Though they prayed and chanted over her, the paralysis continued to spread. Deiu Sanh was devastated.

Then a group of Christians came to the village offering prayer for anyone who needed it. They asked to pray over Deiu Sanh's wife. He didn't know anything about their religion, but he allowed them to come to Han's bedside. The Christians began to pray, speaking strange words about Jesus's love and his saving blood, thanking Him for his healing. Then, three days later, Han recovered.

Filled with joy and amazement, Deiu Sanh and Han searched for the people who had prayed with them. The Christians spoke with them and told the two about the good news of God's Son, Jesus, who had come down to earth to die for the sins of all people. Deiu Sanh and Han were moved deeply by this story of love.

Deiu Sanh and Han came to Jesus soon afterwards and immediately began studying the New Testament. Deiu Sanh longed to share this amazing joy he had received, but in his home region of Hanoi, people didn't want to hear about Jesus. Nonetheless, Deiu Sanh began to preach, standing in the middle of the village and speaking passionately to those who passed by about the salvation Jesus offered. The crowds thought he was crazy. But as they heard him speak tirelessly day after day, a few people began to listen. Deiu Sanh's excitement and zeal was contagious. Now he attracted a small audience, and some among them started to ask questions. He was able to share with them the story of Han's healing.

One night Deiu Sanh lay awake in his bed, considering the possibility of starting a gathering in his home. A sharp knock at the door startled him.

Two police officers stood in the shadow of the doorway, their expressions serious. "We've heard that you have been preaching in the market," they said. "It has to stop."

Deiu Sanh was anxious, and confused. "Why? There is no law against practicing religion..."

"You are stirring up the public and causing trouble," an officer said sharply. "It must stop."

When they had gone, Deiu Sanh sank to his knees and began to pray feeling his heart grow heavy inside him.

Deiu Sanh didn't stop preaching. He went to his regular spot in the market and started to speak to the people. A crowd accumulated around him, and he saw many of the upturned faces watching him eagerly. Then a commotion at the back of the audience disrupted the scene. A black car was pushing through the people; it pulled right up next to Deiu Sanh. He spoke more quickly, trying to keep the people's attention, and still continued to talk even as officers grabbed his arms and dragged him into the car.

Deiu Sanh was put into jail. They told him he could be released right away if he promised to renounce his "false religion." But he would not. After a week in his cell, the police let him go home to his family.

Deiu Sanh talked and prayed with Han, and they both agreed that he could not stay silent. Deiu Sanh went back to the village, found a place in a different part of the market, and preached. Two weeks passed, and then the police came for him. He spent a month in prison this time before being released. Neither time had he been charged—there was no real crime in his behavior—he had only been warned to keep silent. But this he could not do.

Deiu Sanh went to the people whom he had seen listening to his preaching. He asked if they wanted to hear more. Enough people responded for him to start a church that met in his home, and the number of attendees steadily increased.

Several months passed, but eventually the police got wind of Deiu Sanh's activities. He was arrested again.

Over thirteen years Deiu Sanh was in and out of prison for refusing to stop preaching. It was hard on his family, and Deiu Sanh longed to be with them. But he was asked to deny his Savior, and he could never bring himself to do that. His family, though they missed him sorely during his imprisonments, stood by him and supported him.

The police tried to stop Deiu Sanh by throwing him in jail, but Deiu Sanh soon discovered that it was there that his preaching had the most effect. He was able to speak regularly to his fellow inmates, and many of them were saved. When they left prison, they left as children of the King, eager to tell others about their salvation.

As those long years went by, the government began to soften. Some religious groups were given permission to freely share their faith.

Meanwhile, Deiu Sanh was in the middle of his most recent sentence. He sat in his bare, gray cell, praying, when he heard someone come to his door.

"The warden wants to see you," said the guard.

Deiu Sanh was filled with worry as the guard led him to the warden's office. Did they have some new, worse punishment for him?

The warden didn't look angry when Deiu Sanh walked in. Instead he motioned for Deiu Sanh to sit, and he peered keenly at him from behind his desk. "You have been a prisoner here a long time."

Deiu Sanh nodded, not sure where the conversation was going.

"Tell me," said the warden, leaning forward. "If you were to be released, would you continue to preach your Christian faith?"

Deiu Sanh steeled himself. He yearned for his freedom and his family. Desperately, he asked God for strength. "Yes, I would," he said heavily. His whole body drooped with exhaustion and despair.

The warden gave a quick nod and passed a piece of paper across to Deiu Sanh. "Then you are free to do so. Here is your license."

Deiu Sanh couldn't breathe. "What...you mean...I can preach in Hanoi?"

The warden smiled faintly at him. "You can preach anywhere in Vietnam."

When Deiu Sanh emerged from prison for the last time, he was completely overwhelmed. Freedom smelled sweet in the air, and he could feel God's power at work. The whole country was now open for him to share the gospel. He only had to decide where to begin.

Deiu Sanh wanted to bring the salvation story to the villages of Vietnam. As he worked and preached, he met a missionary who told him about a man who was also striving to reach Vietnamese with the Gospel. This man was Taraoth, and he worked with Big Life Ministries. Deiu Sanh and Taraoth got in touch, and soon one of the Big Life directors came to see Deiu Sanh. As all three talked, they recognized God's will in Deiu Sanh being Big Life's "Person of Peace." During the next year, God's used Deiu Sanh to start sixty churches in Vietnam.

A Tiger for Jesus

Francis. It was a strange name for a Muslim. He was an older man, with a long white beard, and clothed in traditional dress. He stood silently beside his nephew, Munshi. Francis's eyes were steady and his gaze firm, as he surveyed the man Munshi had just introduced. They greeted each other, and Francis's handshake was as unyielding as the rest of him.

Aaron nodded to Francis with a smile. "Welcome, friend."

Francis merely bowed his head in return and said nothing. Aaron motioned for Munshi and Francis to come join the small circle of men inside the schoolroom. Francis took his seat beside Munshi with a powerful grace that reminded Aaron of some sort of beast of prey.

"Today," Aaron said to the twenty men seated around him, "this course will come to a close. I have taught you how to share your Christian faith with people whom you may not know, strangers. But the true test of your witness will come when you return to your friends and family, to people whom you know and love." Aaron looked at their faces. These men would risk danger and even death bearing the gospel to their villages. "Now, let us complete the final lesson."

Aaron taught them what to do when a person expressed interest in Christ and wanted to learn more. Francis sat in stoic silence, listening, his eyes intense. Suddenly he turned sharply to Munshi and whispered something to him.

Aaron was in the middle of a sentence when Munshi's hand shot up in the air. Aaron halted, rather amused, and called for him to speak. Munshi's voice was thick with suppressed excitement. "Uncle Francis says that what you say is truth."

After the lesson was completed, Aaron saw Munshi and Francis approaching him. Francis held his hands behind his back watching with cat-like eyes. Though his English was broken, Francis spoke very clearly. "You, baptize me," he said.

Aaron wasn't sure he had heard correctly. "You want me…"

Francis took a step towards Aaron, aggressive in his stance. "You say baptism to follow salvation, soon as possible. Baptize me."

In a jolt of amazement, Aaron realized, Francis had been saved that day—during the class, without any outburst or outward show. But the fierce light in Francis's eyes left Aaron with no doubt that Francis's salvation had been as powerful to him as any miracle.

Aaron slowly nodded his head. "You are—correct. Absolutely right." Francis raised his chin a fraction higher.

Munshi was sent off to buy a plastic kiddie pool—the quickest, cheapest thing that would hold water—and Francis was baptized.

From that moment, Francis would settle for nothing less than being on the front lines of Jesus's army, serving Him in any and every way possible. His manner of attack was simple. "Do you want to hear about Jesus?" he asked of everyone he met. "Let me tell you about Jesus."

A year later, Francis invited Aaron to a very special occasion: the baptism of seventeen of his family members. The baptism was to be held in an open, public place, where everyone could see. Aaron was happy to attend, but he was worried. How would the Muslims react to a Christian ceremony?

The baptism continued for a full hour. Francis wept as he baptized his family, and Aaron remembered the day he had baptized Francis in the little plastic pool. Now Francis was boldly following the same ceremony.

Afterwards, Aaron went to meet Francis. "Baptizing for an hour in front of this audience?" Aaron shook his head, looking wonderingly into Francis's set face and steady eyes. "My friend… are you never afraid?"

Francis bowed his head slightly, and his eyes seemed to glow as he gazed at Aaron. "If you for Jesus," he said in his thickly accented voice, "you must be tiger for Jesus."

Francis continued to spread the gospel of Jesus, gaining friends and followers as well as enemies and persecution. A year after the baptisms, Francis led a seminar much like the one Aaron had run. After a day of teaching, he and two companions waited at the bus stop. A van pulled up, and men whom Francis did not know climbed out. They surrounded the three friends and forced them into the van. A sack was pulled over Francis's head, enveloping him in stuffy blackness.

Hours later the sack was removed, and Francis gratefully sucked in fresh, cool air. A man stood before him. He was angry. "You are causing a disturbance in the cities with your teachings. You must stop."

Francis looked at him keenly, calmly. "Let me tell you about Jesus."

The next morning, Francis and his two friends were found on the outskirts of the city. They were whole and well.

Aaron rushed to see Francis when he heard about the kidnapping. "Did they hurt you?"

"No, hardly at all." Francis smiled his rare smile. "But they did learn a thing or two about Jesus."

Aaron found himself looking on Francis with the now familiar feeling of awe. After a moment he said, "Francis, perhaps you should let the dust settle before you continue your work."

Francis leaned forward, his eyes like steel. "Aaron, I am old. In days I have left, I do something that matters, not just in this life, but eternity. I make difference."

Two years later Francis passed peacefully into glory. He had been a Christian for four years, and in that short time he had personally brought over a hundred people to Christ.

Did You Know...

The book *God's Bottom Line* (that changed John Heerema's entire life) has a study guide for small groups?

The questions in this study guide help you think through what God is doing on a global scale and challenge you to act on His promise to Abraham to redeem people from every tongue, tribe, people and nation.

Discover your global role in His global plan by using this study guide as you read *God's Bottom Line*.

Find out more about the book at: UnveilinGLORY's bookstore: www.UnveilinGLORY.com/ bookstore

A Different Boss

Dilbar strained with the heavy cart he was pulling behind him. It was piled high with bags of grain and corn. The air was cold, and the tips of Dilbar's ears were going numb. Gritting his teeth he walked onwards.

A customer had purchased the bags at a wholesale store, and now Dilbar was hauling them to the truck stop. At the customer's vehicle, he lifted the heavy bags into the car, received his fee, and then took the empty cart back to the store to wait for another customer. The payment was small, but it was enough. He would send it back to his family's farm.

Dilbar pulled up outside the store and set his cart down with a bump, heaving a sigh. His breath made clouds of puffy steam in the air. How he disliked physical labor.

At that instant, the door of the store opened, and Yusef, the owner, stuck his head out.

"Dilbar!" He said with a smile. "We've no more customers. Come inside for a bit. My son has a pot of tea ready."

Dilbar nodded gratefully and followed Yusef into the store. They had struck up a fond friendship during the time that Dilbar had been working as a cart-puller. Dilbar had a great liking and respect for the patient, friendly store-owner, and he always looked forward to days when he would get this invitation to sit with Yusef and his son.

Inside the shop, Dilbar held his hands close to the fire, sighing in pleasure as the icy chill gradually faded from his fingertips.

Yusef's son poured him a cup of tea, which Dilbar accepted with a smile. He always seemed to smile more when he was with Yusef and his son. He wasn't sure why, but it was nice. They made him feel warm inside in a way that was quite different from the hot tea.

"Dilbar," Yusef said. "You are very courteous, and you work hard. What would you say to working for me in the shop?"

Dilbar's eyes widened. "Work—work for you? In the shop?"

"Yes. You could stay upstairs in the spare room, and take your meals with us. What do you say?"

Dilbar was dizzy with happiness. No more pulling carts and lifting heavy loads. No more working outside in the elements. "Sir…" he said breathlessly. "It would be an honor to work for you."

Yusef smiled. "Then you start tomorrow."

Dilbar got a young boy to take over his cart, and he moved into the shop with Yusef and his son. Instead of lifting huge bags of grain, Dilbar greeted customers and made tea and swept the floor. And Dilbar was making twice the amount of money to send home to his family. His father wrote him a letter, saying how proud he was of him. Everything was going well. Dilbar sat down behind the shop counter, breathing in the smell of the fire and of the boiling tea with a contented smile.

Every morning, Dilbar saw Yusef and his son talking together behind the counter. They were bent over something, and one day Dilbar saw that it was a book. Instantly, everything clicked. That was why Yusef and his son were so kind, so caring. They were devoutly religious. They read the Quran every morning. Dilbar found his respect for Yusef deepening.

On the store's off day, Dilbar would sit up in his room relaxing. One afternoon, he saw mounds of papers littering the desk in the corner of his room. Yusef often came up here to work when he had to stay late. He must have done so the night before. Dilbar shook his head, smiling wryly at his boss' untidiness. He would clean up for him.

Dilbar set about organizing the papers. He pulled open a drawer, about to place a sheaf of papers inside, when a pile of books at the bottom caught his eye. Frowning, he pulled one out and looked at the cover. He stared at it in shock. It was a New Testament! The book was strictly forbidden. Dilbar hurriedly dug through the rest of the books. They were all Christian. How could it be? Yusef was kind, thoughtful, loving—how could he be reading such things?

The next morning, as always, Dilbar saw Yusef and his son reading behind the counter. From the corner of his eye, Dilbar peered at the cover. Yes, it was a New Testament. He felt sick. They weren't reading the Quran everyday; they were reading corrupted, Christian books!

At last Dilbar couldn't stand it any longer. "Sir," he said to Yusef. "Why are you reading Christian books?"

Yusef didn't speak for a moment. Then finally he sighed and looked down. "Come with me, Dilbar. We need to talk."

He took Dilbar out of the store, leading him to a small restaurant a short distance away. As they walked, Dilbar felt nervous and awkward. He had always been so close to Yusef. But now—well, Yusef was doing wrong. He should be reported. But how could he betray the man who had done so much for him? Yusef would lose everything, maybe even his life. Dilbar could not do that to him.

Yusef got them a table in the corner away from the crowd.

As they sat down, Dilbar said quickly, "Sir, I mean you no harm. If you want me to leave the shop…"

"No, Dilbar," Yusef said quietly. "I want you to listen."

Yusef began to talk about Jesus. He explained to Dilbar that the New Testament is not corrupted, but truth. Yusef said that Jesus had been sent to the earth to save sinners. This was nothing like what Dilbar had been taught. But it fascinated him. He forgot about the conflict in the morning. All he wanted was to hear more.

Over the following days, Yusef talked long and often with Dilbar. Dilbar read the New Testament searching for answers. Yusef answered Dilbar's eager questions and helped him understand difficult passages. Dilbar realized that what Yusef said, what the New Testament said, was truth. But how could he accept this, since he was a Muslim?

Then one day, a friend came to visit Yusef. A Christian named Musa. Musa, Yusef, and Dilbar discussed everything Dilbar wanted to know. After hours of talking, Dilbar finally reached his decision.

"How do I become saved?" he asked, his throat constricting with tears.

"Believe that Isa died to save you from your sins, and that he rose again," Musa said. "If you repent from your sins, and ask Isa to be your Savior, He will."

"I must do so," Dilbar whispered.

Dilbar was saved that day, and Yusef baptized him. Dilbar kept his job in the shop, working for Yusef with a heart that was even happier than before. Over time, as the years passed, Dilbar started his own shop with the money he had saved. His cousin came to work with him, and as a result of Dilbar's witness, he too was saved. With help from Musa, Dilbar began a Christian fellowship, which he leads to this day—and whose numbers are continuing to grow.

He Tore Their Family Apart

"I'm divorcing you," he hissed.

Uong froze. "No...please. What will we do? How will we live?" Her pleas didn't move him. He just looked at her with such bitter hatred in his eyes that Uong began to tremble.

"I don't know, and I don't care," he said viciously. He turned his back on her. "I don't care about any of you anymore."

She was...angry. It didn't matter that life had been a living nightmare before her husband left. All she remembered were the days that had followed—the days of poverty, loneliness, and anger. Her husband had gone to the arms of another woman, probably someone without children to feed, someone who was younger, prettier perhaps. Uong was left alone. Her children didn't understand what had happened, or why their father had been so cruel to them. Fathers were supposed to love and support their families, not tear them apart.

Her husband had made a lot of money. He had a good job...their family could have been successful, prosperous, rich. But that wealth hadn't gone to his children or his wife, and happiness had never found its way into their home.

But now that he was remarried—oh yes, now his new wife got it all. She had his love, she had his care, and she had his money. Everything that he had withheld from Uong went to her. It made her so, so angry. To see her children poor and forsaken...how could he have done this, not just to her, but to them? Did he really hate his family that much?

Uong tried to be strong, for her children. She held in her bitterness and the stress that weighed heavily on her. But keeping her emotions hidden only made them grow stronger—like trying to trap steam in a pot. Sooner or later it will boil over, or the vessel will crack.

Eventually Uong was exhausted and worried. She couldn't sleep at night. The anger ate at her from the inside making her short-tempered and tense. Soon it was too much for her to bear, and her health began to fail. But there was no money for a doctor. In fact, there was no money for anything.

Uong tried to fight back her swelling emotions, but finally they broke free. She collapsed onto her bed, sobbing desperately. She was alone, she was tired, and she was *scared*. She had tried to keep her children comfortable and happy, but she simply couldn't do it on her own.

A little hand slipped into hers. Uong looked up, hurriedly wiping the tears from her face, and saw her son standing beside the bed. He smiled gently at her. "It's okay, Mommy," he said comfortingly. "Everything will be all right. You don't have to cry."

She gazed into his big, deep eyes, feeling her own fill with tears. "Thank you," she whispered, leaning over to kiss his head. He squeezed her hand and smiled at her one more time. Then he skipped out of the room and down the hall. Uong watched him go, her heart heavy. "Keep believing, son," she said quietly, "because I have given up hope."

There was nothing to do.

A faint knock came from outside. Uong heard feet running to the door, and then the sound of its hinges swinging open. "Mommy!" Uong heard her son call. "There's people here. They want to see you."

Uong got to her feet, smoothing down her clothes. Even the simple movements caused her head to ache, and her limbs felt weak. She rubbed the last moisture from her face and stepped out of her room. It was time to put on a front again. Pretend everything was alright.

Three friendly faces met her at the door. "Hello," one of them said. "We are traveling through the village, and wondered if you would like to hear about Jesus."

Uong exchanged glances with her children. "Okay," she said. "You can come in."

She sat down with a soft sigh of relief. The Christians seated themselves opposite her and began to share. Her children were on the floor at her feet, listening eagerly.

"Jesus is the Son of God," one of the Christians began. "He is our Savior. We are all sinners and cannot enter heaven. We can never earn a pardon for our sins, or live a perfect life. The penalty for sin is death, so we are all condemned. But God loved us so much that he sent his Son, Jesus, to earth. Jesus died in our place, paying the price for our sins. He rose from the grave three days later and conquered death once and for all. Now Jesus offers us the gift of salvation that can only come through His sacrifice. When people believe that Jesus died for their sins, and asks Him to save their soul, they will have eternal life. They are saved forever. God will always be with them."

Uong listened silently. Tears were dripping down her cheeks and she didn't know how they had gotten there. The message of hope made her heart ache.

"Are you alright?" one of the Christians asked quietly.

Uong was motionless, her hands clasped in her lap. Then she shook her head. "No," she said slowly. The words felt heavy in her mouth, like they didn't want to be said. "No, I'm not alright." Suddenly she could breathe a little easier.

Uong shared everything that had happened to her. She told them about her anger, her worries, and now her physical weakness. They listened to everything she said, with the deepest compassion.   When she was finished they asked if they could pray for her. Uong agreed, bowing her head as they knelt around her.

They suggested that Uong attend a fellowship, where she could learn more about Jesus. After one visit, Uong began coming to the Christian services regularly. The Christians there prayed for Uong's condition constantly. Uong was moved by the love she felt there, almost like a tangible force in the room. There was something powerful working through these Christians.

The knowledge of His love and power completely overtook her. As she rested in that love, her sickness left. Uong gave her life to Jesus.

Now Uong's home is no longer a place of strife and anger. There is forgiveness and joy! A fellowship of a dozen believers now packs in there weekly, and fills it with praise and worship to Jesus Christ. Uong's life has been changed completely, from hatred, bitterness, and despair to love, joy, and purpose.

Their Idols were Powerless

Asta and his family were good, respectable people. They were devoutly religious and worshipped many gods. And yet still they had troubles. Asta wondered constantly why his religious practices didn't seem to have any effect on his life. What was the purpose? But where could peace be found if not in the gods? These doubts and questions plagued Asta. He felt lost and confused.

"Asta." His mother called him quietly.

Asta lifted his head and walked into the next room. He frowned in puzzlement as he saw his mother standing alone, her face grave. "What is it, mother?"

His mother took a step towards him, taking his hands in hers. "We must..." she paused and looked down, squeezing her son's hands.

"Mother?" Asta said gently.

She raised her head. "We must offer a sacrifice," she said huskily, "for your father."

Asta stepped back. "So it is true then," he said tonelessly.

She nodded, blinking away her tears. "Yesterday. They said he has a disease of the mind."

Asta stood there, still, silent. He swallowed, and then nodded slowly. "Then, we must perform the rituals."

His mother choked back a sob and covered her face with her hands. Asta took her in his arms, stroking her hair as she wept into his shoulder. He stared at the blank wall behind them.

Was that all they could do? Perform ceremonies and hope that the gods would hear them? Asta glanced down at his mother, crumpled and broken. It was his father's mind and life that they would pray for. It seemed too precious a request to entrust to gods who didn't care.

The whole family participated in the rites. They sacrificed and prayed for the healing of their father and husband. All of them pleaded with the idols desperately.

Except one. She was Asta's sister. And she was a Christian. She gathered with the rest of the family, but she didn't participate in any of the ceremonies. Instead, she talked about Jesus. "Please, these idols cannot help us," she said. "We must pray to Jesus. He can heal Father, and He will."

The family didn't listen to her. They still loved her, but they refused to have anything to do with her religion. It was not Hindu, and so it was false. They continued to pray to the idols.

But Asta's father did not recover. He became worse. Asta's mother was on her knees for most of the day, bowing before the gods. "Please!" she wept. "Save him." She bent her head to her knees, muffling her sobs. Her husband was deteriorating rapidly. Was there anything else she could do? She had completed every ceremony, recited every prayer, but the gods did nothing. She couldn't lose her husband, she couldn't, she couldn't. Asta came up behind her, touching her on the shoulder. "She is here," he said.

Asta's mother took a deep breath and nodded. Asta's sister visited often. She came and sat with her father, watching his face with tears shining in her eyes. Then she talked with her mother and comforted the other family members. She was a source of hope and strength to them all. Asta's mother went out to greet her, and they sat down together.

"He is getting worse." Asta's mother spoke in a low voice. "I've tried everything, I—" she broke off, biting her lip.

"Mother, please," Asta's sister said softly. There was a note of desperation in her voice. "Jesus is the only one who can heal. We must pray to Him."

"No!" Asta's mother began to cry. "This family is Hindu, even if you have forsaken your religion for another. The gods—they will provide." But she had hesitated, and Asta saw the doubt in her eyes.

Asta had begun listening closely when his sister talked about Jesus. The way she spoke of Him, she had such joy, such absolute faith. She had never stopped sharing about Jesus. Asta could see that she believed with all her heart that Jesus could save her father. Why? What power did Jesus have?

But then again, what power did the idols have? It had been many days. There was no answer from the gods, and Asta's father had deteriorated even more. Asta's mother was pale with grief and worry and little sleep. The whole family was tense. They had done everything. They could do nothing more.

The whole family was sitting together, silently. They stared at the floor, at the ceiling, anywhere but at each other. They didn't want to see the sorrow in their eyes.

Asta's sister spoke, very quietly. "Would you mind if we all prayed to Jesus?"

No one said a word. They barely reacted to Asta's sister's request. She went over to sit by her mother. Her mother looked up, gazing at her daughter hopelessly. Asta's sister clasped her hands. "Please," she said. "You've tried everything else."

Her mother pressed her hand to her eyes as if trying to hold back the tears. She nodded. Her voice was barely audible as she whispered, "All right."

Asta's sister prayed over her father's bed, asking Jesus to heal his body. It wasn't a long prayer. But she prayed it earnestly with full certainty and passion. When she finished, she talked with her family about Jesus. She told them the story of His death and resurrection, and how He offers eternal life to sinners. This time, they all listened.

Asta's father made a quick, full recovery. No one could believe it. After so much time pleading with their idols, one simple prayer to Jesus had healed him. They asked Asta's sister to tell them more about Jesus. Asta must have asked the most questions. He had so many stored up from all the doubts he had experienced when no one had been able to dispel his confusion. His sister could answer them all.

Asta's whole family, devoted, religious Hindus, came to realize the truth: *their idols were powerless.* Jesus is the one true God, and the only One deserving of worship. They all accepted Jesus as their Savior. Asta became involved with Big Life Ministries, working to help the Gospel reach many of the villages in his home country.

Asta has found true purpose at last. He has clarity, hope, and joy. Jesus is the reason for everything. Asta now worships a God who loves him, cares for him, and always hears him when he prays. And above all, he serves a Savior who has ransomed his life from the grave and given him the promise of life eternal in heaven.

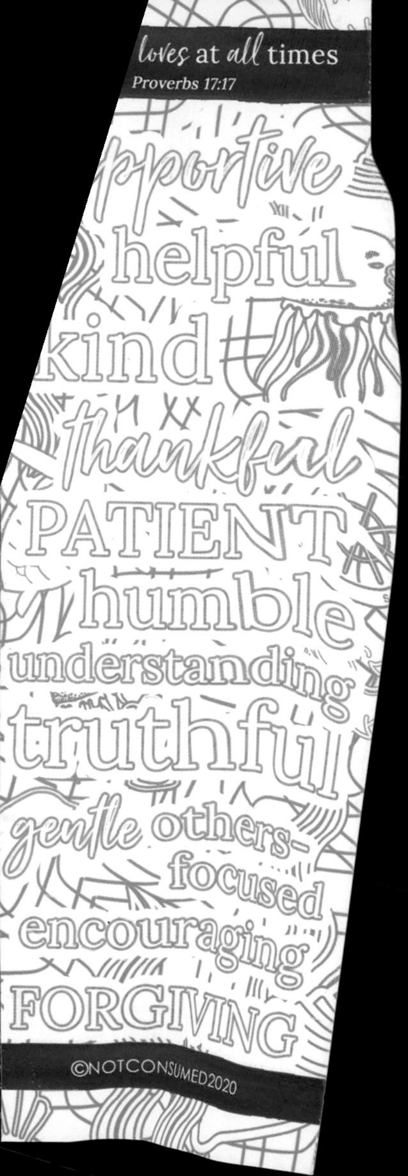

loves at all times
Proverbs 17:17
pportive
helpful
kind
thankful
PATIENT
humble
understanding
truthful
gentle
others-focused
encouraging
FORGIVING
©NOTCONSUMED2020

CAPTA...

FIRST MAT...

SECOND MATE

INNER CIRCLE

OUTER CIRCLE

THE *sweetness* OF A FRIEND COME
FROM HIS EARNEST COUNSEL.
PROVERBS 27:9b

Soul Mate

Dal left home when he was fourteen years old. There was work in India, and he was determined to make his life prosperous. It wasn't easy—sometimes it was very dull and lonely. But he managed to get a good job, and he labored tirelessly at it. There were also gloriously happy moments, like the day when he met the girl who would soon become his wife.

After five years in India, things had settled for Dal. He was no longer alone, and he had a respectable, steady place in his community. But then Dal became very ill. He could no longer do many of the things he had enjoyed before. No doctors or medications could help him. For seven years Dal endured great trial and suffering. He couldn't understand why this misfortune had come upon him. He was young, in the prime of his life, with so many plans that he hadn't yet fulfilled. Dal became frustrated, moody and bitter. He spoke sharply to his wife. She was often in tears, but she continued to be there for her husband.

As Dal watched her loving and patient attitude, he felt guilty. He was letting his miserable spirit turn him against the person he loved most dearly. He didn't want that to happen. Something had to change, and since there was no longer anything for him in India, Dal decided to return to Nepal and his family. There, Dal began thinking about deeper things. He had tried and failed to be prosperous and successful, so if he could no longer do that, what was his purpose? Why was he never satisfied? Deep within him there was a longing—for something, but Dal didn't know what.

"I found out something interesting today," Dal said casually.

His wife was busy nearby, but she looked up curiously as he spoke. "Oh? What was that?"

"My aunt is hosting a Christian fellowship in her home," Dal explained. "She was telling me about their worship services earlier. She invited me to attend sometime. She said they would pray for my healing."

His wife was silent. Dal didn't know if she was angry, shocked, or something else, her face was strangely pale. "Maybe you should go," she said quietly.

Dal nodded slowly. "I've been thinking about it all day, ever since my aunt talked with me. Do you think they could do anything for me?"

She came over and sat by him, grasping his hands in hers. "Dal." Her voice was firm, intense. Dal was surprised by her emotion. "You should talk with them. You might learn something."

Dal looked at her. He stroked her hair, and smiled. "Alright. Maybe I will."

He made up his mind the next week. When he told his aunt that he would be coming to the fellowship that night, she was thrilled. At her house, she introduced Dal to many Christian brothers and sisters, who all greeted him with smiles and friendly handshakes. Dal enjoyed himself immensely. He was moved by the people's passion as they worshipped and sang together, and the pastor's message aroused his thoughts. He only understood bits and pieces. But he wanted to learn more. After the fellowship, Dal approached the pastor and asked to meet with him later that week.

The pastor smiled kindly. "I would be happy to speak with you."

Three days later, Dal and the pastor sat down for what would be a long, intense discussion. "Jesus is the only way of salvation," the pastor said earnestly. "He died for our sins, in our place, so that whoever believes in Him will have eternal life." He leaned forward, looking Dal in the eye. "I know you have been suffering for many years with your sickness. Jesus healed people just like you, even those who were lame from birth. He is more powerful than you or I could ever imagine."

Dal's hands were shaking. "I—I believe," he stammered. "I believe in Jesus Christ." Tears spilled down his face, and he clasped his hands to pray. The pastor put his hand on his shoulder as Dal asked Jesus to be his Lord and Savior.

It was a few hours later when Dal returned home; anxiety was clutching his heart. What would his wife do when he told her he was a Christian? Would she leave him? It would be alright, whatever happened; he had Jesus. But he loved his wife, and he couldn't bear the thought of her rejecting him.

She was in the kitchen.

Dal approached her slowly, his heart pounding against his chest. "I—I need to tell you something." His throat was dry, and the words came with difficulty, reluctant to leave his lips.

His wife turned to him, her eyes questioning, wondering. Dal swallowed. "I have decided to follow Jesus," he said.

For a moment she didn't even move. It was like he hadn't said anything at all. But then she gasped, her hands going up to cover her mouth. Tears sprang to her eyes, and she was sobbing, her shoulders crumpled. Dal felt his heart breaking. He had lost her. He had lost her.

She raised her head, her face bright with shining tears, and Dal watched a smile spread across her face, with a look of pure joy and relief. "Dal," she said softly, "I am a Christian, too."

Dal stared at her, his mouth hanging open. "You? But, what—?"

"I've been a Christian. But I was afraid—if you knew—that you would reject me." She wiped her eyes, breathing out a shuddering sigh. "I hoped if you went to the fellowship and heard what I had heard, about Jesus and his love and power, that you would realize the truth." She looked up at him, now barely able to contain her smile. "And you did."

Dal couldn't say a word. She was smiling at him, and then she laughed, and he laughed, with breathless relief and absolute happiness. And he had her in his arms.

Dal and his wife began walking together in Christ. They prayed daily for Dal's healing, but also that their hearts would be open to whatever God's will was for them. After some time and much prayer, Dal began to recover. The illness that had been with him for so long, eventually vanished completely. Dal praised God for his grace and blessing, and his Christian brothers and sisters rejoiced with him.

But the rest of his immediate family couldn't accept Dal's salvation. They rejected him, as did the villagers in his neighborhood. They made life very difficult for Dal and his wife. Eventually they both decided that it would be best to move to another village. Once again Dal said good-bye to his parents and to everything he knew. Once again he packed his belongings and left for a different place, a different life.

He knew that the way ahead would be hard, but it was mapped out by his Lord in heaven. And he rejoiced to have the soul-mate God had created for him holding his hand. God had a plan for his life. And Dal would do his utmost to be open to God's will and to walk in the works He had laid out for him to do.

Divorce His Wife?

Karan took a deep breath. It was time. *Calm*, he told himself. *It's just another ceremony, just another ritual like all the others.* But he couldn't stop the anxiety knotting his stomach. What would it be like to constantly have to live with a girl? To be joined by marriage? To be the head of a family he needed to provide for?

He felt so young, even though sixteen was the customary age for marriage in the Hindu culture. Karan shook his head. It didn't matter what he thought, or if he didn't feel ready. His parents had chosen this girl to be his wife. He would marry her today, and he would watch over her as long as they were bound together.

Everything passed in a blur, and suddenly the ceremony was over. Karan was a married man.

His new wife seemed just as unsure as he was. She was very quiet, and her hand felt a little shaky on his arm. Karan felt a sudden surge of protectiveness. She belonged to him now, just as much as he belonged to her. He placed his hand over hers and squeezed it gently. "It'll be alright," he said gently. "I'll take care of you."

A small smile crossed her face. Karan could see that she appreciated his words of comfort. "Thank you," she said in a soft, steady voice.

Karan found himself warming quickly to her gentle grace and her firm assurance. He liked her. He liked her a lot.

It had been a few months. Karan was getting used to coming home to his wife and his new daily routine. His wife kept busy around the house, dutifully attending to her tasks, but always greeting Karan with a smile. It made Karan's heart glad when she glanced up at him. Yes, life was good. It was very good.

But one morning Karan's wife didn't get out of bed. She moaned in pain, her breathing shallow and raspy.

Karan knelt by her side. "What's wrong?" he asked anxiously.

She shook her head, barely able to speak. "I—I hurt all over," she gasped, "It's hard to breathe." Her chest rose and fell in weak spasms.

Karan pressed her hand. "I will get help. The doctors will heal you."

He called on many physicians. But none of them could do anything.

"I don't know the remedy for this disease," the latest doctor said simply. "I'm sorry, but I cannot help you."

Karan stared after him helplessly, and then glanced down at his wife. She forced a small smile. "It's alright, there is" she paused not knowing if she should say it, "there's nothing to do."

Karan tried everything. He sacrificed animals to the Hindu gods and sought the help of the priests. He even journeyed to another country in search of a cure. But there was nothing, anywhere. Karan felt powerless. It was his responsibility to protect his wife, this girl who had become so precious to him. He was failing her. But what else could he do?

Karan sat with one of his friends, silently sharing a drink. He gazed off into the distance, his thoughts, as ever, with his wife at home. Her mother was with her now. She had promised to tell him at once if there was any change.

"How is your wife?" his friend asked at last.

Karan played with his glass. "She is no better, no worse," he said at last. "I haven't found anyone who can treat her."

His friend sighed. "Sometimes it is better to let go of things which will hold us down. If she will not recover, maybe you should divorce her."

Karan started in shock. "What?"

His friend shrugged. "It would be for the best."

"But, could I just leave her to suffer alone?"

"It was merely friendly counsel," his friend said. "But I am not the only one who would advise you so."

Karan stared into his glass. Divorce his wife? Just because she had fallen ill? No, he could never do it. None-the-less, he tried to imagine. If she never got well, and spent the rest of her life confined to her bed, what would that mean for him? Would it be better to rid himself of her? Though Karan tried to see the reason in his friend's statements, everything within him rebelled against it. Even if she did live her life in sickness, he would be by her side. She would not be alone.

Karan was heading home when the man stopped him. "Tract, sir?" he asked.

"What about?" Karan asked absently.

"Jesus. The One who gives eternal life to everyone who believes."

Karan looked at this man oddly. "What? How could someone do such a thing? And why would he?"

The man offered the tract again. "Take this. And if you come to the fellowship tonight, I will answer all your questions."

"I can't," Karan backed away. "I have to stay with my wife. She is gravely ill."

The man bowed his head solemnly. "Then maybe you should bring her tonight, if she is strong enough. The Christians will gladly pray for her."

Karan hesitated for a moment. Then he nodded to the man and went on his way, the tract clutched in his hand. He had tried everything else. What could he lose?

Karan carried his wife into the fellowship that night. Her eyes were closed, and her pulse beat feebly against his chest. He gently laid her down, supporting her with his arm. They sat together and listened as the message of Jesus was proclaimed.

"He is God's Son," the pastor said. "He came to earth to die and pay the penalty for our sins, and He rose again from the grave. Without a Savior, we would be condemned to die. But Jesus has given us a way of freedom, and the promise of eternal life. All we must do is call upon Him to forgive our sins and be the Lord of our lives."

Karan was captivated. He felt that the words were being spoken directly to him. There was a Savior who loved him and who could save him. It seemed too wonderful to be true. He glanced over and saw his wife sitting up, watching the pastor preach. Her expression showed him that her heart was being moved in the same way. He reached out and took her hand. She turned towards him, tears shining in her eyes. "Jesus is the Savior, Karan. I believe it."

"So do I," Karan whispered. A lump rose in his throat as he spoke those words.

Together, with the Christians gathered around them, Karan and his wife asked Jesus to save them from their sins and take control of their lives.

All the Christians prayed for Karan's wife. Karan prayed to Jesus constantly, asking Him to heal her. In time, she did begin to recover, and slowly regained her full health. Karan couldn't contain his joy. He praised Jesus's name and His mighty power.

Karan and his wife gave up all their Hindu practices and devoted their lives instead to following Jesus. Karan was baptized. Afterwards, he became actively involved in sharing the Gospel with others. Through a man named Prem, Karan eventually began working with Big Life Ministries to take the good news of Jesus Christ to villages throughout the country.

Did You Know...

Boldly Whispering the Name of Jesus is a 30-day devotion that highlights the powerful testimonies of men and women around the world who have made incredible sacrifices and often face severe persecution to share Jesus.

Download the **free electronic version** at amazon.com

OR

Get a **free printed copy** by emailing: info@blm.org

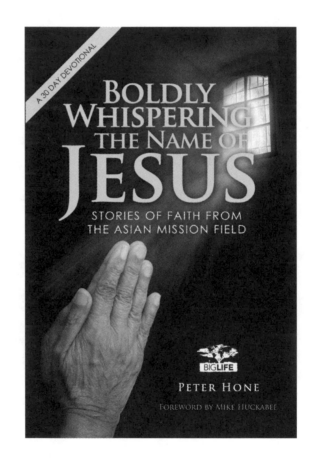

The Turning Baby

Farshad needed a job. His father had died suddenly, leaving the family to struggle for a living on their small farm. Farshad, now the man of the house, took up the responsibility of providing for them. He went to the city to find a job. Over the next few weeks, Farshad found several different work opportunities, but they never ended well. His bosses were either cruel or demanding, and Farshad stopped working for them.

Now he stood in the middle of the noisy, bustling city, without a job—again. His family was counting on him, and he was failing miserably. Farshad suddenly felt a tap on his arm. "Excuse me," said a young boy. "The owner wants to talk to you." He pointed at a shop across the road.

Curious, Farshad entered the shop. The owner, Younis, welcomed him. "Do you seek work? I have seen you at that spot by the road for several days now."

Farshad nodded eagerly. "Yes sir. I will work hard at whatever task you give me."

Younis regarded Farshad, his eyes gentle and kind. "You may start tomorrow, " Younis said. Then glanced at Farshad's dirty clothes and worn shoes. "When did you last eat?"

"Two days ago," said Farshad, his stomach starting to grumble.

Younis shook his head and led Farshad to a back room of the shop, where he fed him a good meal. The next day, Farshad came to the shop to begin his job.

Farshad worked hard, for he saw that Younis was a kind, honest man, and he wanted to please him. Younis had a very successful business, and was quite wealthy. But he was not greedy or arrogant. Instead, he was generous and filled with contentment and joy. Younis paid for Farshad's meals and a small place near the shop where he could stay.

The steady income Farshad received for his labor provided for the needs of his family. For three years Farshad worked for Younis, striving each day to do his job well so that he could re-pay in some small way the kindness Younis had shown him. Farshad now helped Younis manage the shop, and he held sacred the trust that Younis placed in him.

One thing was strange about Younis—throughout all this time, Farshad never once saw him go to mosque or talk about religion. Sometimes, when business was slow, Younis would seclude himself in a small room for a while. One day Farshad had to come for him, and he saw Younis inside reading a book.

"What are you reading?" Farshad asked lightly.

"It is the Gospel," Younis said slowly. "The Injil Sharif."

Farshad looked at Younis in fear. Younis would be in trouble if anyone found out what he was doing. Younis, however, did not seem afraid.

"This Gospel is not just for Christians," Younis said. "Jesus's salvation is for all men."

Though he tried to push it aside, Farshad felt powerful truth in those words.

During the next months, Farshad found himself lingering in that back room with Younis. There was something about his boss, a peace that he carried inside him, and Farshad wanted to know where it came from. Younis began teaching him many things from the Injil Sharif. Far-shad never spoke a word about Younis's activities, even though Younis had never asked him to keep it secret. Farshad loved and respected Younis far too much to turn him into the religious leaders—and the words of Injil Sharif were speaking to him in a strange way. Farshad asked Younis for a copy of the Injil Sharif to read, and as he did so, he found his Islamic faith being tested.

For four years now, Farshad had been providing for his family. They were so pleased with his efforts that Farshad's mother arranged his marriage with a girl he had known since they were children. The two were happily married, and four months later his wife announced that she was pregnant. Farshad and his family rejoiced.

One day, while Farshad was working at the shop, he got a call from his mother. His wife was in labor! Instantly, Younis told Farshad to stop work for the day and go to his wife.

When Farshad arrived home, he was met with worrisome news. His wife was in a great deal of pain. Farshad rushed her to the clinic where they did an ultrasound.

Soon the doctor came in and said, "You have a son. But he is lying in the wrong position." The doctor said that they needed to take Farshad's wife to the big hospital.

Farshad didn't know what to do. The hospital was far away, and his wife was hurting very much. And how could he pay for an ambulance? The doctor told him that he needed to decide quickly. Panicked, Farshad called Younis.

Younis rushed to the hospital. "We need to pray," he said when he walked in the door.

Farshad was confused, but he followed Younis to his wife's beside. Then Younis began to pray. It was like nothing Farshad had ever heard. Younis spoke to God as if he knew Him. He begged for God's almighty power to save Farshad's wife and son, in the name of His Son, Jesus. Suddenly, Farshad's wife cried out and lay quiet. Younis finished his prayer, and led Farshad from the room.

A few moments later, Farshad's mother came running. "She wants to speak with Farshad," his mother said. Farshad rushed to his wife. She was sitting up weakly in bed, and as Farshad came near she grabbed his hand fervently. "When that man prayed," she said. "I felt something turn the baby around." The doctors didn't believe it. Farshad asked them to take another ultrasound, and when it came in they were dumbstruck. The baby was in position to be born. Farshad knew that it was Jesus who had moved his son.

The baby boy was born without issue, and Farshad, his wife, and his whole family came to know the Lord. Suddenly, Farshad understood Younis' peace and fearlessness. He began sharing the gospel with customers at the shop and with the people in his village. Because of his witness, many came to salvation. Now Farshad's family hosts a fellowship in their home, continuing to grow in their faith in Jesus.

He Kept all the Rituals

Smoanh was raised in a traditional Buddhist family. As such, he grew up worshipping evil spirits and performing all kinds of religious rituals. However, even though he followed Buddhism devoutly, the rest of his life was a mess. Smoanh did many wrong things and never stopped to think about how his actions might affect his family. All he cared about was doing what he wanted. He drank a lot and went out at night, leaving his family alone and wondering where he was. When he finally came home, his wife would weep in distress. But her tears meant nothing to Smoanh. He ignored the fact that he was steadily destroying his relationships with his family and his friends. As long as he kept to the Buddhist rituals, he thought, he would have good fortune.

Then Smoanh became ill. It wasn't just a simple disease—he was very sick. His wife took care of him, trying to make him comfortable and ease his pain. Smoanh pushed away her kindnesses. He knew that as soon as he made the proper sacrifices, he would be healed.

"We must...perform the rituals..." he gasped, trying to sit up in bed. His wife pressed her lips together and nodded sharply. The family offered up sacrifices, praying for Smoanh's healing. Afterwards, Smoanh lay down to wait. But days dragged into weeks, and his health did not improve. Smoanh prayed constantly to the evil spirits, begging them to lift this illness from him. He made more offerings. Still he remained sick. Smoanh was shocked and confused. Didn't the beings he worshipped have power? Hadn't he been faithful? Why were they refusing to help him now?

But there was nothing more Smoanh could do. Months went by, and Smoanh began to give up all hope. The sickness clung to him. He was weak, thin, and weary. His wife faithfully attended to him, and Smoanh came to realize how much she loved him. It was a miracle that after all he had put her through, she still cared for him so deeply. He had lived a fruitless life and done many terrible things. He did not deserve the kindness she showed him. As his body failed, Smoanh felt his heart softening.

So when someone came to his village preaching about Jesus' love, Smoanh was ready to listen. This man, a Christian, spoke of the healing power of Jesus Christ and the salvation which He offers to all people. Smoanh found himself wanting to hear more. He had continued in the Buddhist rituals as he had been taught, but he lacked zeal. The ceremonies were just routine, without power or purpose. But this story about Jesus—it thrilled his nerves and set his spirit alight. There was something, something in that name.

A few days later, Smoanh gathered what little strength he had and left his bed to talk to the Christian. "I have a sickness," Smoanh began hesitantly. "I would like you to pray for me."

The Christian readily agreed. He asked Jesus to touch Smoanh's life and bring him not just healing but understanding and faith. "Only faith in Jesus will heal you," The Christian said to Smoanh. "You must believe." He shared the Gospel message with Smoanh, telling him about Jesus, God's son, who loved mankind so much that he had come to earth to die for their sins. Smoanh listened, tears starting to sting his eyes. He didn't deserve anyone's love. But Smoanh's wife had showed him unfailing kindness, even while he was doing so many bad deeds. And Jesus had loved him, Smoanh, a sinner—enough to give His life for him.

"There is nothing you must do, no ritual you must perform," the Christian said. "Only believe in Jesus and ask Him to save you."

This short conversation sparked a great desire in Smoanh's heart. He longed to find out more about this Jesus. Though very weak, Smoanh began attending a Christian fellowship. After hearing his story, the Christians there started to pray devotedly for Smoanh's salvation and his healing. At church, Smoanh studied the Bible, drinking in the knowledge of God and Jesus Christ. The more he learned, the more certain he became. He had found the truth. Jesus was the Son of the one true, all-powerful God, and He was the only way to eternal life.

Smoanh confessed his sins, and accepted Jesus as his Savior. At once his life was transformed. He turned away from all the bad things he had been doing and stopped worshipping evil spirits. Instead, Smoanh began living according to Jesus' teachings.

The prayers of the Christians were answered. With God's power, Smoanh recovered from his sickness. Now, he was desperate that his wife and family would come to know Jesus as well. He prayed ceaselessly for them and shared the Gospel whenever he could. His wife couldn't believe the change in him. Smoanh was kind, patient, honest. He had quit all his filthy habits, and when he spoke to her his voice was full of love. She laughed and cried with joy—overwhelmed by this incredible change in her husband. She had to know what had caused it.

Soon Smoanh's wife and the rest of his family were saved. Smoanh rejoiced that his prayers had been answered, and that he could now share his newfound hope and joy with the ones closest to him.

Smoanh devoted his life to serving Jesus. When he heard about Big Life's mission to plant churches, he was eager to help. He knew that Jesus had called his followers to take the Gospel into the world and make disciples in His name. It was Smoanh's desire to answer that call.

Come

Everything Dessaiah did seemed to go wrong. He would drink too much, become drunk, and then commit acts he regretted. It was an endless cycle, for when Dessaiah didn't drink, his body couldn't function. He was addicted. And the more he drank, the deeper his need became, and the greater his acts of violence.

Dessaiah became a trouble-maker in his village, and he did many awful things. Finally, drunk again, Dessaiah did something so foul that his village couldn't ignore it any longer. Full of rage, they dragged him into the middle of the village and beat him viciously.

When Dessaiah crawled back to his house, his body was a mass of ugly bruises. He slumped through the door and collapsed on the floor. This was all he was. A cowardly, quivering man, worthy to be beaten like a dog. Had he ever done anything in his life that he could be proud of? Dessaiah started to cry like a child, gripping his head. It was splitting with pain. No one would care if he was gone. In fact, the people of the village would probably be happy.

Maybe ending it all was the only thing he could do to somehow redeem his life. It would be better for everyone, including himself. He was stuck in a lifestyle of filth, lawlessness, and immorality. To continue in this way would destroy him eventually, slowly and painfully. But he could stop everything, right now, on his own terms. It was the only way to be free. Dessaiah sat crumpled in a ball, rocking and sobbing, all alone. He would do it.

Then a man named Phillip interrupted his plans. Phillip came to Dessaiah's village, preaching about Jesus Christ and his gift of salvation. Dessaiah listened silently. He huddled in the shadows where no one could see him staring in desperation at this man who spoke of hope and freedom.

Dessaiah walked up towards Phillip when everyone else had left. "Who, who is this Jesus?"

Phillip smiled. "He is the Savior of all mankind." Deep relief stirred in Dessaiah's heart. *A Savior.* Phillip looked concernedly at Dessaiah.

"What is your story, my friend? You look like you need hope."

Dessaiah nodded, and suddenly he was telling this man everything; about his addiction, about the terrible things he had done, about the beating, about the way every villager, young and old, looked at him in disgust. Weeping, he poured out his loneliness and the fact that he was planning to take his own life.

"No one can help me," Dessaiah said in a low voice. "No one wants to help me." Dessaiah swallowed, his voice barely a whisper. "And I don't blame them."

"You're wrong," Phillip said gently, putting a hand on Dessaiah's shoulder. "Jesus can help you. He can free us from any chains, and cleanse us of all wrongdoing. If you believe in him, He will give you a new life."

Dessaiah smiled grimly. "I do not think anyone can cleanse me."

"Would you let me pray for you?" Phillip asked. Dessaiah hesitated, but he nodded.

"Lord, please reveal your power to this man," Phillip prayed, "and free him from the sins holding him captive."

It was the simplest, most meaningful prayer Dessaiah had ever heard. It was nothing like the prayers the Hindus offered up to their idols or the other religious rituals they performed. Phillip prayed earnestly, but as if he was talking to a dear and close friend. The tears flowed anew as Dessaiah listened to his loving, compassionate words. How could this man care about him? It was amazing.

When Dessaiah went to sleep that night, his mind was in doubt. He no longer knew the right road to take. It had seemed that ending his life was the only way to rid himself of his mistakes, but now that choice seemed more like surrendering to them. Could Jesus really free him? Was it even possible?

Dessaiah tossed in his sleep, mumbling under his breath. There seemed to be a voice whispering to him, through the dark corridors of his mind…*Come*, it said. Dessaiah strained to hear from where the voice was speaking. "*Come*," the voice called louder and nearer. "*Come.*" Dessaiah turned in every direction, searching through the blackness. "Who are you?" he shouted at last.

A brilliant white light filled his eyes, chasing away the shadows and bathing Dessaiah in a peaceful warmth. *Come*, a man said. The single word held more love than Dessaiah had ever known, or ever would; the light pierced his soul as well as his eyes. *Come*, the man whispered, one last time. Already the light and the voice were fading, back into darkness, back into silence.

"Wait!" Dessaiah called. "Wait!" He was running, arms outstretched, to where the light was disappearing into a tiny pin-prick like a star—then falling, *falling*. Dessaiah jolted awake in his own bed. For a moment he lay there, panting, his mind dizzy. Then he closed his eyes. It had been Jesus. He was sure of it. Jesus had called to him.

"Phillip! Phillip!" Dessaiah dashed down the street, running towards the place where Phillip stood. He turned as he heard Dessaiah shouting his name.

"What is it?" he started to ask, but Dessaiah interrupted him.

"Jesus…" Dessaiah gasped for breath, "He, He spoke to me. He called me to come to Him."

Phillip laughed out loud, in pure joy. "And will you answer him, Dessaiah?" he said excitedly.

Now Dessaiah was grinning too, immense joy and eagerness pounding through him. "Yes!" he shouted. "I believe! They prayed together, and Dessaiah accepted Jesus as his Savior. Immediately, he shared the news with his family.   They too believed seeing an instant change in his life and were all baptized together.

Dessaiah understood the meaning of new life. Jesus broke all the bonds that held him to sin, and had washed Dessaiah's heart clean with His blood. Dessaiah stopped all his bad habits. His only desire was to live for Jesus, his Rescuer, and to spend his life serving Him. Phillip discipled Dessaiah in the Word, and taught him how to tell others about the Gospel. Dessaiah knew that he finally had a purpose—he would share Jesus with those who were lost.

Dessaiah's village had been angry with him earlier, but now there was greater anger. Dessaiah had left the Hindu religion and practices to follow Jesus! The villagers beat him again, brutally injuring him, and forced him to pay large amounts of money. Dessaiah was badly wounded, and he had to sell a portion of his belongings to pay the fine. But unlike before, he didn't lose hope. In fact, there was joy! He knew that Jesus was with him, and that He would take care of him.

And as Dessaiah grew in his faith and preached Jesus's love to his people, many of them believed. Now, Dessaiah is himself training young Christians to witness to the villages of India. He has a new life, and he is forever grateful to the One who set him free.

Drug Sellers

As a young boy, Kou Rath approached the bamboo hut with a curious joy inside him that he had never experienced before. There was singing inside—beautiful singing with the harmonious blending of several voices. He was sure this was the hut his friend Chenda had told him to come to. Kou Rath was entranced. He slowly approached the hut, and eased open the door. The song flowed out to meet him, welcoming him inside.

As Kou Rath's eyes adjusted to the low light, he made out a group of people sitting on the floor. They were singing with their eyes closed, smiling peacefully.

Chenda looked up as Kou Rath entered the room and eagerly gestured for him to join the circle. The gathering was a wonderful time for Kou Rath. The songs the people sang were full of joy and praise for the one they called their Lord. Later, as the group began to read from their Bibles, Kou Rath heard that this Lord was the one true God, and that His Son, Jesus, had come to save people from their sins. Kou Rath became aware of his own sin. He realized that he needed Jesus to save him, but he was not yet ready to ask.

That night, when Kou Rath returned home, he couldn't wait to share the experience with his mother. But she wasn't happy. She said he couldn't go back to the hut with Chenda. Kou Rath was sad, but he obeyed and stayed home. Thankfully Chenda would come to visit him. Each time he came, Chenda told Kou Rath what had been spoken at the most recent gathering and taught him the songs that they had sung. Soon Kou Rath was humming the songs of worship everywhere he went. He thought on the lyrics, and his desire for Jesus grew.

One day when Chenda and Kou Rath were walking down a dirt road, a car came racing up behind them and skidded to a halt a few feet away. Clouds of dust sprang into the air all around them. Through the dust, several men jumped out of the car. They seized Kou Rath and Chenda, and although the terrified young boys fought with all their strength, the men overpowered them. Beating Kou Rath and Chenda brutally, the men shoved them into the car and drove away. Kou Rath and Chenda huddled together in the back of the car, shaking with fear. They were both covered in blood and bruises; whenever they tried to speak to each other their kidnappers would strike them again. So the two friends sat in silence, listening to the men speak in a foreign language and wondering where they were being taken...and why.

They found the answer in a dark, smelly basement, somewhere in the heart of Bangkok, Thailand. The men who had captured them pushed them inside the room with eighteen other boys. None of them spoke to each other; they were all numb with fear. Kou Rath was the farthest away from home he had ever been. He was so scared.

The kidnappers had captured Kou Rath, Chenda, and the other boys, to work for them selling drugs. If they sold enough drugs each night to the people on the streets, they were given a bowl of rice to eat. If they didn't, they were beaten and went hungry. Kou Rath often went hungry. The city was dangerous, and once his supply of drugs was stolen from him while he was out on the streets. He still bore the marks of the beating he had received from his kidnappers as punishment. Kou Rath was weak from not having enough food. There had to be some way to escape the horror of this life. But two boys had already tried to get away, and both of them had been caught. After that, they had never been seen again.

Kou Rath began to lose all hope. There was no light, no rescue, nothing...Then Kou Rath remembered, like an echo in his heart, the beautiful praise songs to Jesus. Jesus could save him, couldn't he? *So why hasn't he?* Kou Rath thought angrily. *Why did he let me and Chenda be kidnapped?* Instantly, Kou Rath felt guilty for his thoughts. He remembered that he had never asked Jesus to forgive his sin, yet he also felt the overwhelming love of Jesus. Tears slipped down Kou Rath's face. He realized that he needed to ask Jesus for rescue, not from this drug den, but from his own sin.

It was the middle of the night, but Kou Rath crawled across to where Chenda was sleeping and woke him up. Together they prayed. Kou Rath sobbed, as, brokenly, he asked Jesus to be his Savior. Every day afterwards, Kou Rath and Chenda prayed together, and they both gained strength from it.

It was several weeks later. Kou Rath was on the streets, peddling his drugs. He glanced to the side, where the gang watcher always stood. The watcher would make sure that none of the boys tried to escape. But tonight...he wasn't there! Kou Rath looked again to be sure. No, the post was empty. Kou Rath hardly dared to believe that a chance of escape was before him.

Slowly, he began to walk away through the shifting masses of people. Then he began to run, picking up speed. The crowds flashed past him; his bare feet struck the stones and his breath came in short, quick gasps. Miraculously, he ran straight past Chenda. "Run!" Kou Rath shouted.

They both ran as fast as they could through the noisy confusion of the streets, their legs shaking and burning with the effort. But they didn't stop running, not until the city had faded away behind them. Neither of them knew where they were. All they could do was keep traveling east. They came to a bus station, where they used the last of their coins to get a ride to the border of Cambodia. But they were still lost, hungry, and exhausted, and now without any money.

Kou Rath and Chenda stumbled onwards, their feet were cracked and dusty from walking. At last Kou Rath cried out to Jesus once again. "Lord, you have saved us from our kidnappers. Now please, let us find a way home." They had dragged themselves a little further, when Chenda spotted something white hanging from a tree. They pulled it down, and found, to their amazement, that it was a bag full of rice! At the bottom of it was another bag, this one full of money. Starving, they fell upon the food, and were able to use the coins to buy bus fares to their home villages.

As they rode, they praised God with tears in their eyes. He had saved and preserved them, and now they were going home.

Kou Rath joined the fellowship at Chenda's village. He told everyone the story of how Jesus had rescued him and Chenda. But he wanted to tell even more people about Jesus— throughout all the villages of Cambodia. Through Big Life Ministries, Kou Rath received the training he needed to begin fulfilling this mission.

Did You Know...

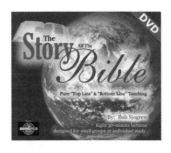

The book *God's Bottom Line* (the same book that changed John Heerema's entire life) has a DVD series that parallels it?

Eight one-half hour lectures help you to see your Bible as one book, with one introduction, one story and one conclusion. (It also comes with notes.) You'll never read your Bible the same after watching this series!

Think about getting this for your next Sunday school class or small group Bible study.

Find out more about the book at: UnveilinGLORY's bookstore: www.UnveilinGLORY.com/ bookstore

It's Too Simple

Midnight. The moon was hidden behind the clouds, just a faint glow in the sky. There wasn't a breath of wind.

It was the perfect night for stealing.

Chea crouched low to the ground, his knees aching from the uncomfortable position. The house lay directly ahead. He cast a quick glance behind him, and then darted forward a few paces. These people were wealthy. They would have riches to spare.

An hour later he was slipping away, as quiet as a shadow, a small treasure tucked inside his coat. There was only one more place he had to visit tonight. Chea went to the Buddhist temple and laid the stolen goods before the idols as an offering.

Chea worshipped many gods. Not just the gods of the Buddhist religion, but also the Chinese idols. He hoped that at least some of them would hear his prayers. In exchange for offerings and sacrifices, Chea asked for good fortune and peace. But his lifestyle was unsteady, and he often ran out of money. When this happened, Chea would steal. He reasoned with himself that his actions were justified if the things he stole were offered in worship. Yet he still felt uneasy. The choices he had made terrified him sometimes—and it wasn't just the stealing. In the name of his numerous gods, he had done many deeds of which he was not proud.

And his family—he had brought hardship upon them that they didn't deserve. Chea was scared. He needed the gods' protection and provision, and they wouldn't give it if he didn't offer them something in return. If they were pleased, he and his family would be safe—wouldn't they? Chea did everything he could to ensure that the gods would watch over them. If it meant following a hundred different religions, if it meant stealing, or even hurting other people, he would do it.

Then Chea's children fell sick. All three of them, deathly ill.

Chea panicked. What had he done wrong? Had he offended the gods in some way? He stole twice as much and offered them double what he normally gave, begging them to heal his children. But there was no answer.

Chea was confused, tormented by doubt and fear. Was there some other idol he had to worship? Had he missed a ritual, not sacrificed enough? He couldn't understand. Why were the gods not answering his prayers? Chea watched by his children's bedside as their health worsened. He was pale from exhaustion. Dark circles rimmed his eyes, and his lids drooped heavily. He hadn't done anything these past days except pray. He had prostrated himself on the floor, crying out in desperation. And still, *still*, there was no reply. *Why?*

Chea stroked his children's foreheads gently, one by one. They were so young. "Please," he whispered. Tears spilled down his roughened cheeks, bright and gleaming. "Oh, please...." He covered his mouth with a hand. Sobs began to rack his body and he slumped down into a chair, his eyes squeezed shut.

The next morning, one of his children died.

Chea slammed the door hard on its hinges. His wife was back in the bedroom, holding her child's hand and crying. Chea couldn't weep. He was too angry.

He threw his head back. "Why are you doing this?!" he shouted at the heavens. Silence greeted him, mocking him. "I did everything for you!" He screamed his accusation at the heavens, and his throat burning. With a roar of rage he kicked the ground, then the house. He threw whatever he could get his hands on. Finally, sweating and gasping, he fell to his knees. He wrapped his arms around his head, tearing at his hair and grieving. But none of his gods could do a thing.

He had always worshipped the gods faithfully, and now they had failed him. He had spent his whole life adoring the idols, which had let his child die. Now what was left for him to trust? Could he really trust anything? Chea didn't know what he might have done. Maybe he would have hurt someone, or reverted to drinking—he didn't know. But it didn't matter.

The next day changed everything. That morning a pastor came to visit.

"Jesus came to save sinners," Pastor Smoanh said. Chea and his wife and their two children were all listening to him. Pastor Smoanh smiled at the children who were watching him with big brown eyes. "He loves everyone, especially the little children. He loved everyone so much that he died for them. Because He has paid for our sins, anyone who believes in Him will live forever and have their hearts washed clean."

Chea shook his head slowly. "It can't be. It is too simple. Only believe and you will be saved? What god has ever offered such a gift?"

Pastor Smoahh turned to Chea. His eyes were gentle and kind, as if he knew that Chea was breaking apart inside. Chea was desperate for something to cling to, something that wouldn't let him down.

The pastor continued. "No god ever has given such a gift, except the One true God," he said solemnly. "It is that simple. Jesus came to save, and He doesn't ask for anything but your faith. If you put your trust in God, He promises that no one can snatch you out of His hand."

Chea looked at his wife. She took his hand, wiping away the tears that were gathering on his cheeks. "I want Jesus to save me," he said huskily. "I—" he paused, taking a deep breath. "I trust Him."

It was that surrender that changed Chea's life. He asked Jesus to forgive his sins and promised to love and serve Him forever. No longer did he participate in any of the bad activities, no longer did he steal. His wife joined him as well. Through their prayers their two remaining children got better. Then he and his family had contentment and happiness such as they had never known. Chea began a Christian fellowship at his house leading other believers in worship and study. Now he starts each day with hope and doesn't fear the future—for he knows that Jesus will always be there and will always hear him when he calls.

He Never Lost Hope

Namanthya's family was Christian. His father was a pastor. But Namanthya, he was something entirely different.

He had grown up being taught the Bible and being told about Jesus's love and power. His father had hoped that one day Namanthya would grow up to be a pastor also and that he would reach many people with the Word of God. He prayed that God would use his son for great things. But though Namanthya had heard all about Jesus, he didn't follow His commands. He wanted to live his life the way he wanted, and he didn't care what God's will was for him.

He began drinking constantly, and became increasingly violent and angry. When he came home late at night, drunk and dirty, he hurled insults and curses at his family members. Sometimes he even struck them.

His presence at home brought a large amount of conflict and strife, and he hurt his family deeply.

They tried to advise him against his aimless lifestyle, warning him of the danger in which he was putting himself. Namanthya sneered at their caution and turned even farther away from them and God.

One night Namanthya threw the front door open, stumbling inside. His father and mother looked up as he entered. Their faces were strained, tense. His father was kneeling on the floor, his hands clasped. His eyes looked tired as he turned to face his son.

Namanthya shut the door. He stood for a moment in the doorway, gazing into his father's eyes. They held such pity, such sorrow. Namanthya felt ashamed, then angry. He was angry because he knew that he was making wrong choices, but he couldn't humble himself enough to face that fact. Instead he struck out at the one who had aroused his guilt.

"Still praying?" Namanthya sneered. He stepped into the room towards his father. Slowly his father rose from his knees.

"Every day," he said calmly.

"You should give up," Namanthya said bitterly. "Your God can't change me."

His father came a little closer. He looked so burdened, so fragile. "Yes, he can. If you surrender your life to him..."

"Stop preaching to me!" Namanthya spat.

His father flinched as if he had been struck. But he didn't step back. "I will not. I will never stop loving you, and if I love you, I will always tell you to do what will bring you happiness and peace. You are angry all the time. Do you really want this life you have?"

Namanthya clenched his fists. He glared at his father with fire burning in his eyes. With a great effort he turned away.

His father stayed where he was, looking into the distance. His lips moved in prayer as tears shimmered in his eyes.

The next night Namanthya's head was splitting in two. He had drunk even more than usual. The world was spinning around him making his stomach twist unpleasantly. Namanthya held a hand to his forehead and stumbled forwards. He needed to get home. He needed to sleep.

Nothing felt right. He could barely keep on his feet or even think. He felt the door handle under his fingers and heard the hinges creak as he leaned against the door, pushing it open. He almost fell inside. Again, his parents were waiting for him. Why did they still hope? He was gone; he was so far gone. His stomach lurched, and he gasped. He saw his father coming toward him. Blearily, Namanthya looked up. "Stay...away," he muttered. With difficulty, Namanthya straightened up, fighting back the dizziness and the nausea.

"Namanthya," his mother said gently.

"Stay away!" he shouted. Anger surged through him and he wanted to hurt someone. He hated everything and everyone.

"Calm down, please," his mother pleaded.

"Shut up!" He raised his hand and struck her across the jaw. She choked, collapsing to her knees. His father came running towards him, shoving Namanthya away and putting his arms around his wife.

Namanthya swayed, staring at the two of them. His heartbeat pulsed in his ears. With a retch he turned away and emptied his stomach onto the floor. The ceiling flipped upside down and he was falling. As his head struck the floor, he tasted blood on his lips.

Words. Voices, murmuring softly. Namanthya felt cool air creep into his lungs. Slowly, painfully, he breathed in, then out. There were blankets beneath him and a pillow under his head. People were close by. He could hear their small movements and their breathing: in, out, in, out. He lifted his eyelids. They were so heavy. Light penetrated the darkness, sending piercing pain through his head. He groaned, finally opening his eyes completely.

He was lying on a bed with white all around him—white floors, white walls, white ceiling. Faces hovered anxiously over him. He blinked and saw his family. His father, with his jaw set like it always was when he was worried. His mother, a bruise spreading over her face. He remembered everything then. The anger, the blood in his mouth—striking his mother to the ground. And yet as she bent over him her eyes were concerned and compassionate, full of love.

Namanthya took a sharp breath and sobbed. He put a hand over his eyes, scalding tears soaking his face. He had done this. His family knelt around him, their hands and voices offering comfort. Comfort he didn't deserve. His wretchedness churned inside him like some vile creature wanting to tear him apart. He cried like he had never cried before.

Never before had he seen himself so clearly. He was worthless, ruined—so selfish, so proud. He was a sinner. And he needed Jesus.

Namanthya made a choice that day. In a fresh humility he asked Jesus to forgive his sins and make him new. And Namanthya vowed to follow Him.

Recovered, he left the hospital and soon was baptized. Immediately he became involved with Big Life Ministries bringing the Gospel to the lost villages across the country and planting churches for believers to gather in together.

His father had never lost hope. God did have a plan for his son, and he would use Namanthya to bring great glory to the Kingdom of God.

A Martyr?

Shabbir wanted to die. He longed for it so much that the thought consumed every waking moment.

He didn't want just any death.

Shabbir was a trained Islamic teacher. He loved studying and teaching the Quran to his devoted village. But more than anything, he wanted to die in holy war as a martyr. Shabbir was convinced that this was his calling. If he died fighting against the infidels, he would go straight to paradise to be with Allah.

So when the Russians attacked, Shabbir left his village and his students and went to be a soldier. The people in his village loved him very much; he was an excellent teacher. They asked him not to go, but Shabbir was deaf to their pleas. He prayed constantly that Allah would count him worthy to be slain in his service.

Shabbir received military training, but just a short while afterwards, the war ended. Shabbir had to leave without fighting any infidels. He was confused and conflicted. He had been so sure that this was the path Allah had set out for him. If he couldn't be a martyr, what could he be?

Shabbir returned to his village, where he eventually married and had two children. But the peace and contentment of his home life did nothing but torment Shabbir. He wanted to be fighting. He could feel the passion, the desire, simmering beneath his skin. All he wanted was to serve Allah. Wouldn't Allah let him?

Then came the news: war had erupted between India and Pakistan. Shabbir rejoiced. Finally his time had come! Shabbir knew that his wife wouldn't want him to go to war, so he arranged to have her and the children visit a relative in another village. Then Shabbir would leave while they were away, and tell them by letter that he had joined the army.   As Shabbir planned, a sense of panic nagged at him. What if the war ended again before he could get involved? What if he wasn't killed? "As soon as I get into battle," Shabbir determined that night, "I will go where the fighting is most dangerous, and kill as many infidels as I can before they kill me." Resolved, Shabbir closed his eyes to sleep.

While asleep, Shabbir had a vivid dream. There was a man dressed in white. He stood on a hill, and thousands of people were crowded around him. They were all gazing towards him as if unable to look away. The man was glowing with purity and power. Shabbir spoke to the person at his elbow. "Who is that man?"

"That is Isa," the person replied, his voice awed and hushed.

Isa! Shabbir was filled with amazement. Isa, the prophet! Shabbir had to get closer to the man in white and ask him all the questions that were burning on his tongue. Shabbir squirmed through the crowd, until he stood before Isa. "Isa," Shabbir said, "What must I do to gain eternal life?"

Isa turned towards him. His eyes...they were so deep, so full of love. "Pray to God, and seek His will. You must love all men."

Shabbir felt a horrible twisting in his stomach. He bent over, retching, and felt something dark and awful, something evil, come flooding out of him. Shabbir staggered, taking in a deep breath. He was clean. He was free. Shabbir's eyes burned with sudden tears, and he couldn't speak for the joy and relief welling up inside him. He fell to the ground at Isa's feet, knowing that he owed it all to Him....

With a violent start, Shabbir woke up. He was shaking, drenched with cold sweat. What had the dream meant? He remembered it so clearly: the evil darkness that had come out of him and the overwhelming freedom he had felt when it was gone. His tears of joy were still damp on his cheeks.

The dream haunted Shabbir. He thought and thought, trying to discern its meaning, until he even forgot about his longing for war. What was that horrible thing inside him that he had vomited? His sin, clearly. But what had he done wrong? He was a devout Muslim, following all of Allah's ordinances. "Pray to God, and seek His will," Isa had said. Shabbir did so daily, praying to Allah and asking for knowledge. But Isa had also said, "Love all men." That Shabbir had not done. In fact, he had hated the infidels and dreamed of slaying them. Shabbir felt ashamed and guilty. Then he felt afraid. What was happening to him? Was his solid faith being shaken by a mere dream?

Shabbir confided in a friend, telling him about the dream that was plaguing him. His friend shocked him by saying, "You need to go to a Christian. They're the only ones who can tell you what your dream means."

Shabbir couldn't believe it. A Christian? An unbeliever?

"Please, Shabbir," his friend said. "Write to this address. They can help you." He offered Shabbir a slip of paper.

At last, Shabbir relented. He wrote to the address, detailing his dream and asking for help.

A little while later, a package arrived. Shabbir opened it eagerly, hoping to finally have the mystery of his dream explained. But inside the package was nothing but books—Christian books, including a copy of the corrupted New Testament. Angry, Shabbir threw them away.

Then he began to think. He was a learned scholar. He knew the Quran very well. He was allowed to read the New Testament as long as he was able to discern what was true and what was corrupted. And it was Isa who had spoken to him in his dream. Maybe answers could be found in the New Testament.

Shabbir pulled the book out of the trashcan and studied it for a moment. Then, reaching a sudden decision, he opened the cover and began to read.

The words changed everything. Shabbir read of love and forgiveness. He realized that the evil inside him was sin that could only be taken away by Isa. With tears dampening his face once again, Shabbir confessed his sin. Immediately, brilliant, glowing joy poured through him; it felt like he could breathe freely for the first time in his life. The terrible darkness inside him had fled, and his heart now belonged to Isa.

Shabbir relocated his family to another village where he could start his life as a Christian. But just a short while later he found his new faith tested. His wife fell gravely ill. Shabbir prayed to God, begging him to save her. God did; Shabbir's wife recovered her health completely.

From then on, Shabbir spent his days studying Isa's word. His scholar's mind drank it all in, and each day brought new revelations and new teachings. Shabbir felt a deep peace enter his soul. He wanted to serve Isa in whatever way was needed.

When Shabbir heard about Big Life Ministries, he knew that he had found the place where God wanted him to be. Shabbir spread God's Word among his fellow countrymen in the very villages where he had once taught Islam. Now he preached the love of Isa, and he prayed every day that God would use him to reach the lost.

An Angry Mob

Jadab took a deep breath and looked toward the building. A Christian gathering was happening inside, this very night. Jadab decided to attend.

There would be answers here, he hoped. And peace.

When Jadab entered the building, he was immediately surrounded by music. The Christians were in the midst of a praise song, their hands lifted, their voices raised in melody. Jadab felt a faint smile cross his face. He slipped into the midst of the people, hiding himself in the crowd. The Christians all sat down for the message, and he sat down with them.

"Good evening," said the pastor with a smile. "I don't know if there is anyone here who has never heard about Jesus. But if there is, I would like to share with you, for a moment, what He has done for me." He began to walk back and forth before the people. "I was a sinner, lost and condemned to death. I had nothing to offer God. But then I learned that Jesus had come to earth and died in my place for my sins. Three days later He rose from the grave, victorious forever over sin and death. I couldn't believe it. God's only Son had died for *me.*"

Jadab was gazing at the pastor, but he saw nothing. His eyes were filled with tears. The pastor's message was speaking to him, deep down. *Jesus loved—sinners? He loved them?*

"I wept in shame. Trembling I bowed before my Lord, and asked that he forgive my terrible heart. " The pastor paused, a smile crossing his face. "He did," he said softly. "That night I was saved, and I have never stopped thanking Jesus for it every day since. Now I want others to know Him, too. I want sinners to realize that there is hope in Jesus Christ, there is power in Jesus Christ, and there is *salvation* in Jesus Christ!" The pastor's voice grew stronger with each phrase, and the church began to cheer and clap.

Jadab found himself clapping with the rest and sobbing. Hands were laid on his shoulders. People began to pray softly for him as Jadab sank to his knees. "Please," he whispered through his tears. "Please save me. Forgive my sins, Lord Jesus, and save me." A pressure suddenly released. Jadab took in a huge breath, laughing and weeping. Peace and joy flooded through him, like pure, clean water. He was free. Jesus had saved him!

Jadab was baptized and immediately began reaching others. He traveled from village to village, sharing the Gospel, mentoring Christians, and starting churches. People were listening. Jesus was moving in powerful ways throughout the villages, and their time there had already been fruitful.

Now Jadab and his family were in Orissa. One calm, cool night, as Jadab lay awake in bed, a faint noise registered on the edge of his consciousness. Like muffled voices, a long way off, there was shouting. Jadab frowned and threw off his blankets. Barefoot he made his way to the door and opened it. The village was quiet. A few lights were beginning to turn on; apparently he wasn't the only one to have heard the noise. Jadab peered up and down the street. Everything seemed to be fine, then a terrible scream pierced the air. Jadab jumped. Doors began to fly open, voices calling anxiously. In the distance, a plume of fire leapt into the night. A roar of fear rose from the villagers, and Jadab ran back into the house.

"Quickly!" He shook his wife and children awake. "We have to get out of the village. Take only what you can carry," he said as they stumbled out of bed, their eyes wide with fear.

The little group slipped out into the village street. The noise had grown louder. Already more houses were burning, and Jadab could hear angry chanting. It was a mob.

A lone figure, merely a shadow in the night, came running down the street from the source of the chaos. "They're looking for all the Christians!" he panted, pointing behind him. "They're going to kill them all!"

Jadab felt his blood run cold. His wife clutched at his hand. They had to leave, now. Jadab turned away from the villagers and pulled his family into the darkness, away from the destruction and the screams—the terrible screams.

They ran out of the village, into the forest. Jadab heard others fleeing nearby, wordlessly, their heavy breathing the only sound besides the scuffle of their feet through the underbrush. Jadab kept tight hold of his wife's hand, who in turn held fiercely to her children. Their little girl was sobbing in terror. Jadab's own heart pounded in time with his running feet. He felt fear of the night, fear of the unknown, and the fear of pursuit. At every moment he thought he heard shouts behind them, yelling for them to stop. He ran faster.

It seemed that the forest and the fear would never end; that the night would keep going, like a nightmare from which he couldn't wake up. But the dawn came, and at last Jadab and his family stopped to rest. They could see the sky in the distance painted orange and black, reflecting the light of the flames that still burned in their village. There would be nothing left. Jadab's wife rested her head on his chest, fighting back tears. "What's going to happen to our children?" she whispered.

Jadab kissed her forehead. "We must trust God," he said. "That is all we can do."

For three days they had continued to stumble through the forest, covered with dirt and sweat, scratched by brambles and twigs. The children were exhausted. Even Jadab didn't feel like he could go much farther.

Then the trees cleared. Jadab lifted his eyes wearily and saw a camp ahead. A refugee camp. His shoulders slumped in relief, and he managed a faint smile. "We're safe," he said to his family. Other bedraggled groups were beginning to emerge from the forest as well. The guards hurriedly ushered them inside the camp, looking anxiously over their heads at the trees beyond.

As his family passed through the gate, the knowledge of safety swept over Jadab like a wave of warmth. They would have protection from the mobs here. His wife smiled up at him, and his children huddled close to his legs. God had provided, as He always would.

The mob was beaten back at the camp, and the Christians inside were kept safe. As for Jadab's home, it was impossible for him to return there. When they left the camp, Jadab and his family relocated to a different village. There, Jadab continued his ministry for the Lord. Despite everything they had lost, Jadab was content. Jesus had been with them throughout their ordeal, and He had kept them safe. Now Jadab is sharing the Gospel in his new neighborhood, where God has enabled him to plant nine churches made up of one hundred forty-nine new Christians.

The Perfect, Empty Life

When she was still very young, Sunita was married. Her husband loved her dearly; she was happy to be with him. And yet...there was a sense of something missing. The love that surrounded Sunita didn't feel right. Even with her husband's love her happiness was shallow and fragile. There was no peace in her heart. It was as if a breath of wind could blow it all away at any time.

The older she got, the more Sunita was tormented by these thoughts. On the outside everything seemed perfect, but on the inside she was deeply depressed. She needed answers or some assurance that this anxiety wasn't all simply in her head. Was there a way to peace? Or was this meaningless, drifting existence what life was? She shuddered. No. There had to be something more.

"Good morning!" the young man called cheerily. He passed by Sunita's house, lifting his hand in greeting. Sunita slowly returned his gesture. Her face was downcast. The man could see it, for he stopped walking and turned back towards her. "Are you alright?"

Sunita pressed her lips together. No, she wasn't alright. She longed to spill out all her troubles and doubts on someone who would just listen—someone who wouldn't scorn her or reject her. She had kept silent for so long. She couldn't talk to any of her Hindu family and friends; they wouldn't understand. They would tell her that she should be happy.

"Excuse me..." the young man said softly, sensing something was deeply wrong. "Do you need anything?"

Sunita raised her head to look at him, her eyes shining with tears. She had seen him passing by before. He traveled regularly to a church that was only a short distance from Sunita's house. He was a Christian. Sunita knew that they listened when people had problems. It would be safe to ask one of them her questions. And maybe this young Christian could help.

Sunita told him everything. It gave her such relief to share her burden with another soul. He listened attentively until she was finished, and then he didn't laugh or shake his head. "There is something missing from your life, Sunita," he said seriously. "Jesus."

Sunita stared at him. He was the first person she had ever met who actually agreed with her—her perfect life wasn't complete. But did he really have the answer? "Jesus?" she asked.

"Yes. Inside every person is a God-sized vacuum that only God can fill. We are all empty without Him," the man said earnestly. "Jesus is the Son of the one true God. He is the Savior of the world. He can forgive you of your sins and fill the void inside of you."

Later, sitting alone in her house, Sunita thought about what he had said. The world suddenly seemed huge and full of questions. She had to know the truth. She needed something to hold on to. She closed her eyes, listening to her breath slowly ease in and out. "God," she whispered. Her voice sounded thin in the silence. "Please tell me, can I find true peace?"

Tears seeped from beneath her lashes.

Then she felt it...a voice, quiet, but so real. A still small voice filled with power, whispering back to her soul. *I give peace and joy.*

Sunita put a hand over her mouth. Her heartbeat was racing and she began to weep. It was God. He had spoken to her, to *her*. To a lonely, lost little girl...He had given her the answer. He was the answer.

A few days later, Sunita started attending the little church nearby. She learned more about God and his Son, Jesus. She heard the Gospel shared yet again, and soon she believed. She accepted Jesus's free gift of salvation and asked Him to forgive her sins. It was instant. For the first time in her life she felt complete. There was a deep, powerful love, and peace—at last. Jesus was what she had been missing. Now she vowed to follow Jesus and live her life according to His will.

Sunita stepped into her house closing the door gently behind her. She was glowing with excitement and joy. Gathering with the other believers at church always made her feel more alive. She looked up, and saw her husband waiting for her. He was standing, gazing at her. His eyes, normally tender and loving, were hard. Sunita felt a chill run through her.

"Why would you do this?" he asked coldly.

"Do what?" Sunita asked shakily.

"Become a Christian!" His voice rose to a shout. He walked towards Sunita, his face twisted with rage. "You have betrayed all of us!"

He raised his hand and struck her to the ground. Sunita cried out, covering her head with her hands. He had never, *ever* done anything like this before. "Please," she sobbed, "Please, listen..."

He continued to beat her. There was such hate in his face, in his voice, in his eyes. It terrified Sunita more than anything. He loved her, didn't he? How could he hate her so fiercely now? Finally her husband stepped back. His chest was rising and falling heavily, and his jaw was clenched. Sunita shrank away from him, wiping away her tears.

"You have to choose," he hissed. "Do you love Jesus, or do you love me?"

Sunita's voice trembled. "I love you both," she breathed. "Please—I love you both."

Her husband glared down at her and then turned swiftly and strode away. Sunita bowed her head, pressing her hands to her face. She didn't think to get up. Alone, crumpled on the floor, she sobbed.

It was strange. All at once her life had been shattered from its ordered, peaceful bliss. But in the midst of the trouble, Sunita felt more at peace that she ever had before. Her husband's anger hurt her, deeply. But instead of retreating into herself, she began to pray desperately for him. Constantly she asked that Jesus would touch his life and let him see the truth. It seemed that her prayers had little effect. Her husband continued to despise her, ridiculing her for her faith. Sunita thought he would never look at her in love again.

But suddenly everything changed. Sunita knew it could only be the power of God. One morning her husband approached her, quiet and subdued. Softly, he asked, "Can you tell me about Jesus?" Sunita felt weak with shock and joy. She shared the Gospel with her husband. As he listened, his brow furrowed in concentration. Sunita could see he was thinking about every word she said.

God answered Sunita's prayers, and her husband came to know the Lord. Now she, her husband, and their three children are sharing God's love in their home country of Nepal. They have a good life—not because of nice circumstances or wealth, but because they have the immeasurable joy of Jesus Christ.

Two Charging Boars!

Kirrin began drinking alcohol when he was a small child. With the drinking, he smoked and used drugs. The substances affected his actions, and soon he was stealing and getting into fist-fights.

Then a group of men came to his village. They were Christians. They showed the villagers a film on a big screen. It was about Jesus, who had come to earth as a man to save sinners. Kirrin watched it with the rest of his family. He was captivated by the story, by this man who was so full of love. When Jesus was brutally crucified, he felt tears sliding down his cheeks. He sat with his knees hugged to his chest, trying to understand the conflict in his heart.

After the movie, the Christians sang songs about Jesus. One of the songs spoke about how fleeting life is, here one day and then gone. Kirrin knew that he was ruining his life by drinking. He realized that Jesus was the way to eternal life. But he could not surrender to Him. He had done too many wrong things—things he was still doing. How could someone like him ever bring glory to God?

Kirrin went back to the liquor that could make him forget everything. But it was not true happiness, he knew that. Often he thought of Jesus, and the joy he had seen in the Christians. Every time he did so, he felt horrible guilt and shame for what he had done. But he had become addicted to alcohol. He didn't know how he could ever stop.

Kirrin grew up, married and had two children. Somehow he managed to have a successful career, which made him prideful. Yet he was still drinking and often, he beat his family when he came home.

One day his mother came to speak to him. "Kirrin, I must tell you something." Her face broke into a radiant smile. "I have accepted Christ as my Lord."

Kirrin's eyes hardened. He saw the happiness in her, and he hated it. He hated the powerful sense of loss he felt inside as he watched her smiling at him. "Get out of my house," he hissed.

His mother stepped back, her smile fading.

"Go!" Kirrin shouted.

His mother turned and hurried out the doorway, trying to hide the tears in her eyes.

As she closed the door, Kirrin collapsed to his knees, sobbing. He despised what he was. He was trapped in sin that was fast closing over his head. He could never get rid of his sins. He had done too many wrong things. Kirrin wrapped his arms around his head, gasping for breath through his tears.

With no hope, Kirrin drank more and more. Nothing else mattered but the next bottle. Eventually Kirrin abandoned his job and his family and wandered to another village.

But God wasn't finished with Kirrin yet. While in the village, Kirrin heard of a Christian fellowship being held nearby. Without knowing why, he went. He stank of alcohol, and he was shaking all over. He was hideous—but the Christians welcomed him into their midst, speaking gently and lovingly to him. Kirrin was amazed by their kindness. He sat silently, listening to the worship songs and the messages. Again, that sense of emptiness tore at him. But it seemed to lessen as he closed his eyes, letting the name of Jesus wash over him.

When Kirrin fell asleep that night he had a dream. He was standing in the middle of a bridge. It was weak and poorly made, and it swayed beneath his feet. Kirrin clung desperately to the ropes on either side. Peering over the edge, he looked into the ravine below—but the bottom was so far down that Kirrin could not see it. He gulped in fear.

Then the bridge shook violently. Something big had stepped on to it. Terrified, Kirrin looked up. A huge wild boar was standing at the far end of the bridge. It snorted aggressively and pawed the bridge, lowering its four lethal tusks. Kirrin whirled to run, but saw the other end of the bridge blocked by a second boar, just as large as the first. The boars gave a great roar, and charged down the bridge, heading straight for Kirrin. Trapped in the middle of the bridge, Kirrin panicked. He looked wildly for a way of escape, but there was nothing but the bottomless drop on either side. The boars were rapidly galloping closer, their rattling hoofs deafening in his ears.

"Kirrin!" A powerful voice called out over the noise. Kirrin searched for the person who had spoken. But there was no one—just a brilliant golden cross that appeared in the air over the side of the bridge. Kirrin shielded his eyes before its blinding light, as the voice said, "Come to the cross!"

The boars were closing in, their small eyes red with fury. Kirrin cowered in fear. "Come!" The voice boomed.

Kirrin shouted in terror, and then ran to the edge of the bridge and leapt out into thin air, towards the cross that grew so bright he could see nothing else....

Kirrin awoke with a start, his heart pounding. He knew it had been Jesus. Jesus had actually spoken to him. Kirrin's heart ached with emotion. He knew that Jesus loved him and wanted him to come. He knew Jesus was the only one who could take away his sin and fill that emptiness inside him.

For a week Kirrin didn't touch a drink. It was the longest he had gone without alcohol since he was thirteen. He was dumbfounded by the realization that Jesus, the Son of God, had called him. What did it really mean to "come" to Jesus? No one had ever told him how to get to know Jesus personally.

Kirrin attended another fellowship. He shared his story with the people there and Kirrin found himself weeping brokenly. They told him all about Jesus' love for all people and coming to Jesus meant yielding his life to Him. Kirrin needed to let Jesus be the Lord of his life.

It finally clicked in Kirrin's heart. He now knew how to jump to the cross in this life. He whispered a prayer. "Here I come Lord Jesus. I yield my life to You. Be the Lord of my life."

At that moment Kirrin was saved. The change in his life was radical. He went home to his family and asked for their forgiveness. He broke his addiction to alcohol and began living for Christ. The leader of the fellowship he attended, Robert, trained Kirrin to share the gospel. Kirrin told others how he had been saved by Jesus' mercy. He told them that no one is too far gone for Jesus to be able to rescue them. All anyone has to do is come.

Did
You
Know...

You can learn more about the ministry of
Big Life by visiting our website:

www.blm.org

You can also follow us on social media:

www.facebook.com/BigLifeMinistries

www.twitter.com/BigLifeOnline

A Paralyzed Mother

Uma was a Buddhist. In order to be accepted in her tribe, she was required to perform many expensive rituals. This was hard on Uma, a widow with three children. She was not rich. But as a Buddhist, she had to practice her religion—there was no choice. She needed the close-knit family of her tribe, and the care they would give her.

The high cost of the celebrations and rituals put Uma in debt. Times were hard on their family, and Uma was often lonely and worn out. But she pressed on. Yet one trial after another kept coming, one hardship following close on the first—would the problems never cease? Her family managed to scrape by for several years. Then, without warning, Uma was gripped by paralysis.

Uma tried again and again to get to her feet, but she no longer had any control over her body. She could not walk.   Uma stared fixedly at her immobile limbs, trying to be calm, clear-headed...but her breathing was quick and panicky, and tears were already falling. Sobs rose in her throat. With a cry of despair, Uma let fear claim her. What had she done to deserve this? She thought she had been so faithful.

Uma's community gathered to carry out rituals and ceremonies for her healing. Uma lay in bed, unmoving, hoping and praying that their sacrifices would save her. But there was no slow regaining of strength and no faint touch of life in her deadened limbs. The practices Uma had followed all her life did nothing for her now.

When Uma heard that her father-in-law was coming to her house to see her, hope arose again. He was a witchdoctor. He called upon witchcraft to heal Uma, and performed many rites over her bed. Nothing changed. Uma was still paralyzed. Her newly discovered hope evaporated immediately. The religion that had taken so much from her over the years had failed her. What had been the purpose of all those required celebrations and ceremonies? And even witchcraft was powerless? There was nothing else to try. She was doomed.

"Mother," her son said softly. "I hate seeing you so sad. There must be something to do."

"There is nothing," Uma said bitterly.

Her son hesitated for a moment, and then said, "There, there is a church. Maybe they could pray for you."

Uma considered what he had said. Though Christians were seen as outcasts in the village, what did she have to lose? If there was even the slightest chance that she could be healed, she would take it. "Where is the church?" she asked.

Her son smiled in relief. "I'll take you."

When Uma arrived at the church—a Christian church—the members welcomed her inside. She told them her situation, and begged them to pray over her.

"Please, stay here with us for fifteen days," they said earnestly. "We will pray for you all the while."

Uma agreed. The Christians did as they had promised; day and night there were people praying urgently for Jesus to bring healing to Uma's body. During those fifteen days, they shared the story of Jesus Christ with Uma many times. They told her that everyone was a sinner, and for anyone to receive eternal life, one must ask Jesus to save them and forgive his/her sins. They told her that Jesus is the only way. Uma listened eagerly. She felt amazingly loved, continually wrapped in prayer and kindness. Those fifteen days were like living in a different world.

When the time had elapsed, Uma tried once again to move her legs. She felt a little surge of strength in her muscles. Her heart beating fiercely, Uma slowly raised herself up from her chair, and moved her leg forward in a tiny step. She walked. Uma laughed breathlessly, her eyes wide with wonder. She barely remembered what it felt like to have movement in her legs, to feel them responding…and walking. There was power in these Christians' prayers! It wasn't just another ritual. Their God was alive, and He had worked a miracle for her. The Christians gathered around Uma, cheering and clapping as she took a few more baby steps. The healing had begun.

Uma stayed at the church for 40 days, at the insistent pleas of the Christians. They all continued to pray for her, and by the end of 40 days, Uma was walking and running and living a normal life. She was overwhelmed by the kindness of the Christians. They had been praying constantly, and had rejoiced with her as though she were their own. What kind of love was this?

It was the love of Jesus living in them. They shared the Gospel with Uma once more. She wept as she realized that Jesus had loved her, a sinner, enough to give His life in her place. Uma, with the family of believers around her, prayed to Jesus and asked Him to save her from her sins.

Uma couldn't thank anyone enough. She overflowed with gratitude to the Christians for their unfaltering prayers, and to Jesus, who had given her more than she could ever repay. He lived in her! She could feel His vibrant power already changing her life. He had healed her body, and now he was working a miracle in her heart.

She told her story to the entire village, proclaiming Jesus's power and love. They listened in amazement. Uma had been healed from a disease that none of their Buddhist practices had been able to touch. They continually asked, "What was this power that had released Uma from her paralysis?"

"It is Jesus!" Uma exclaimed.

The villagers nodded, looking at each other in astonishment. "Yes," they said. "It must be Jesus!"

Uma's whole village, including her family, was saved as a result of Uma's healing. They recognized that Jesus is the one, true, all-powerful God.

Uma was baptized and made a promise to her Lord that she would serve Him in any way He asked. Now, through Jesus' strength, she is doing just that and the entire village is living in a different world—the tribe of Jesus Christ!

Thanking God for Evil Spirits

Asif and Marium were husband and wife, a content couple with three children. They took pride in being Syed Muslims, directly descended from Mohammed's bloodline. This meant that they were respected, high-class, and successful. Their home life was peaceful, for Asif was a good husband and father and Marium obeyed him devotedly. But one day, he started to change.

Asif became short-tempered, sometimes brooding and other times yelling at Marium. He wasn't the only one acting differently. The children were fighting amongst themselves and waking up in the night, unable to sleep because of frightening dreams. The whole house was filled with a dark presence—something *evil*.

Marium spoke with Asif for a long time, and eventually he agreed with her—there was an evil spirit in their home. Asif had the village religious teacher pray over the house. But nothing changed. In fact, the strife in their family got worse.

Finally, Marium called her brother, Shah. Shah was the family member she trusted the most. He was a bright scholar and respected at the religious school he attended. He would know people who could banish the evil spirit.

Shah was happy to talk with her. He listened to everything she had to say, and then was silent.

"Please, brother," Marium pleaded. "Will you send someone to help?"

He hesitated. "Yes I will," he said at last. "But listen to me, Marium." A hint of urgency had crept into his voice. "The men I will send can—and will—help you. They are my friends. But you must know that they are Christians."

"What?" Marium burst out. "Christians? But brother—"

"Trust me," Shah said. "They can fix your problem."

Mairum spoke to Asif. At first he, too, was taken aback.

"Just this time," said Mairum desperately. "Let them come and try to help us, and then we'll never have to see them again. What harm can it do?"

Reluctantly, Asif agreed.

When Shah's two Christian friends arrived at the house, both Marium and Asif felt themselves warming towards them. The men were simply dressed, well-mannered, and gracious. Marium and Asif told them what had been happening. They listened carefully, and then shared passages from the Bible with Marium and Asif about Jesus' power to cast out demons.

"Now, let us pray with you," said the first man. His prayer was passionate and filled with faith. He spoke as though he was absolutely certain that God would fulfill his request.

A few days after the Christians had visited, Marium felt the presence vanish from the house. The whole family sensed the change. They began to smile and even laugh again.

Mairum called Shah to thank him. As they talked, Shah told her about Jesus. "I believe He is the one true God," Shah said.

Mairum refused to accept it. "No, it can't be true. Christians are infidels."

"Mairum," Shah said softly. "Could infidels have cast the spirit from your home? You have already seen the power of Jesus. Now will you let that power work in you?"

Mairum wept. She was a Muslim, how could she believe? But as Shah continued to speak with her, she felt her heart being changed. Shah sent her a New Testament in the mail. She eagerly read through it, and then called Shah one more time. "Brother, I believe that Jesus is the only way to heaven." Shah rejoiced with her at the news.

Mairum wanted to be baptized. One day when Asif was gone, Shah's Christian friends returned to the house.

Smiling happily, they asked her, "Do you believe in Jesus, the Son of God, and have you accepted him as your Savior?"

Mairum's face was glowing. "Yes," she replied.

Then she closed her eyes tight as they poured a bucket of water over head. She was free, free from sin and finally alive in Christ.

Mairum thanked God that He had allowed evil spirits to come to her house. They were what God had used to point her to Him.

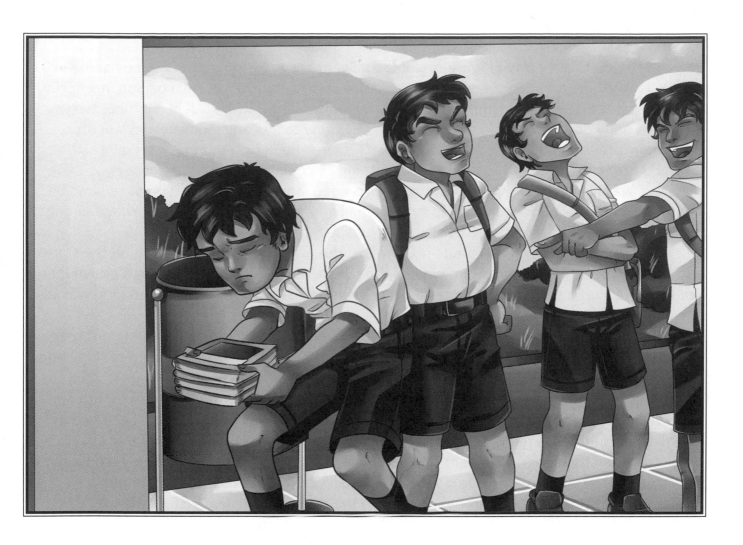

Standing Tall for Jesus

Lal tried to shut his ears to the jeering taunts. But they followed behind him like weights tied to his limbs, dragging him down and making each difficult step even harder. *Can't you even walk straight? What's wrong with you? Come on, stand up like a normal person!* Tears slipped down Lal's cheeks and he hobbled forward even faster. They couldn't see him breaking. *Crybaby*, they would taunt. *Weakling.*

"Where you running off to?" someone called after him gleefully.

"Nowhere fast," his friend chimed in. A smattering of laughter greeted his comment. Lal bit his lip and kept walking. If he kept his back to them and didn't respond, the teasing wouldn't get worse. He just had to ignore it.

But it was hard, so hard, when every word they spoke stung him like a lash. When their laughter made him want to shrink down and cover his face with his hands. He knew he was a freak, deformed and hideous. He knew it all too well.

Lal finally limped through the door of his house. His mother greeted him, but he hurried past her and into his room. He shut the door and took a deep breath. Then the sobs came, like water breaking from behind a dam, unable to be bottled up any longer. Lal slid down to the floor, shaking. It *hurt*. The jeers and insults were lodged in his heart like knives that penetrated deeper with each moment. Lal choked and gasped for breath. He clasped his hands tight over his mouth so that no one could hear his grief. It would only show them how frail he really was.

He couldn't fix it—any of it; he couldn't change the way he looked. His spine had been crooked all his life. It meant he would never stand up straight like a normal person, never run, and never work. It was hard enough to walk. He looked pitiful with his feet shuffling awkwardly and his body doubled over like a hunchback. He drew taunts and mockery and laughter. How many times had he longed to escape from his wretched body, tearing at his own skin as if he could break free from it? But there was nothing he could do.

This was his life. This was how it had always been, and this was how it would always be. They had tried—his back could not be straightened. Lal slowly wiped the tears away, leaning his head back against the door. There was no escape for him.

Twenty years went by. Lal made his slow, painful way in life, trying to shrug off the stares and the whispers that followed him wherever he went. It still hurt. Lal was now a grown man, not the lonely little schoolboy who cried himself to sleep at night; but when the world was especially harsh and cold, sometimes he still wept into his pillow and tried to hide his tears.

It was hard for him to find jobs because there were few tasks which he could perform easily. It was hard for him to find relationships because of his deformity. It was hard to find happiness. And it was impossible to live a normal life.

Then the rumors began to reach him. He heard tales carried from mouth to mouth and from village to village. These stories claimed that people had been miraculously healed of diseases and injuries in the name of Jesus with a healing power surpassing anything imaginable. Lal dared to let himself dream. What if these miracles were true? Could it even be thinkable that he, too, might be healed? Would he actually be able to take a step without wavering, to stand tall and straight with his head tipped to the sky, to run, to live, to breathe free air at last?

But Lal was a Hindu. Jesus was the Lord of the Christians. All of a sudden Lal realized that he didn't care. He had to see if there was a chance; he simply had to. And if there wasn't, well, it was better than having done nothing.

Lal went to meet with a group of Christians. He came only to ask for prayer, but as the Christians shared their teachings with him, he found himself being affected deeply. Their faith amazed Lal, and their kindness moved him. They didn't scorn him for his physical deformity. They talked with him like a friend, comforting him and asking not only about his disability but about the condition of his heart. For the first time in his life, Lal cried in front of complete strangers. He felt no shame, for they weren't ashamed of him. Instead, they laid their hands on him and prayed.

Soon Lal was attending a fellowship, where all of the Christians prayed faithfully for him. Lal listened intently as the Word of God was shared. The pastor spoke about Jesus, His love, His forgiveness, and His sacrifice. It was like nothing Lal had ever learned before. He came to understand that he was a sinner and he deserved death—there was nothing he could do to earn salvation. Jesus was the only way, and Jesus had loved humanity enough to die on the cross in their place, rising again to reign in glory. A short time later, Lal tearfully asked Jesus to forgive his sins and save him. He accepted Jesus's free gift of eternal life.

Lal's Christian brothers and sisters rejoiced in his spiritual healing. But they continued to pray for Lal's physical body as well. And in time, Jesus worked a miracle in Lal's life. His power did what no witch doctor or medical doctor had been able to do—slowly Lal's spine straightened. Lal couldn't believe what was happening. Each day he was able to lift his head a little higher. It really was happening; it was God's will to heal him. He was being healed! Lal laughed and wept in joy, thanking God with every breath he drew.

Now Lal stands completely straight. He walks as strongly as any young man his age, and at last he is able to run freely. He has a new life—both on this earth and in eternity. Working with Big Life Ministries, Lal shares the Gospel in his area so that more and more of his countrymen can hear the name of Jesus.

A Proud Heart

Buddhi had a big family, with lots of sisters and brothers. All of them followed the Buddhist religion faithfully. Buddhi's father, as the leader of the family, offered two large sacrifices each year and was involved in witchcraft. Their family believed this would make them prosperous.

But when Buddhi was young, his mother was paralyzed. They tried many different treatments, saw many doctors, and tried using witchcraft to heal her, but nothing helped. Then a man came to their house. He said that only faith in Jesus Christ could heal Buddhi's mother. As he shared the gospel, Buddhi's family believed. They asked Jesus to be their Savior, and a few months later, their mother was able to move again. It was a miracle! Buddhi's siblings and parents praised the Lord, rejoicing in his mighty power. Buddhi felt like he was watching them from a distance. He had seen everything that had occurred, just like the rest of his family. But he alone did not believe.

This had all happened many years before. Now Buddhi was grown and married. He moved away from his Christian home and family to another district in Nepal. He wasn't a happy man, he barely ever smiled. He lived a life without peace—drinking and smoking to satisfy his emptiness. People didn't enjoy spending time with him because he was always so grumpy and discouraging. He brooded constantly. He thought about his family, happy and content, and the miracle they had all witnessed. Sometimes he wondered why he hadn't believed as they had. Maybe it was the proud heart he always had. Even as a child—he had never wanted to admit that he was wrong.

Buddhi sat alone outside his house, a cigarette between his lips, watching the world through narrowed eyes. The passersby avoided his gaze. *They hate me*, he thought. *They all do. So why should I care about them either?* Recently there had been a lot of these thoughts running through his head. He was moody, troubled, and hopeless. He didn't care about anything or anyone anymore.

"Buddhi!" his wife's scream split the air. Buddhi jerked his head up, startled. Shoving his chair back, he turned and ran into the house. His wife was kneeling on the floor, bent over their daughter. She lay motionless, eyes closed, a trickle of blood seeping down her forehead. Buddhi stood rigid in the doorway, staring.

"She fell," his wife said anxiously, gingerly touching her daughter's head. She tried to lift the girl up off the floor.

Buddhi came and gently moved his wife aside. He cradled their young child in his arms, carrying her towards her bed. She was so light, so fragile. He cupped her limp head in his hands as he slowly lowered her on to the blankets. "Will she be okay?" his wife whispered. Buddhi didn't answer. He didn't have an answer. He stroked his daughter's forehead, feeling his heart beating painfully against his ribs. So there was still someone he cared about after all.

She lay there for three days. Three days of silence, fear, and grief. Buddhi called upon the doctors and witch doctors, eerily reminded of that time, so long ago, when his religion had been powerless, when the name of Jesus was the only thing that could heal. His anger flared, and Buddhi dismissed the thoughts. But they would not leave. And when, one by one, the doctors sadly shook their heads, Buddhi felt himself trembling. His daughter was pale—lifeless.

When they had tried everything—when the rituals and practices of Buddhism had failed yet again—a Christian came to their village. The woman visited their house, and she spoke those same words: "Faith in Jesus in the only thing that will save her." Buddhi felt his blood run cold, like he was watching a dream come to life. Could this really be happening again? He sensed that he was being given a second chance to see the truth and forsake his pride. But his pride was too great.

"I would like to pray for your daughter," the Christian said. Buddhi stared into the distance, as if he could see his mother lying motionless on a cot, and a family kneeling to pray. His pride broke just a little.

"O.K. You can pray for her," he almost whispered to her.

The woman prayed over their daughter for two whole days. Buddhi was amazed at her tenacity. She wouldn't give up. He watched over his child constantly, searching desperately for any sign of life. On the night of the second day, Buddhi and his wife both slept by their daughter's bedside, while the Christian continued to pray. At last the sun rose, fingering the horizon with beams of rosy light. The glow washed into Buddhi's house, into the bedroom where the three adults were slumped in exhausted sleep. Three adults and one child—a child who blinked and opened her eyes.

"Daddy?"

Buddhi snapped awake, adrenaline coursing through his limbs. He turned to the bed and found himself looking into his daughter's big, clear eyes. She was watching him calmly, curiously. "Daddy?" she repeated.

He scrambled to his feet, the quick motion waking his wife and the Christian lady. They stirred, yawning and rubbing their eyes blearily. Then they too saw the little girl sitting upright. Buddhi's wife gasped, tears of happiness filling her eyes.

The girl looked oddly at each of her parents and at the strange lady, all standing around her bed. "Can I have some milk?" she asked. Her mother laughed in relief, running and pulling her daughter into her arms. But Buddhi stood back. He was watching, as if from a distance, those happy faces, the awestruck tears. He hung on the edge, teetering yet again between his pride and what was really true.

Smiling, his daughter turned towards him and stretched out her hand. It was if her outstretched arm beckoned him, *"Are you going to give up your pride?"* His wife and the Christian turned to look at him as well. Buddhi stood alone, silent.

With a breathless sob he burst into a smile, tears flooding down his face. His pride finally broke. He believed in the power of Jesus. He ran to his family and hugged them close.

Together, Buddhi and his family accepted Jesus as their Lord and Savior. Buddhi's life became purposeful, driven, and full of joy—a far cry from the miserable, hardened man he had been before. He determined to leave behind his old life completely and grow in his walk with Christ.

One day he met a pastor named Prem, who was involved with a ministry called Big Life. Buddhi felt the Lord's call to serve. Now he works with Big Life to plant churches in the many villages throughout his home country.

Millions of gods

Lolita was taught to follow the Hindu religion. She worshipped many things, from gods and goddesses, to stones, water, fire, even mud and anthills. All of the Hindus followed these practices. All of Lolita's family did so as well. Lolita knew nothing else. It was tradition, and Lolita did everything just as she was supposed to do.

When she grew older, Lolita was married in the manner of her culture. She and her family lived within the customs as devout Hindus. Each year, they were required to pay a considerable sum of money for witch doctor rituals. This was a standard practice to bring good fortune and health to a family. Lolita knew it was the proper thing to do. But it cost so much money, and she had to provide for her family. However, she couldn't refuse to participate in the religious ceremonies—that was unthinkable.

Lolita recognized that something needed to be done to raise the money. She and her family went to work at the factories, laboring for long, exhausting hours to earn enough money to live on. Times became very hard for them. The whole family was tired and stressed, but despite their efforts, their finances continued to dwindle. Soon, Lolita would be expected to buy the witch doctor's services. There was no way that she could find the resources to pay for the Hindu rituals as well as continue to feed her family. They would have to choose one or the other.

Lolita shied away from the thought of forsaking the traditions with which she had grown up. It was against everything she had been taught. But, could she bear to watch her children grow hungry and faint? The witch doctor promised good fortune. Surely that was what they needed now, but would not good fortune come quicker if they saved the money? Lolita was in an agony of doubt and indecision.

It was morning at the factory—early, gray, and cold. Lolita could barely keep on her feet. Her eyes were rimmed with dark circles. She hadn't slept well the night before. Constantly she was thinking about her family's troubles, trying to find some way to fix them. But the solution evaded her. Now she stumbled through a day of work and wondered how she could go on. What she wouldn't give to just lie down and rest.

A voice, raised in passionate emotion, echoed across the factory. Lolita lifted her head with a puzzled frown and turned in the direction of the noise. A single man was standing in the middle of the work station, surrounded by a small crowd of factory workers. He was speaking earnestly to them, pleading with his hands and his voice for them to listen to what he was saying. Lolita cast a quick glance around and began walking towards the speaker intending to pass by just close enough to catch what he was saying.

"Salvation is found in no other but Jesus Christ alone," he proclaimed. "Whoever believes in Him will be saved!" He lowered his voice gently. "If you are hurting, weary, and heavily burdened, Jesus will bring you true peace, joy, and rest."

Lolita stopped in her tracks, forgetting about everything else. The words struck her somewhere deep down in her heart. A few moments before, she had been longing for rest and a way to cast off her burdens. Then this man spoke of the exact thing she was hoping for. But this rest was in a man named Jesus.

"We are all sinners and deserve death. But God sent His only Son, Jesus, to die in our

113

place. He paid the penalty for our sins and rose again from the grave. Now He freely offers us eternal life. We do not have to do anything but believe in Him and call upon Him to save us."

Lolita wanted to hear more. At the end of the work day, she caught up with the man and asked to talk with him. The more she listened, the more his words rang true in her heart. She began to realize that there was only one God, not millions like Hinduism teaches.

At the end of their conversation, Lolita asked excitedly, "Will you come and speak with my husband?"

The man—Prem—agreed.

That very night, she and her family were saved. They recognized that they needed Jesus to save them from their sins and that He was the only one who could bring them peace, order, and rest. Suddenly, Lolita was free from all the traditions and customs that had been bearing her down. An anthill was now just that, an anthill. There were no gods living inside of it—nor were there millions of gods. There was just One God who loved her and would give her the rest she longed for.

She now knew that God was the only One who deserved her worship. Lolita became part of a Christian fellowship where she could gather with other believers and share her faith.

Her Hindu neighbors and friends saw the new joy in Lolita's life. They were affected by the story of salvation which she shared with them. Some believed as she had, and Lolita's family was able to begin a church in their village.

Lolita now works with Big Life as a church planter, taking the Gospel further into her region. Like that one voice in the crowd, she tells of freedom and salvation which is only to be found in Jesus Christ.

The Mysterious Book

Hammad and Hassan were cousins. They were both shepherds—each with a flock of sheep that they led out to graze every day. Shepherds often went out together, for there were many predators wanting to attack the sheep—wolves, bears, tigers, and snow leopards. Life up in these cold, windy mountains was difficult, but for shepherds like Hammad and Hassan, it was home.

Today, Hammad herded his family's flock of thirty down onto a plain of short grass. These sheep were a huge part of the family's income; thus, the job of a shepherd required someone responsible. Hammad thought he was just that. He didn't care much for reading and learning; Hammad much preferred the sweeping view of the mountains and the grassy hills that sloped away from him on either side. He didn't even mind the cool wind too much. It somehow gave him a sense of freedom.

Then his sharp eyes noticed one of his sheep wandering away from the flock. Hammad whistled for it, but the sheep ignored him and trundled still farther. Grumbling to himself, Hammad hurried after it, and with some difficulty succeeded in herding it back with the group. The flock seemed very restless today, roaming off with ideas of their own, or fussing with the other sheep and causing disturbances. As the day wore slowly on, Hammad stopped noticing the cold for he got quite warm running after the wayward sheep.

He nudged one of the animals with his staff, looking over at his cousin, Hassan. Hassan was sitting where he had been all day—curled up on a rock, reading intently from a book. Hammad noted with considerable envy that none of Hassan's sheep were straying. They all grazed contentedly in one big, happy group.

"Why am I having so much trouble today while your sheep are all so calm?" asked Hammad, with not a small amount of grumpiness.

Hassan looked up distractedly. "I don't know," he said lightly. "Maybe I am a better shepherd than you?" Hassan laughed, turning back to his book.

Hammad didn't let the matter drop. "But you have done nothing today—nothing except read. Your sheep seem to be doing all the work themselves."

Hassan laughed again. He seemed completely content and at peace, just like his flock.

Hammad looked at him oddly. His cousin seemed different lately, like he had found something for which he had been searching very hard. "And what is this book that has taken you away from us all day?" asked Hammad.

Hassan shrugged casually, not looking up from the pages. "Just a storybook." Hammad finally turned away, leaving Hassan to become completely absorbed in his reading once more.

Over the days that followed, Hassan continued to read his book. His flock continued to mind themselves, never once causing trouble or giving Hassan any reason to get up and put his book away. On the other hand, Hammad had never been busier. He was starting to get very cross about the whole thing, especially when he noticed that not only were Hassan's sheep more well-behaved than his, they were also getting fatter and larger! Both flocks were being fed on the exact same grass, and nothing had changed in the shepherd's care of them, yet somehow Hassan's sheep were healthier than Hammad's.

Then came lambing season. Hammad watched in shock as Hassan's seventy sheep birthed twenty-two lambs, while his flock of thirty birthed only five! That was too much for Hammad. He went over to his cousin's house right away.

"Why are these strange things happening?" Hammad asked Hassan. "Why is your flock doing so well?"

Hassan wrinkled his brow, thinking. "I do not know, cousin, truly."

"Then answer me this," said Hammad. "What has changed you? You are different than you once were."

Hassan looked into his cousin's eyes, and Hammad could almost see the joy radiating from inside him. "I feel like myself," Hassan said simply.

As Hammad was about to leave, feeling more confused than when he had arrived, Hassan suddenly reached for his book. "Maybe," Hassan said slowly, looking down at it, "This is what has changed me." He handed the book to Hammad with a smile. "I've finished it. Why don't you read it now?"

Hammad was wary of the book at first. He didn't enjoy reading—he had learned that well in his Islamic classes. But thinking about the flocks' strange behavior got him to open the cover. As he read Hammad realized that this was no ordinary book. It was full of stories, like Hassan had said, but they were stories about a great, all-powerful, and merciful God—a God who loved and cherished His people. Hammad brought the book with him as he tended his flock, and found himself becoming wrapped up in the words on the pages.

Hassan's familiar, merry laugh interrupted him. "Look at your sheep, cousin!"

Hammad jerked his head up. But there was no wandering or missing sheep. Instead, his whole flock was quietly grazing, without a single one out of place. Hammad was amazed. He looked down at the book in his hands. Could it be…?

He left the book at home the next day. By the end of it, he was sweating, having had to repeatedly round up his suddenly unruly sheep. Hammad brought the book out every day after that, and never did he have to get up from where he sat. Hammad read about Jesus, God's Son, who came to rescue sinners and give them eternal life. The message of the book spoke to him like nothing he had ever read before.

He spoke with Hassan about what he was experiencing. His cousin's smile got even wider. "I have believed in Jesus ever since I read this book. His words have blessed me and have brought peace to my heart. I know that it is only through Jesus that I can have salvation."

Hammad nodded, as if finally understanding. "Yes," he said. "It is true." And a smile began to spread across his face.

Hammad now shepherds a growing church, but he still continues to care for his father's flock of sheep. The flock has now grown to a hundred and fifty—a hundred and fifty of the fattest and healthiest sheep in the entire region.

Did You Know...

The book you are reading is a follow-up to the book *I Heard Good News Today*?

UnveilinGLORY sold this book for years, but when the publisher ran out, we were told, "We're not printing any more."

Upon hearing that news, we bought the rights to the book and have been printing and selling them ever since.

Because families loved the first book so much, we were motivated to write this new book. We hope it becomes a series with other agencies!

Find out more about the book at: UnveilinGLORY's bookstore: www.UnveilinGLORY.com/ bookstore

The Search for Truth

When Butta was a boy, his favorite time of day was the early morning when his father would take him to the temple to pray. Afterwards, they would sit together and Butta's father would teach him about our god. "Our purpose as men is to seek truth," Butta's father would say. "And truth can only be found in god. As you seek him in your heart, you will eventually find him."

Butta bowed his head, fervently praying. *Please. Please, let me find Truth.*

Butta's father was a Sikh, carrying the name 'Singh' (lion)—a title of complete commitment to god. One day Butta hoped to be just like him.

As Butta grew older, his search for Truth became more and more important to him. He studied the Sikh scriptures constantly, and spent much time praying and meditating. The people of his village began to expect that Butta would succeed his father as the Granthi, the reader of the scriptures at the temple. Everyone loved and respected Butta's father, and they welcomed the idea of his son following in his steps. His father was very happy. But Butta felt discouraged. He didn't know why. This was the dream he had been longing for all his life. But now that it was within his reach, when he should have felt fulfilled, he felt empty.

Becoming a Granthi meant first becoming a Sikh. There was no particular age when this would take place. It happened when the person was ready to fully commit his life to the pursuit of their god. But because Butta was from a strong Sikh family, and the son of a Granthi, he began to feel the building pressure to become a Sikh. He couldn't wait too much longer. But why did he want to wait?

Then, suddenly, his father passed away, and at last the request became official: "Butta, please step up and take your father's place." Butta didn't know what to do. His wife expected him to accept; the village expected him to accept. The decision troubled him day and night, and still he could not figure out why. The meaning of his life was to find Truth. He knew that. He had always known that. But...was Sikhism really the way to find it? Was this all there was to life? It just couldn't be.

Ashamed and confused, he finally rejected the position as Granthi. Everyone was shocked. Butta tried to escape his troubled thoughts by taking his wife and son to another part of Punjab. His wife couldn't understand why Butta had rejected his life-long religion, and she argued with him frequently about it, questioning him.

Then late one night, in the dark hours of midnight, Butta heard screams echoing through his house. His son's screams. Terrified, Butta rushed to his son's room. The boy was having a terrible dream, and when Butta woke him from it, the boy sobbed and clung to his neck. "Voices told me," he said. "They said that our family would be destroyed." Butta comforted him, but over the next few weeks the nightmare continued to steal into his son's dreams, waking him in terror. At last his wife convinced him to seek the prayers of the Sikhs, but they did nothing. Butta's son's nightmares got worse, until the dream came every night. Desperate, Butta even took his son to the Hindu temples, but they too, could do nothing to heal his son.

Butta had nowhere else to turn. His son was haunted by the dreams and afraid to go to sleep. Then Butta's friend told him about a mighty healing he had witnessed in a city. His friend said it was at a Christian church. Butta had never heard of Christianity, but he was willing to try anything to make his son well.

Butta, his wife, and his son made the journey to the city, and at the church service Butta brought his son forward. He told the pastor what was wrong. The pastor put his hands on Butta's son and began to pray. His words were filled with power as he asked Jesus, by the power of His blood and authority, to heal the boy and drive away the evil spirits that tormented him. As he prayed, the pastor began to quote John 14:6: "I am the way, the truth and the life...."

The words lodged deep in Butta's heart. Truth. In a single, glorious moment, Butta knew that he had found what he had been searching for all his life. His confusion became clarity. He had found the true God. He had searched, and he had found *the* Truth. His son would be healed—Butta believed it.

At his side his wife knelt to the ground, crying. She, too, had heard and understood.

Butta's son was healed completely by Jesus' power, and Butta and his wife eagerly began learning more about Jesus Christ. Today Butta shares his faith with the Sikhs, hoping to lead them from their traditional, deep-rooted beliefs and bring them to the One who is the truth for which they are looking.

A Small Scrap of Paper

Faizal had been given the greatest honor that a Muslim could receive—he had been asked to become a Taliban warrior. Faizal was chosen because he was completely devoted to Islam and the word of the Quran and was prepared to kill for those beliefs. His father was extremely proud.

Faizal was excited to begin his training. He would have a chance to fight the infidels and if he died, he would be guaranteed his place in Paradise. He would be revered by the common men. It was the opportunity of a lifetime.

At the Taliban camp, Faizal was trained in guerrilla warfare and in the use of many different kinds of weapons. He learned about survival skills, explosives, spy techniques, hand-to-hand combat, how to operate modern war machines—and how to destroy them. The training was intense, but Faizal's mind and body became hardened by the exercise; he was fit, sharp, and ready to fight.

When the camp was completed, their commander sent them home with an impassioned speech. "When you are called again, you are called to war!" he cried. "Come ready. It is your duty, your privilege, to be fighters in the holy war against the infidels. They seek to destroy Islam. Will you let them persecute and kill your countrymen? Or will you wipe them from this earth?"

Faizal screamed his response with the rest of the recruits. His blood was hot in his veins; his heart throbbing with passion.

He returned home to wait for the summons to war. Every morning Faizal awoke to the commander's words ringing in his ears, calling the warriors to their holy purpose. Faizal knew that his destiny was drawing near. He could feel it—a stirring in the atmosphere, in his soul.

Faizal had much spare time now that he was home. He sat outside a little tea shop one afternoon drinking a cup of the dark brew. The low hum of the market around him soothed Faizal, and he leaned his head back and closed his eyes.

A sudden breeze swept over his face. Faizal sighed with relief enjoying the cool touch of the wind. The breeze grew stronger. Faizal sat up and saw a tiny dust-devil swirling through the sand a short distance away. It was barely taller than Faizal's knee and a deep red color. He watched as it spiraled towards him. A strange flicker of white glimmered in the dust-devil's funnel.

Gently, the wind died down, and the dust-devil dissipated at Faizal's feet. The piece of white fluttered to the ground—a small scrap of paper. Curious, Faizal picked it up. The paper was battered and sandy, but Faizal could clearly read the small words printed on it.

"Blessed are the poor in spirit, for theirs is the kingdom of heaven." Faizal jerked his head up, unconsciously checking to see if anyone was watching him. There was no one. Faizal slowly turned his eyes back to the paper. He didn't know what it was, but the teaching was not from the Quran. He should throw it away and not look at it anymore. But—the words, they spoke to him. He had to read more.

Quickly, Faizal read the next line. "Blessed are the merciful, for they will be shown mercy."

What was this? Mercy? Faizal had been taught that mercy has no place in a warrior. He was to kill his enemies without hesitation. Faizal rubbed the thin paper between his fingers as his thoughts ventured to places they had never gone before. What did this mean?

Faizal got to his feet leaving his tea forgotten. He slipped the paper into his pocket.

Over the next few weeks, Faizal read the paper countless times. "Blessed are the merciful…" It was strange—and beautiful. Faizal didn't understand why the words were affecting him so. But he couldn't deny that his heart was changing.

Faizal was summoned to war a short while later. He packed, said good-bye to his family, and walked out the door. But he couldn't take a step farther. The glory and excitement of war suddenly meant nothing to him. All that mattered was a single scrap of paper and a message of mercy and peace.

Instead of going to the Taliban camp, Faizal went to a friend's house, where he stayed alone. He sat in his borrowed bedroom, agonized and confused. What had happened to him? Those words on the paper had been the cause, he knew. But what did they mean? He had to find out, before it drove him mad.

Faizal asked his friend if he knew anything about where the paper might have come from.

His friend squinted at the small writing. He shrugged. "I'm not sure. But the kingdom of heaven sounds like what the Christians teach." Faizal thought about that. Christians were unbelievers. But he would gladly go to anyone who could answer his questions.

Faizal arranged to meet with a Christian, a convert from Islam. It would be on the edge of the city away from anyone Faizal knew. The Christian agreed to come.

"You can't go!" insisted his friend as Faizal prepared to leave the house. "You can't meet with a Christian! It's too dangerous. You know they can't be trusted."

Faizal smiled at his friend, perfectly calm. He even felt excited. "I am a Taliban warrior. I do not know fear." With the paper clutched in his hand, Faizal made his way to the arranged meeting-place.

The Christian was nervous. He had no idea what to expect from this Muslim. After all, he was a Taliban fighter. But something had told him that he needed to come meet with Faizal—that it was very important.

The two sat down, and Faizal got right to the point. "Do you know," he said, pulling the paper out of his pocket, "what this is?"

The Christian unfolded the scrap and read it. "This is from the New Testament," he said slowly. "They are the words of Jesus."

Faizal's head was spinning. The words of Jesus—Jesus had spoken to him. Faizal was overwhelmed by the presence of a powerful, powerful love, pressing in around him, thickening the air. He cried out and fell to his knees, tears spilling from his eyes. He had been so wrong. He was so full of sin. And yet Jesus Himself had called to him.

The Christian knelt beside Faizal. He gripped the young warrior's hands, and together they went to Jesus in prayer. Faizal sobbed uncontrollably as he confessed his sin and accepted Jesus as his Savior.

From that day, Faizal's life, his very identity, was completely changed. He now followed the call of his Lord, Jesus, and the passion in his heart was deeper and more intense than anything he had felt before. Faizal began pointing other Muslims to the truth. He spoke to some of the most radical Islamic groups in the country, preaching about mercy and love and Jesus. Many young Muslims came to salvation as Faizal had.

What Faizal was doing was extremely dangerous, but he wasn't afraid. If you asked why, he would say with a smile: "I am a warrior for Christ. I do not know fear."

The Unexpected Tiger

Twenty pairs of frantic feet pounded the earth. Twenty people ran for their lives, clutching their children's hands, pulling them headlong through the forest. The only sound was their breathless gasps and the noisy crackling of the leaves. Phillip led the villagers on, constantly glancing over his shoulder. He could hear the shouts in the distance, the screams of anger and hate. They were gaining on them.

Ever since darkness had fallen the day before, Phillip and his Christian friends had been living a nightmare. Angry mobs descended upon their village, vowing destruction and death on all Christians. Phillip and twenty others managed to escape to the forest. For what seemed liked ages they huddled in the undergrowth, the mothers trying to comfort their children. Everyone was confused and terrified. Phillip could feel their eyes on him, looking up to him as an elder of their village. They expected him to know what to do. They needed him to lead them. But he was just as lost as they were.

Then as dawn began to break, a boy had burst into their clearing. His hair was wild; his eyes crazed with fright. His feet were bare and scratched by the thorns. "They're coming," he cried hopelessly.

Twenty people ran for their lives.

Phillip gritted his teeth and ran faster urging his villagers onward. He dared not think about what would happen if the Hindus caught them. They had to get away, they *had* to. He whipped his head around to search the trees. There was no one in sight, not yet. One of the little girls clapped a hand over her mouth, stifling a frightened whimper. Phillip set his eyes back on the forest ahead. For now the trees shielded them. No one could see far in the thick forest and that gave them an advantage. "Hurry now," Phillip whispered urgently. He took the little girl's hand.

They plunged onward and burst out into openness. Phillip staggered to a halt, disoriented by the sudden clear sky above them and the sun shining brilliantly after the dimness of the trees. A wide clearing lay before them. Empty. Phillip glanced at his friends, his jaw tightening grimly. He saw in their eyes that they understood. There was no cover anymore.

"Run!" he shouted. They ran as they had never run before. Every ragged breath left in their lungs—every bit of strength in their limbs poured into their flight. Phillip kept his gaze fixed on the forest at the other side of the clearing. In it was safety, refuge, and perhaps a chance at life. If they reached that side of the forest they could keep going. If they didn't, life would be no more. The clearing seemed to stretch farther and farther with each step they took, holding safety just out of their reach.

Running, Phillip heard the triumphant roar of their pursuers. They had broken into the clearing, and the forest was still thirty yards away.

Phillip slowed, then stopped, turning to face those who wished their death. The other Christians stopped with him, their faces pale. They knew it was over. At the other side of the clearing, the mob was racing towards them, brandishing their weapons with cries of wild delight. There would be no mercy. Phillip was shaking as he moved in front of the women and children. "Oh, Father," he whispered, as the villagers pressed close behind him. The atmosphere was thick with fear; Phillip could feel it weighing on his heart. "Protect us." The Hindus screamed their war cries. He could see their eyes now, narrowed with rage, the faint lines creasing their faces—the white knuckles gripping their weapons.

Phillip closed his eyes and prayed for strength.

A mighty roar shook the air. Phillip's eyes snapped open. Its origination wasn't from the mob. The Hindus froze where they were, staring off to the side—afraid. Phillip slowly turned his head to follow their gaze.

A massive tiger had emerged from the forest. It was a full-grown male, muscled and lean, the sunlight dappled on its sleek black and orange coat. Both the Hindus and the Christians watched it, motionless. The tiger began to pace across the clearing, the grass parting in waves before its heavy paws. Phillip felt a new fear—a suspenseful, fragile fear—spread over him. At any moment the tiger could choose to viciously and violently attack them. He would be active and alert during mating season, and this tiger's breed preferred to hunt and kill during the day. The two groups were in his territory. They had disturbed him. Any movement, any distraction, would send the tiger into a fury.

Phillip swallowed hard, watching the tiger glide smoothly through the grass. He passed right between the Hindus and the Christians. Maybe he would simply continue on and enter the forest again. The Hindus were waiting, their hands tight on their weapons, longing to continue their attack. Phillip stood his ground, trembling.

The tiger slowed as it reached the center of the clearing. Then he stopped. It lifted its magnificent head, and yawned leisurely, his razor-sharp teeth gleaming white. He seemed to know that he owned the moment. As the humans watched, the magnificent creature stretched, looking for all the world like some over-grown house cat. It flopped down onto the ground, rolling playfully over onto its side and then upright again.

There the tiger stayed. He twitched his tail, watching the Hindus with alert, focused eyes. He showed no sign of leaving. The Hindus shifted uneasily. They didn't dare try to push past the tiger. Phillip's legs were aching with tiredness, and at last he slowly seated himself on the ground. The other Christians followed suit. Some of the little ones slumped tiredly against their parents' shoulders, closing their eyes. The tiger licked a paw with its brilliant pink tongue.

The minutes passed by with agonizing slowness. As the sun rose higher in the sky, the Hindus began to glance at each other, undecided. They had lowered their weapons. The un-checked rage that had twisted their features faded, leaving behind the faces of tired, worried men. They whispered quietly amongst themselves. Then, slowly, they withdrew. Keeping their eyes fixed on the tiger, the Hindus backed away until they had reached the other side of the clearing. There they turned and went back the way they had come.

Phillip took a deep breath, feeling tears of relief spring to his eyes. Their pursuers had given up the chase. But the tiger still remained. As Phillip watched cautiously, the animal turned its head, looking straight at the Christians with its deep brown eyes. It rose to its feet with one flowing movement and easily moved off through the grass. Phillip's eyes followed the tiger, shocked, as it loped back into the forest. Its task was finished.

The twenty villagers made it to the other side of the forest and then to a refugee camp where they found shelter and food. There, other Christians welcomed them. When they told their story, the Christians were amazed and praised God for delivering them from a seeming-ly impossible situation. Phillip knew that he had seen God's hand working that day. God had protected His children.

Wanting to Die

Hari was brought up in a Hindu community. He believed that Christianity was bad and was to be avoided by all Hindus. Hari was only in 6th Grade when he first heard about Jesus. But from that moment on he had hated Christians.

It was that very same year, in 6th grade, when Hari became very sick. He had agonizing pains in his stomach, so intense that he was curled up on his bed, howling and sobbing. He couldn't go to school that morning, or the next morning, or the next. Hari had to be removed from school. His family hoped that with time to rest, Hari would heal.

But the illness only worsened. The piercing aches in Hari's stomach started to spread through the rest of his body. Hari was in constant pain with no way to get relief. Hari's family took him to many different hospitals, but the doctors did not know what was causing Hari's suffering. Then Hari's family tried witchcraft and other Hindu rituals. But even as the witch doctors worked their craft, Hari continued in pain with sweat and tears soaking his skin.

There was nothing else to do. Hari's parents looked at their son, lying exhausted on his bed. They were crying. The more they went to the witch doctors, the more Hari suffered. Unless a miracle happened, Hari would have to live with this terribly painful disease for the rest of his life.

Hari knew that all hope was gone. It had been a long time since the last treatment, and his pain had only worsened. A deep depression had fallen over him. He couldn't live like this. It would be better to die and have peace than to feel the agony he was experiencing now. Hari had to have relief; he couldn't go on. *It would be better to die.*

When Hari was a teenager, he decided to kill himself. Soon. In just a few days, this pain would vanish. Hari had no desire to live. His heart had become strangely heavy; joy seemed to have left him. It felt as though he was being pressed in by some dark presence, and the life was being squeezed out of him. Hari gripped his bed sheets, stiffening as another jolt of pain lanced through him. He gritted his teeth, a faint moan escaping his lips. Then it was gone. Hari went limp, his chest heaving. He began to cry. Soon this torture would be over.

Hari's father closed the front door behind him. He hated leaving his son crying and his wife in distress, but he had to go to work. He just had to keep on going. At last the lunch break came. Hari's father slumped into a chair and buried his face in his hands. His thoughts kept going back to his home where his son lay in bed, racked with pain and without a will to live. What could he do for his son? Was there any way to help him?

His friend walked over and slowly sat down beside him. "Are you alright?" he asked.

"I don't know what to do," Hari's father said softly. "I've tried everything." He rubbed his hand over his face, trying to conceal the tears burning in his eyes.

The man beside him was silent for a moment. Then he took a deep breath and turned towards Hari's father. "There is a church in the next village," he said haltingly. "You could take him to the fellowship."

Hari's father looked sharply at his friend. "But they are Christians—they are evil."

The man dropped his eyes. "I'm sorry, but I think it is your only hope."

Hari's father thought on what his friend had said. It pained him deeply to see his son so weak and in so much pain. And it was true, there had been many stories of miraculous healings

127

by the prayers of these Christians. But if his millions of gods couldn't heal Hari, how could only one God of the Christians heal him? It didn't make sense. But what did Hari have to lose?

Maybe these Christians could help him.

His family decided to go. Hari's father carried him into the fellowship, and explained to the Christians there how Hari had been suffering. They knelt around Hari, every face compassionate and anxious. Hari found it hard to hate them. The Christians rested their hands on Hari and began to pray.

They prayed in the name of Jesus, for His power to bring healing to Hari's body. As they prayed, Hari tensed; sudden, overwhelming terror and depression gripped his mind. He cried out gulping for breath. The Christians continued to pray louder, speaking Jesus's name. Hari felt pure evil touch inside his mind, making him twist in revulsion and fear. He screamed for it to stop. He heard the prayers growing louder, full of power, until they were the only thing he could hear.

Hari gasped and opened his eyes. He was lying on the floor with the Christians huddled around him and multiple hands touching him. His parents were by his side, their eyes frightened. His hands were still trembling. Hari took a deep, calming breath.

It was then that Hari realized that the evil presence had been demonic spirits. And he now realized that the Hindu rituals and witchcraft that Hari and his entire community practiced had left him open to more attack. No wonder it had been getting worse.

Hari and his family returned to the fellowship many times, where the Christians continued to pray earnestly over Hari. His pain lessened greatly each day, and he no longer thought of death. Hari had hope again.

The power of the multiple spirits gradually lost its hold over Hari's mind and body. After a month, Hari was fully healed. Hari and his family were amazed and overjoyed. The Christians told them that Hari's healing had come from Jesus, the one true God and Savior. They shared the gospel, telling of Jesus's death on the cross, his resurrection, and his gift of salvation to sinners. Both Hari and his whole family accepted Jesus Christ as their Lord and Savior. He was the One and true God over their millions of gods. They praised him for the miracle He had worked in Hari, and for the forgiveness which He had given them now.

The Hindu village in which they lived was horrified. Their gods had been outdone. This enraged the Hindu leaders of the village. They called for an emergency meeting and came to a clear decision: Christians could not be allowed in their community. They forced Hari's family to leave the village. Hari didn't want to leave his schoolmates and his house, but he knew that something bigger awaited him. He vowed that he would serve the Lord in his life, however Jesus would ask, and wherever He would call.

Her Sister-In-Law

Bhim grew up with a harsh understanding of the world. When she was a young child, she was constantly sick and spent much of her time in various hospitals. After she had become a little older, Bhim was married to a man named Shyam. He didn't make her life easier or happier. Shyam was addicted to alcohol. He fought with Bhim often, until she was frustrated and in tears.

"What can I do?" she wept. "I haven't been happy in so long." Maybe, if she and Shyam moved out of the country, they could start a new life elsewhere. Maybe, with a fresh beginning, things would get better. Shyam agreed. The two moved from Nepal to India and settled into a home there.

But Shyam didn't change his ways. While Bhim was trying to manage the household and the money, he would spend large amounts of their savings on drink. Bhim was stressed to her limits. She now had two children to look after as well as the rest of the family's affairs. Shyam wouldn't take any of the responsibility. He didn't help Bhim, even when she stayed up into the morning trying to cover the work of two people and fell asleep on her feet the next day. Bhim would break into tears without warning. Many times she was overcome by exhaustion and loneliness. She longed for rest, peace, joy. So many things she wanted, but she could never see them becoming a part of her life.

There was one occasion when Bhim felt a little relief. Her sister-in-law, a Christian, would come to visit. Bhim took some time to sit down with her, sip some tea, and talk. The conversation soothed Bhim's nerves. By the time her sister-in-law left, Bhim felt like she could make it through a few more days. Maybe it was her sister-in-law's sweet smile, or the genuine love in her actions towards Bhim. Maybe it was the stories she told—stories about Jesus. Bhim always liked listening to those tales of miracles, sacrifice, love, and joy. She didn't really understand them, but she wanted to hear more.

Bhim's sister-in-law told her the story of Jesus's death on the cross. "He died for everyone," she said. "If we believe in Him, He will save us from the penalty of our sins and give us eternal life."

Bhim was confused. "I," she paused trying to gather her question, "I don't know what you mean by that."

Her sister-in-law smiled gently. "Then I will tell you the story again, tomorrow." She prayed with Bhim, asking this Jesus to touch Bhim's heart and give her understanding.

Bhim's sister-in-law did come back, and she told Bhim the salvation story—again, and again. Bhim paid close attention. She wanted to understand. She wanted Jesus. But how?

"You must believe and accept His sacrifice," her sister-in-law said.

Bhim nodded, realization slowly clearing her mind. "I do," she said breathlessly. "I do believe." In that moment, she realized it was true. She believed that Jesus was Lord, *her* Lord.

Soon afterwards, Bhim prayed to Jesus and asked Him to forgive her sins. Bhim had never been happier in her entire life. She had joy—such joy! And there was peace in her hectic, flurried life. Jesus would take care of her, and hold her in His arms. All she had to do was trust in Him.

Bhim began talking to her husband about Jesus. Shyam was as confused as Bhim had been, but he listened. Bhim shared the Gospel with him, many, many times. Then, gradually, Shyam started to change. He stopped arguing with Bhim, and he spent more time with his children. He tried to help out around the house. He didn't go drinking as often. Bhim was overjoyed. She could feel their life being renewed as Jesus entered into it.

She sensed joy in every morning and peace every time she lay down to sleep. At last, Shyam came to understand Jesus' sacrifice. Shyam accepted Him as his Lord. He quit drinking altogether and his life was entirely transformed.

As for Bhim, she could laugh again. She rejoiced in her children and in teaching them about Jesus. She smiled at the housework. She found happiness in Shyam. Their relationship grew and strengthened each day with Christ as their center.

Bhim and her family now share the salvation story with those around them. Bhim prays that the people they witness to will come to understand the power of Jesus's love and the joy that can be theirs through Him.

Poisoned Tea

Raban closed his eyes. He took a deep breath, allowing the dusty, sweet taste of the air to fill his lungs as his shoes scuffed along the dirt road. The walk had been peaceful and quiet, giving him plenty of time to pray and think back along the journey that had brought him to this point.

He was heading to a little church that he had planted. Raban's desire to start churches had first emerged when, as a new Christian, he found himself becoming a mentor and leader to many young believers. Big Life had trained him in this and he loved doing helping young believers.

He saw the small building appear in the distance. Soon Raban was welcomed inside by the leader of the fellowship and the owner of the house in which they met—Dinesh. Raban was overjoyed to see Dinesh again. Dinesh, too, greeted Raban enthusiastically, but his face was oddly tense and shadowed. Raban could tell that all was not right.

"What is wrong, Dinesh?" Raban asked, frowning.

Dinesh hesitated a moment, and then said. "It is the priest Ratai Mandi. He is causing trouble for us. He wants us to stop meeting."

"Do you think he would let me talk with him?" said Raban. Maybe he could get Ratai to change the way he felt towards the fellowship. After all, they were not doing any harm.

"If you don't meet with him, he'll come to you. He's been demanding to speak with you."

Dinesh took Raban to Ratai's house. As they approached, Raban saw a tall, muscled man standing stock-still in the doorway. He was dressed in rich traditional robes with his arms folded imperiously.

Trying to fight back his nervousness, Raban approached the priest with a friendly smile on his face. But even as he opened his mouth to say hello, Ratai cut him off.

"Your fellowship must stop. You must leave this place."

Raban was slightly taken aback by the aggression in Ratai's voice. Recovering himself, he said in what he hoped was a calm, steady voice, "We are doing no harm. As Christians, we treat everyone—"

The priest lashed out, slapping his hand hard across Raban's face. Raban staggered backward in shock. Ratai shouted insults and accusations at Raban and Dinesh beginning to advance upon them while shaking a heavy staff.

Frightened, Raban and Dinesh retreated. They hurried quickly away knowing that the meeting had gone horribly.

Raban went home after the fellowship that day, but his thoughts remained back at Dinesh's village. He worried about the fellowship there. Ratai was a violent man, and he was also a very important one. If Ratai wanted to—and he clearly did—he could bring a lot of hardship upon the group of believers.

Raban prayed daily for the fellowship and visited again to encourage Dinesh and the others. But while he was there, Ratai met him again. This time, Ratai's rage seemed to have doubled. His face was twisted with anger, and when Raban tried to reason with him, Ratai pulled back his fist and punched him. Raban cowered in pain as Ratai struck him three more times—twice with his fists and finally with his heavy stick. Ratai was shouting all the while. Finally, as Ratai continued to rage at him, Raban left the village.

On his way home, Raban prayed desperately for the fellowship's protection. Bruises were already beginning to show on his body, and he remembered all too well the towering form of the priest and the angry light in his eyes. Maybe he should stay away for a while. Every time he had gone to the fellowship, it seemed to make Ratai worse.

So Raban decided to stay away. But the longer he stayed away, the more Raban felt guilt growing in his chest. He tried to push it away, making excuses, but he could not. Every time he closed his eyes he saw the faces of the church he had started...the church he had abandoned. He had received word from Dinesh that the group was still meeting, but they were now doing so in hiding. Though Dinesh didn't say it, Raban could hear the pleading in words: Come back. Help us. We need you.

Even though the church needed him, Raban didn't come....because he was afraid. As he realized this, Raban's prayers changed. He continued to pray for the fellowship, and also for Ratai's salvation, but now he began to pray for himself—for courage.

A few days later, Raban returned to the village. He was wary, but Ratai didn't turn up. Raban was able to worship joyfully with his fellow believers. They were all delighted to see him and greatly strengthened by his presence. When Raban left that day, his heart was full of worship.

But as he stepped onto the dirt path away from the village, he saw Ratai standing a little ways ahead blocking the road. Raban breathed a silent prayer and continued walking. He drew level with Ratai, bracing himself for violence and abuse. But Ratai was silent. His face unreadable, the priest jerked his arm in a gesture for Raban to follow him.

Ratai turned sharply and walked towards his house. Raban hesitated before finally trailing along behind him. When they arrived, Ratai pointed toward a seat at the table.   Raban slowly sank into the chair. Ratai still hadn't spoken a word.

The priest silently made a pot of tea and handed Raban a cup. Thoroughly confused, Raban stared at the steaming tea cup in a state of shock. Was the tea poisoned? He didn't know what to do and just sat there.

Ratai poured himself a cup of tea and sat down across from Raban. There was silence for a moment longer, and then Ratai spoke in a low, gruff voice. "I want...to apologize."

The tea almost dropped out of Raban's hand.

"For beating you and shouting," said Ratai. "I was wrong."

Raban was speechless. He could only stare and force his head into something resembling a nod.

Then Ratai spoke again. "Tell me about your God."

Raban couldn't believe that this was real. It was too amazing. But Raban knew that his God worked in amazing ways, and he knew that this opportunity was an answer to his prayers.

A few hours later, Dinesh saw Raban and Ratai walking towards his house. They were walking side by side and both wore peaceful smiles. But if this was surprising to Dinesh, he was still more surprised by what Raban said next.

"Dinesh," Raban said, barely able to control his grin, "Ratai will be attending your fellowship next week. He wants to learn a lot more about Jesus." Dinesh was speechless and just nodded his head in agreement.

Ratai began coming regularly to the fellowship, and it was there that he received Christ as his Savior. Afterwards, Ratai started a fellowship of his own. He was stirred with a passion that everyone in his village should know the good news of Jesus.

Did You Know...

When asked their greatest need, Big Life's indigenous partners (including those in this book) always reply with two requests: prayer & Bibles.

If you feel lead to pray for these men and women, go to www.blm.or/prayer for an opportunity to partner with them in prayer.

If you feel led to provide a Bible for these men and women in their local language, the cost to print, transport and disciple each recipient is only $5.

Visit www.blm.org/donate and write "Bibles" in the comments section.

Hold on to Your Faith

Whenever Chheng felt sick, he would offer a sacrifice. He worshipped spirits, and he believed that if they received a sacrifice, they would cure his pain. But it never seemed to work. Instead, it seemed to get worse and Chheng was overcome with depression, anger, and worthlessness. Although Chheng was not aware of their power, these spirits were evil and they ruled over Chheng. His wife and children were forced to bear the consequences of his dark moods.

For years Chheng lived this way—always feeling unclean deep inside. His health was poor, and he was constantly short-tempered, but he didn't know why. He felt like something was pressing down on him as a heavy weight slowly crushing him.

Chheng became sick again—worse than ever before. As was routine, he made an animal sacrifice, but nothing changed. Chheng was in a lot of pain, and he was scared. Why weren't the spirits helping him? At last Chheng went to a doctor. The doctor examined him, but shook his head helplessly. He couldn't find anything wrong. There wasn't anything he could do for Chheng.

Then a group of Christians arrived in Chheng's village. Chheng hated Christians—every one of them. They were unbelievers. They didn't follow the true religion. But they spoke of healing.

Almost against his will, Chheng went to listen to them. He was drawn by the hope of something that could deliver him from his sickness. The Christians talked about Jesus, who was the Great Healer. And suddenly Chheng was calling out, "Please!" The Christians turned towards him. "If Jesus can heal me, I will follow him," Chheng said.

The Christians smiled sadly. "You must follow Jesus because you believe. Not just because you want healing from your illness."

Chheng was angry. He went home and slumped onto his bed, staring up at the ceiling. He was a fool. This Jesus couldn't have the power to heal him. No one could.

Unbidden tears sprang to his eyes. Chheng sobbed into his bed sheets, thinking about his life—the one that he might soon leave behind. What had he done with it? He had lived in hatred and anger, despising everything around him. Chheng thought about what the Christians had said. "You must follow Jesus because you believe..."

Chheng became sicker and sicker. Just as he had feared, he was dying. Chheng was terrified. There was nothing he could do, nowhere to turn. But constantly the words of the Christians came into his mind, "You must believe...."

How could he believe? What proof did he have that Jesus had any power at all? "You must believe..." But—he was a Buddhist. Jesus was the God of the Christians. *You must believe.* Chheng was unwilling, but he realized that there was only one hope left. He had to go to Jesus.

He decided to go to the Christian fellowship nearby. As he left the house, he commanded his family, "Hold on to the Buddhist faith. I only go to the Christians because I have no other choice."

Chheng entered the fellowship reluctantly. He hated being so helpless, having to seek the aid of the very people whom he had loathed for so long. "I want you," he said heavily, "to pray for me."

The Christians gathered around placing their hands upon him. Chheng listened in amazement as they prayed. Their voices were so tender, so full of love—for him, a person they barely knew. They prayed to Jesus, asking for his healing power to touch Chheng. The air seemed to grow thicker as they prayed. Chheng felt his throat contract, tears blurring his eyes. There was something moving in the midst of these people—an undeniable presence. There was *power* in the room.

Chheng began trembling. Still the Christians prayed, their hands firm upon his shoulders. Chheng was weeping, tears turning to sobs as he felt an infinite, overwhelming peace settle over him. It was Jesus.

When Chheng returned home, he started praying every day. He would read the Bible, and then bow his head before Jesus, the Almighty God. He asked for healing. But he also asked for forgiveness. Chheng felt at peace. There was a hope and a joy inside him that he couldn't explain. Even though he was still sick, Chheng wasn't frightened, not now.

Days passed—turning into weeks, and then months. Chheng prayed constantly, feeling the presence of Jesus close about him every moment. He was no longer close to death. In fact, he was slowly, steadily, recovering.

One day, several months after he had first attended the fellowship, Chheng arose in the morning—and he knew that he was completely healed. He hadn't offered any sacrifices. No doctors had treated him. It was all Jesus. Chheng fell to his knees in gratitude and joy, thanking the Lord for working His awesome power in Chheng's own life. Chheng wanted more than anything to give something back. He knew that nothing he ever did could repay what Jesus had done for him. He had only one thing to give and that was himself. Chheng devoted his heart, his mind, and his life to Jesus, the one, true, living God, the Great Healer.

Despite Chheng's warning to them, his family didn't continue in the Buddhist religion. But by this time, Chheng didn't want them to be Buddhists any longer. He wanted them to believe in Jesus as he did. Seeing the miracle of Chheng's healing and changed life, they, too, came to know Jesus as their Lord. Together the family destroyed all their Buddhist relics. They forsook the practices of sacrifice and spirit worship. Now Chheng and his family are serving Jesus and telling others about Him. Chheng follows Jesus *because he believes.*

She Never Felt so Alone

Samantha (Sam) had never felt so alone.

Some years had gone by since her husband had passed away. The pain of his loss gradually lessened, but there was always the emptiness. Sam's two sons comforted her and stood by her, vowing to support the family. They were Sam's pride and joy, her hope when she had none. So often she could see her husband's characteristics and habits showing in them. It made her smile.

But when life had just begun to return to normal, more trouble came. Sam's savings were thin, and she was forced to borrow money from her neighbors. The loans helped, but Sam worried about how she would ever repay them.

Sam was in the kitchen, trying to make dinner, but she couldn't focus as she worried about the debt. What was she supposed to do? She didn't know how to provide for her family, and she was anxious about them. She wanted to give her sons the opportunity for a good life, but she had no money to spare. They would have to take on the responsibilities of the men of the house. Sam looked down into the pot she was stirring, her vision suddenly blurry. How she wished she could care for them like she wanted to. She hoped they knew that. Tears spilled from her eyes and quickly she brushed them away. She had to stand strong—and stand alone.

The next day dawned bright and sunny. Sam took a deep breath and felt a smile touch her lips. There would be a way through these hard times. It was strange how a new day could bring such a different perspective.

Sam started her daily duties with new hope. She worked diligently, until sweat was beading on her brow. There would be a way…. A knock came at the door. Sam wiped her hands and went to answer the door.

"Hello!" Sam smiled, recognizing one of her neighbors. "What can I do for you?"

Her neighbor's face was solemn. "We need to talk to you."

Sam swallowed nervously. "Please, come in." She backed up, allowing her neighbor into the house.

When they had seated themselves, her neighbor took a breath and began. "You have borrowed a considerable amount of money from many of us. We need to know when you can repay it."

Sam looked down, her hands suddenly clammy. "I…"

"And if you can't pay," her neighbor rushed on. All at once she paused, looking troubled. "We will have to take your house," she said quietly.

Sam jerked her head up, shocked. "No. Please…"

Her neighbor stood up, avoiding Sam's eyes. "We have no other choice. If you cannot pay us by the end of the week, you will have to move out."

Her neighbor hesitated, glancing at Sam. She was staring down at her hands folded in her lap, unmoving. Sam's neighbor watched uneasily as Sam's shoulders began to shake in silent sobs. Then with a sigh, her neighbor turned and left the house.

Sam couldn't repay her debts. They were too large. She and her two sons had to hurriedly pack up all their belongings and move to a rental house a little ways away. Sam wept constantly, remembering all the memories that had been stored up in the home that was now lost to them.

Maybe it was too much for one of her sons. Maybe he had been struggling for a while, Sam didn't know. But she soon found out that he was addicted to drugs. Sam didn't understand. Her precious, beloved son...her hope...he didn't get along with his brother anymore, he shouted at Sam. He fell into a dark and dangerous lifestyle, so far from the helpful, happy boy he had been. Sam felt no reason for living. Even her children, who had always kept her going, had turned away.

She had never felt so alone.

Someone knocked at the door of their little rental house. Sam wiped her eyes and tried to regain her composure. When she opened the door, she saw one of her friends, a Christian. She smiled at Sam. "I thought I would come visit you." She peeked inside the house. "You have a nice place here."

Sam managed a smile; the kind words lifted her spirits. "Thank you. Please come in."

They talked for a long time. Sam poured out all her troubles, her despair, and her loneliness, grateful to just have someone who would listen. Her friend put her arm around Sam's shoulders. "I know someone who will never leave you," she said gently. "Let me tell you about my Lord Jesus."

Sam's friend told her how Jesus had come to save sinners and that anyone who believed in Him would have eternal life. She told Sam that those who were saved by Jesus' grace became his children. "He will help us through all of our troubles," she said. "And He will give us hope."

Sam looked at her friend with cautious hope. Could it be that there was someone who loved her that much? She began to weep. Her friend held her, rocked her. "You must only believe," she said softly.

"I do," Sam sobbed. "I believe in Jesus." She said the words before she realized that they were true. "I want..." she said haltingly, "to be saved."

Her friend grasped her hands. "Then let us pray."

Sam bowed her head. "I-I know that I am a sinner, and that You are the only way of salvation," Sam pleaded through her tears. "I believe that You died on the cross for me and rose again. Please, please forgive my sins and save me."

From that exact moment, Sam was never hopeless again. Always she felt Jesus's presence beside her, supporting her, encouraging her, and giving her joy. Sam prayed daily for her son's addiction and for their financial situation. Over time, Sam's troubles did begin to resolve. Her son overcame his addiction and quit using drugs returning to the family as a loving son.

Sam knew that God would continue providing for them. Even if they didn't have material riches, Sam had an unfailing hope that would always sustain her. She eagerly shared her salvation story with others around her explaining the beautiful message of love and hope that is the Gospel of Jesus Christ.

Renounce Your Faith or I Will Divorce You

How could his heart change like this? Hafiz had been raised a Muslim; he had learned the Islamic customs and studied the Quran. But now he was listening to a Christian preacher—and finding his faith shaken by the man's words.

Munshi, the Christian, was a friendly man, and Hafiz felt comfortable around him. He felt safe discussing difficult questions about Islam. He respected Munshi. So when Munshi began to tell him about Jesus, he listened.

"Jesus is God's Son. He died to save us from our sins," Munshi said earnestly. "Jesus is the only way to get to heaven."

Hafiz was worried. He had to know. And the words just slipped out: "What must I do?"

Munshi smiled. "Only believe."

Hafiz knew that Munshi spoke the truth. The realization was like a beam of sunlight piercing the fog; Hafiz could finally see clearly. One beautiful day, he accepted Jesus's gift of salvation and was saved. Hafiz was baptized and received instruction on how to share his faith with his countrymen. All the while, Hafiz read the New Testament. He couldn't get enough of it. Every time he read a passage, the words seemed to blaze with life, speaking directly to his heart.

Hafiz knew it was dangerous, all of it—reading the New Testament, training with other believers, even living as a Christian. He was careful, especially around his family, all devout Muslims. Hafiz guarded his New Testament closely. He thought that if he hid it at home, it would be safe.

He lived with his new wife, Rashida, in a room that adjoined his parent's house. When Hafiz was alone in his room, he read his New Testament and took time each day to kneel and pray.

Hafiz closed his eyes and felt the world slip away. It was just him and his Savior. Quietly, Hafiz whispered the praises gathering on his lips with the New Testament laying open on the bed before him.

"Hafiz!"

Hafiz's eyes snapped open, and he jumped with shock. Instantly he knew his reaction had given him away. "Rashida?" he said, turning.

Rashida stood trembling in the doorway. Her voice was forceful. "What is that book? What are you doing?"

"Rashida," Hafiz said again, getting to his feet and stepping towards her.

She pulled away, her cheeks glowing with emotion. "What is going on? Tell me, now!"

Hafiz hesitated, the air falling heavily around him. "I have become a follower of Jesus," he said softly.

Rashida stared at him. "*What?* You can't—you are a Muslim. You cannot forsake your religion for another!"

"Please, if you just listen, I can tell you how Jesus changed my life," Hafiz pleaded. "And he can change yours too."

"No!" Rashida screamed. "I am a Muslim, and our children will be raised as Muslims, not under your false religion! Renounce your faith," she said, her voice dropping. "Or I will divorce you."

Hafiz stood, stunned.

"Renounce your faith!" she shouted.

Hafiz heard the pound of footsteps on the stairs, and his family burst into the room.

"What's going on?" Hafiz's father demanded.

"Father, I can explain—" Hafiz said hurriedly, but Rashida cut in.

"Hafiz says he is a Christian."

His father looked at Hafiz, anger and shock warring on his face. "Son?"

Hafiz took a breath, realizing that this moment had been approaching ever since he accepted Jesus as his Savior. "It's true. I am a follower of Jesus."

His father's face twisted with rage. Yelling in fury, he swung a punch into Hafiz's face. Hafiz staggered back, pain exploding behind his eyes. His brothers advanced upon him, snatching up Hafiz's cricket bat and striking him with it. The blows were hard, so hard that Hafiz wrapped his arms around his head, crying out with pain. He shrunk down until their fists drove him to the ground. There he lay, helpless, as his family struck him; his brothers wielding the bat with all their strength.

Hafiz's mother had been watching all this time, but now she ran forward and seized her husband's arm. "Don't kill him!" she cried out.

Hafiz's father stepped back from his son, who lay, bleeding, on the floor. Hafiz quivered, and then was still. Hafiz's father motioned for everyone to leave the room, and then he locked Hafiz inside.

Hafiz blinked and slowly opened his eyes. Everything hurt; he was a mass of bruises, and he tasted blood in his mouth from the many injuries to his face. He was still alive. But what for? He had just lost everyone he loved. They all hated him for becoming a Christian, and Rashida didn't want to be with him anymore, even as they expected their first child.

Tears burned Hafiz's torn, bloody cheeks. He still loved them so, so much.

Creak. It was the next day. The door softly swung open, and slow footsteps advanced across the room. Hafiz, still on the floor and in pain, squinted, trying to see who was approaching. A slim figure knelt beside him, and Hafiz finally could make out his younger brother's face. It was Naadir—gentle, kind-hearted Naadir. He had not beaten Hafiz with the rest of his brothers.

Naadir hesitated; he seemed to be struggling to speak. "Father died last night," he said at last.

Hafiz stiffened with shock.

"Heart attack," Naadir said. He kept his eyes on the ground, his hands shaking. "Everyone is blaming you. They say it is your fault he died. They say you must be killed." He raised his eyes and stared at Hafiz, his gaze pain-stricken. "Our brothers have said they will do it."

Hafiz swallowed, his mind blurred. "When...?"

Naadir bit his lip. "After the funeral." He rose abruptly and retreated to the door, where he paused, glancing back. "I can't see you again. They won't allow me." Naadir bowed his head. "Good-bye, Hafiz."

He slipped away again, closing the door, and Hafiz was left completely alone. Hafiz lay there on the floor, disoriented by sorrow and fear, his wounds cracked and sore. Hafiz could do nothing, except pray. He prayed that when the time came, he would face death bravely, and that his Lord Jesus would give him that courage.

He lay alone until three days later, when his brothers burst into the room and pulled him to his feet. They had come to fulfill their duty.

Hafiz was dragged outside into the glaring sunlight. As Hafiz staggered from his house, he heard indistinct murmuring and the pressing closeness of a large crowd nearby. His brothers shoved him down into the dust in the center of the crowd. Hafiz looked up and saw all the villagers standing around watching solemnly. Hafiz's ankles were lashed together and tied with a rope to the crossbeam of the village well. Then his brothers heaved him over the side.

Hafiz jerked to a halt, bobbing upside down with his head dangling into the well and the rope cutting into his ankles. The blood rushed to his head until he thought it would burst. The agony was blazing, filling his mind, pushing all thought aside until it was just the pain—and then soft, soothing black. Hafiz breathed a prayer through his lips and let himself pass into darkness.

Hafiz awoke. He breathed in, appreciating the feel of fresh air entering his lungs. Such a simple action—but what a luxury—to breathe. Hafiz suddenly opened his eyes, memory crashing in on him. Why was he alive?

Hafiz was back in his room on the floor. His head was throbbing and his body ached, but he was alive. Hafiz tried to sit up, but could not. Instead he rested his head on the floor, wincing, and closed his eyes.

A loud *crack* jolted him awake. As Hafiz puzzled over the sound, a single knock came at the door. It was Naadir. He stayed at the doorway this time, nervously clasping his hands. "Our uncles are shooting at the house," he stammered. A second crack split the air, and Naadir jumped. "They are angry that our brothers did not kill you. Now they are threatening us with guns, if we will not kill you." He stared at Hafiz with a look of fear.

"But why did they not kill me at the well?" Hafiz asked.

Naadir looked distracted by the continuing gunshots; already he had one foot out of the room. "Our mother begged them not to kill you. They brought you out of the well after you had fallen unconscious." He glanced over his shoulder, and his voice cracked. "Please, I must go. They will beat me if they find me here."

"Thank you, Naadir," Hafiz said softly. Naadir looked at him for a long moment, and quietly nodded. Then he was gone.

A short time later the door opened again, but no one came into Hafiz's room. A small bowl of rice was pushed in through the doorway. It was steaming faintly, and suddenly Hafiz remembered how hungry he was. Hafiz slid across the floor and grabbed the bowl of rice, shoveling handfuls into his mouth. It burned his fingers, and tasted rather strange—almost bitter—but to Hafiz it was wonderful. He finished the rice and had just laid down the bowl with a sigh, when a sudden flash of pain lanced through his stomach. Hafiz clutched at his stomach, and then the pain came again—deep, slicing into his intestines. Hafiz collapsed to the floor, doubled over with his forehead pressed against the ground. He was sweating. With every fresh jolt the pain grew worse, and he cried out in torture. He retched, vomiting over and over onto his bedroom floor.

He remembered little from then on except terrible fever. He saw shadows and faces in the distance, and occasionally sensed someone's touch on his body or the echoing murmur of a voice. More often he was shaking with pain, tossing and turning and yelling into the air. He felt like a fire was burning beneath his skin. Then there would be a gentle flow of water into his mouth, and a cold, damp touch on his forehead. Momentary relief, but not enough to ward off the fever.

It all seemed like a dream when Hafiz finally came to himself. There was Naadir, by his side. He was clutching a wet rag.

Hafiz looked at him through bleary eyes. "What happened?"

"You were poisoned," Naadir said shortly, wringing out the rag with a sharp movement. His face was troubled. "Please Hafiz," Naadir said, his voice softening. "You must leave here! Soon, one of them will kill you."

Hafiz closed his eyes. He was so tired. "You are right," was all he could say.

Hafiz escaped from the house and made his way to the city, where friends gave him shelter. For some time he stayed there, trying to keep himself from going insane. His life had crumbled before his eyes. He had left his wife and his unborn child without a single good-bye, and for all he knew Rashida hated him. He might never see his son. His father was dead from shock. His brothers had tried to kill him, and his uncles wanted him dead. What had he done to his family? Had he made the wrong choice? His decision to follow Jesus had brought terrible trouble upon his house.

Hafiz wept and prayed, struggling to remember that Jesus was his Lord, that He is in control. "Please, keep me close to You," Hafiz cried out. He was horrified and hopeless, and all he could do was simply *trust*.

For two years he saw nothing of his family. He lived a quiet, lonely life; his only contact was with Naadir—and only every few months. Hafiz thanked God constantly for Naadir and his kind, open heart and prayed that God would protect him from harm.

Hafiz spent many days in doubt and gloom. He was shunned in his culture and his country. He had heard nothing from his family. Would he have to spend the rest of his life alone, hiding? But then, if he went back to Islam, he could have his wife back and his little baby son. He could see his family smiling at him again and feel their loving arms around him.

Hafiz pushed away those thoughts and opened his Bible. He went back to Romans, the book that he had first heard Munshi read. The passages in Romans had always comforted him in hard times, and now he went back and read a few of his favorites. But as he read, it was a different verse that grabbed his attention: "Who shall separate us from the love of God? Shall trouble or hardship or persecution or famine or nakedness or danger or sword?"

Hafiz burst into tears over his Bible, weeping onto the pages. Jesus had never left him, and here He was reminding Hafiz of it now—that nothing, and no one, would ever take the love of Jesus from him. Hafiz was filled with courage and hope. He decided that he would go and see his family.

Naadir was nervous when Hafiz told him of his plan. "Are you sure you want to do this?"

"Please, just tell them. I'll be in the village for three days, and I want to see them all."

His family met with him: his mother, brothers, and his wife and son. They were all very quiet.

Hafiz held his son for the first time. A lump grew in his throat as he watched the tiny hands reaching into the air. Rashida stood nearby, a single tear running down her cheek.

Hafiz spoke to his whole family when they had gathered. "You tried to kill me, but my God protected and preserved me. He is the only reason I am here today. He saved me, from your hands and from my sins. Since he has forgiven me, I also can forgive you for what you have done."

Now he spoke directly to his wife. "Rashida, I still love you. I cannot return to Islam, but I want to care for you and our son and be a family once more. I want you to come live with me in the city. But if you do not wish it, that is your choice. Consider my proposal for three days and then give me your answer." Rashida gazed at him, cradling their son in her arms. Her eyes were shining with tears.

Hafiz looked at his family one last time, embraced his mother, and then he left, dashing the tears from his face as he walked away.

Three days later, the phone rang. Hafiz's stomach lurched with nervousness as he answered it. It was Naadir.

"I have Rashida's answer," he said.

Hafiz closed his eyes, his breaths quick and shaky. "What did she say?"

There was a pause. Then: "She said she will come!" Naadir cried. Hafiz could hear the smile in Naadir's voice. "She still loves you, and she and your son are coming out to live with you!"

Hafiz sat down in the nearest chair, clutching the phone. He ran a hand over his face, and suddenly he was laughing, even as tears flowed down his cheeks. "Thank you, Lord," he breathed.

Rashida and her son, Najid, did come to live with Hafiz. Their life was not easy at first. Hafiz had trouble finding work because of his religion, but at last he was able to get a low-paying, but steady job. Hafiz worked long and hard, and made enough to support his family.

Hafiz was also sharing his faith with those around him, and he started a discipleship group with ten other former Muslims. Through his continuous witness, Rashida eventually came to salvation. She had seen the way he had gone through everything that had happened to him, and she knew that the change which had appeared in him must have come from Jesus.

One day, Hafiz ran into Munshi, the man who had brought him to Jesus. Their meeting was a glad one. Munshi had heard of what had happened to Hafiz and had been wanting to see him again. Munshi helped train Hafiz and his small group of Christians to reach even more people for Christ.

Now Hafiz works with Big Life, traveling at the head of a group of Christians who spread the gospel and plant churches in villages all throughout Pakistan.

Please, Just Stop

Looking back, even he didn't know how his life had gone so wrong.

It had been the gambling first. He became addicted to the lifestyle of the taverns and spent all his money on drinks and games. He rarely came home on time. He would stumble through the door—his legs weak, his brain foggy, and his temper violent. He couldn't remember all of what he did when he was drunk. The things he did remember, he didn't want to. There had been some terrible nights.

He didn't know why he kept going back to the place that corrupted him. He hated it, and yet he loved it at the same time. Though it was killing him, he couldn't live without it.

Boeu was a Buddhist. He worshipped his ancestors and idols and performed religious sacrifices, as he had done all his life. A great deal of money had to be spent on those rituals. Boeu paid it without a thought. He did save his money for these sacrifices. But with what was left, he bought several drinks. The rest of his coins he gambled on a bet. Sometimes he won—but more often, he lost everything. There wasn't enough money for Boeu, let alone for his family at home. Boeu began selling his possessions. Every coin was another sip of drink or another chance at winning a wager. He thought nothing of his family or of saving the money for them. Boeu sold everything he owned, and everything his family owned. They were helpless to stop him.

Boeu's carelessness had already weakened the family. Now poverty was attacking them from all sides. If Boeu continued to spend their money, how could they go on? And when would he revert to borrowing and falling into debt or even beginning to steal?

Deep down, Boeu knew the truth. He could see his reality as sharp and clear as a glass knife and it was chaos. He tried to tell himself that he could pretend everything away—that by forgetting about his troubles they would disappear. But that was a lie, a weak and pitiful lie. Boeu didn't want to quit his addictions because he didn't want to face the trouble that he had caused. He already knew it, but to acknowledge that fact would make it too painfully real.

One night Boeu pushed himself up from the gambling table. His head was swimming and his feet felt like wooden blocks, clumsy and heavy.

"Leaving already?" slurred the man beside him. He smiled at Boeu, hoping he could win some more money from him.

"Got to," Boeu paused, trying to put cohesive words together, "get home." It was a mumble barely audible. He drained his glass and set it aside, then made his way to the door. Finally he managed to stumble out of the tavern and into the quiet night.

His wife was waiting up when he returned. She stood silently, watching him walk unsteadily through the doorway.

"Boeu," she whispered.

He looked up, squinting. Her form was blurry and indistinct. Who was talking to him?

She walked towards him, her voice pleading. "We are in hard times—we need you. We can't survive if you continue like this, spending all our money and coming home drunk. You need to stop this!"

Boeu stared at her. *Stop this? She's telling me me to quit?* Anger built up inside Boeu like boiling water, blistering hot and rising steadily. How dare anyone tell him to stop. He took a step towards his wife.

She stopped where she was, a glint of fear in her eyes. "Boeu, please, just stop."

Boeu roared like an animal and swung his fist at her. She screamed, leaping backwards. "Beou!" she cried. "Beou, please!"

He staggered towards her. Rage coursed through him, telling him to fight, strike, hurt. He saw his wife dodging away from him. She was speaking, but Boeu heard nothing. Only anger controlled him now. Boeu took a swing at her slight figure. He heard her scream of terror and felt the shocking jolt as his hand struck her jaw. She collapsed to the floor, moaning in pain.

Boeu froze as if he had been paralyzed. His knuckles were throbbing, and his wife's sobs echoed in his ears. Slowly he sank downwards, until his knees met the floor with a sudden thud. He had beaten his wife. *What have I turned into? How have I come this far?* Boeu stared down at his hands, horrible shame creeping over him. "What have I done?" he whispered. He lowered his face into his hands as his wife stumbled away from him, weeping in fear.

Boeu awoke the next morning on the floor. This time, he remembered everything that had happened during the night. He remembered the terror on his wife's face and her piercing scream. He remembered striking her to the floor. Boeu clutched his head, his chest beginning to heave. He had destroyed himself by his addictions, and he was destroying his family, too. He had to find a way to fix his life.

It was just at this time that the answer arrived. A man knocked on Boeu's door. He was a Christian.

Boeu staggered as he got up from the floor and opened the door. Shielding his blood-shot eyes, he managed to say, "Can I help you?"

"I wanted to know if you would like to hear about the Savior," the visitor said with a smile.

Boeu was silent for a moment, staring at this man. He leaned heavily upon the door so as not to fall over. The words hit him hard. *A savior, could it be? Was there truly someone who could help him?* "Who is this, Savior?" Boeu asked.

"Jesus Christ," the man said. "The Son of the one true God."

Boeu took a deep breath. He was wary, but his heart was beating with excitement none-the-less. It was the message he needed to hear, right at this moment. "I want to know about Him," he said quickly. "I really, really do." He invited the visitor in and they sat down.

The man shared the Gospel with Boeu. He told him how Jesus had died to save us all from our sins. "We deserve death, every one of us, for what we have done," the man explained. "But Jesus paid the penalty for us. If we believe in His sacrifice and ask Him to save us, He will forgive all of our sins—and give us new life."

Boeu listened with tears streaming down his cheeks. He couldn't understand this love—that God's Son would give His life for a wretched soul like him. Boeu knew he could never escape his sin alone. He needed Jesus.

The man left a Bible with Boeu, and Boeu read it constantly. He began to understand more and more about God, Jesus, the Holy Spirit, and salvation. And with every word he became more convinced. Jesus was the real, true God—not the Buddhist idols he worshipped. Jesus was the Savior, the only way to eternal life. Boeu prayed to Jesus on his knees, begging Him to cleanse his sinful heart and save him. "I have nothing but my life," he prayed, "And that I offer completely to you."

Jesus transformed Boeu's life. He gave Boeu the power to overcome his addictions and begin walking according to God's Word. As his wife saw the change, she no longer feared Boeu, but loved him and gave her life to Jesus, too.

Now Boeu lives every day with joy and hope, knowing that he has been freed forever from the power of sin. In answer to the call of his Lord, Boeu is traveling to various villages throughout his country telling others how they can find salvation as well.

When Death Leads to Life

Poverty was a daily trial for Ruos and his family. Hardship was normal. Ruos worked himself to the point of exhaustion, trying to scrape a living from the meager coins he received, but it was barely enough to provide one meal a day for his family. Though things were steady, Ruos needed to find a way to get more work.

But the fragile balance took a turn for the worse. Both of Ruos' two children became sick. Ruos panicked. He had no money; he certainly couldn't pay a doctor—he couldn't even feed his children properly! What was he supposed to do? He couldn't just let them die—but there was simply *no money*.

His wife tried to hide her anxiety, but it was impossible. Ruos found her weeping by their children's bedside. Her voice broke as she whispered tenderly to her children, stroking their hair. Ruos turned away, tears stinging his eyes. How could he call himself a father? He was a failure. And now he was watching his children die. It was his fault, all his fault. If he could have worked harder, made more—maybe they would be healthy. Ruos fell to his knees, crying out in despair. There was only one thing left to try. Ruos called out desperately to Buddha, praying for his children's healing. He spent many hours on his knees, alternately weeping and praying, trying to find hope. But none could find him.

It was a still, quiet morning. Ruos rose from his bed, walking slowly across to where his children lay. The silence of the house weighed on his chest, constricting his lungs and making it hard to breathe. His two precious ones lay asleep, peaceful. Ruos felt his legs trembling. He knelt beside them; his eyes were misty. The faintest of hopeful smiles alighted on his lips. Had Buddha answered his prayers? Ruos reached out his hand to brush his little one's cheek. It was icy cold.

Horror jolted through him; he jerked his hand back in terror. He stared at his child's face, suddenly so still—too still. Ruos's eyes widened. "No, no, no, no—" He was clutching the bed sheet, his fleeting tears of joy were replaced with tears of sheer terror.

He heard his wife come up behind him with her own heart-wrenching gasp of realization. Then she was sobbing beside him, holding their lifeless child in her arms. Ruos looked across to the other bed. The small chest rose and fell, breath still passed between those whitened lips. He stood in the middle of the still house, the sound of his wife's grief drowned out by the silent screaming of his heart.

A short time later, Ruos's second child passed away. Ruos couldn't find the tears to mourn. He felt nothing and didn't speak a word as they folded the sheets over his child's empty face. His wife went about the house like a shadow, thin and pale, tears flowing silently down her face.

The funeral was a short, somber affair. Ruos couldn't afford anything special. He stood alone in the crowd; his gaze fixed straight ahead. His children had deserved more. They should have had better—in death and in life. He had let everyone down.

Someone came up beside him and put an arm around his shoulders. Ruos swayed from the contact, continuing to stare into the distance.

"I'm sorry," a man's voice said quietly.

Ruos didn't respond.

The man was silent. For a moment Ruos stood stiffly, and then it all fell away. He sobbed. His heart was broken. Tears came from where he'd thought there were none left. The man embraced Ruos, supporting him as he wept, offering wordless comfort and strength. "Jesus loves you," Tharoath said gently. "He will be with you and your family, if you believe in Him. His hope will not fail you."

Ruos let this message of love sink into him. With the funeral over, he remembered those words days later when his house was too empty and the food was too plentiful, and when his wife cried in her sleep. He was reminded of Tharoath's comforting words when he remembered his children's sweet smiles and the sound of their voices. And at last, he remembered this message of hope when he knelt in prayer, asking this Jesus, this God of love, to save him from his sins.

Ruos's heart was instantly transformed. Suddenly the pain and the poverty didn't matter as much—not when he was filled with the passion and love of Christ. He got in touch with Tharoath and begged to learn more about this Jesus. As Tharoath began to meet with him and teach him God's word, God began to reveal Himself in amazing ways in Ruos' life. Even though he still had much hardship, God brought Ruos much joy. Each day gave Ruos a new understanding of Jesus' love and a new desire to glorify Him.

Over time, Tharoath's teaching brought Ruos to a point of committing his entire life to serving the Lord. Now he leads a Christian fellowship in his home, where believers can worship together with their family in Christ.

As his faith continued to grow, Ruos could finally look back on the pain and the loss that he had gone through and realize that God had been working even within that terrible time. For it had taken Ruos' heartbreak to cause him to look to the one true God—the one who can heal both body and soul.

Bullets Hit the Car

Musa was born into a devout Muslim family. As he grew older, he learned the Islamic teachings and eventually went to university in Pakistan. Musa's English professor there was a humble, loving man, who treated his students with respect. Musa admired him very much, but he knew that he was a Christian. Musa believed that his professor wouldn't go to heaven, and that pained him deeply.

At last Musa found the courage to tell him about Islam. After the professor listened to Musa's words, he smiled and said gently, "Thank you for your concern for me, Musa. But I have security and joy in my heart. If you read the Injil Sharif (The New Testament), you will understand."

When Musa left the university, he joined his father's business in the city. Though gone from the university, Musa's professor's words never left his heart. What did the Injil Sharif have to say that gave the professor such peace?

A church near his workplace had a library inside, and one day he went in and found a copy of the Injil Sharif. Musa began returning to the church day after day to read. The pastor of the church met with Musa and helped him study the Scriptures. As he read further, Musa became more and more convinced that Isa (Jesus) was the only way to eternal life.

One day the church's pastor introduced him to Pastor Sheer Shah, a highly educated man who knew both the Quran and the Bible and who firmly believed that Isa was the Son of God.

Shah's zeal and conviction were contagious. Soon after they met, Musa introduced Shah to a group of scholarly, Muslim men, who had often answered Musa's questions about Islam. As Shah talked regularly with these men, several of them came to faith in Isa. At last Musa, too, surrendered his heart to Isa's powerful love and was baptized by Pastor Sheer Shah. Shah proceeded to mentor the eager young Christian. But Musa was forced to live his new life in secret from his family—or else be rejected as a traitor to Islam.

With an overwhelming need to tell others about Christ, Musa joined Sheer Shah in his ministry to the Afghani refugees on the border hoping to flee to Pakistan. Shah and Musa shared Isa's love for three years and saw over three hundred people saved. When the new Afghani government was established, they also took the gospel back into the heart of Afghanistan.

But not long after starting work there, Shah and a disciple vanished on a drive to the city. A few days later, their bodies were found. They had been brutally killed by radical extremists. Shah's close followers fled, and Musa went into hiding. He knew that Shah's computer had been in the car with him when he was captured—on it were the names and pictures of many disciples, including his own. Musa was scared and stricken with grief for his beloved mentor and leader. How could it be that Sheer Shah, so filled with Isa's love and power, was gone? And who could Musa go to for help? He was all alone.

But an unexpected discovery brought Musa hope. Having returned to his home near the Afghanistan—Pakistan border, he discovered his brother was also secretly a Christian. Both of them had been following Christ at the same time but had not told anyone about it. Now Musa's brother took him in. They embraced each other in joy, suddenly realizing that they were now not only brothers by blood but also in Christ.

Musa's brother and another believer hid Musa for a time, but soon they had to move him to another place. They hid him in a car and drove out of the city. As they traveled down the road, Musa's brother suddenly slowed the car. A truck was blocking the road ahead; it was filled with men carrying guns who were checking the cars as they went by. The passengers exchanged fearful glances. How could they get by without Musa being discovered? Their car crawled towards the blockade. It was the next one to be checked. In desperation, Musa's brother sent the car zooming forwards, and as they sped past the truck, the guns went off. Bullets hit the car, and then one struck Musa in the back with a jolt of red-hot pain. Several more followed. Blood pouring from his wounds, Musa lost consciousness.

Musa awoke in a hospital bed. At his side were his brother and father. The rest of his family was nowhere to be seen. His brother told him quietly, "The newspapers have printed your picture and announced that you are a follower of Isa. The clergy have declared you a traitor." Musa's stomach clenched in fear. He was alive, but for how long? And what would happen to his father now that the authorities knew his son was a Christian? There was only one way to protect him. So Musa told his father that it was a mistake—he was still Muslim.

Later, Musa was released from the hospital and returned home to his wife. When he did, she looked at him with tears in her eyes and asked, "Are you a Christian?" As his beloved wife stood there before him, Musa was unable to lie a second time. "Yes," Musa said, his heart aching. "I am a Christian." Since he had rejected Islam, his wife left him. But because she loved him, she promised to keep Musa's faith a secret.

For several years, Musa lived quietly. By God's protection he was still alive, but he had lost both his wife and his mentor. Sheer Shah's followers remained scattered. Musa's brother and cousin had received salvation, but they were the only family with whom Musa could share his faith.

Then in 2009, Musa was invited to a Big Life seminar, where missionaries were training believers to evangelize their people. Musa remembered the times when he and Shah had spread the gospel among the refugees. Though he still mourned Shah's tragic loss, Musa felt the passion that had burned within him then stirring once again. He could not remain silent.

Musa contacted Sheer Shah's disciples. Slowly, they came forward. As he told them the fire that burned in him once again, they too began to be encouraged by the Holy Spirit. They too realized that they *had* to speak of His wonderful glory.

They set out to do the impossible. They asked God to use them to plant churches among the Muslims of Afghanistan. God heard their prayers and answered them zealously.

Within the first eighteen months, their team has been used by God to raise 200 churches in Afghanistan as 1,200 former Muslims attended worship within them. They are no longer silent.

Did
You
Know...

Gerald Robison wrote a second book titled, *Crocs Eat Rocks*?

It has 101 more glimpses of God's glory in the animal world. It is exactly like *Because He Liked It* but with new interesting facts reflecting the glory of God.

Find out more about the book at: UnveilinGLORY's bookstore: www.UnveilinGLORY.com/ bookstore

Pack Your Belongings and Go

Meaningless. Everything was meaningless.

Naresh had grown up worshipping the Hindu idols. He believed doing so would bring him peace, happiness, and good fortune. But instead he was filled with doubts and fears. He was a young man, preparing to make his own way in the world, and he didn't feel ready. He didn't know where his place was or what he was meant to do.

The Hindu gods should have been able to help him. But Naresh had never once heard them speak.

Naresh's life steadily darkened. He became depressed, searching for hope and finding none. His religion didn't give him peace, neither did money or relationships. There was nothing that could satisfy that yearning in his soul. The emptiness consumed him until finally Naresh had to have relief. He began taking drugs and drinking. For a while they made him forget his restlessness and his pain. They gave him a false sense of joy. But when the effects faded he was worse than before. Naresh found that he needed more and more to maintain his sanity. Gradually, he was becoming powerless to an addiction that threatened his life.

Peace had never seemed farther away.

Naresh walked down the street alone. His head was bowed; his eyes were red from lack of sleep. He felt worn and wasted, like a rag that had been wrung out one too many times. He knew that he was in trouble. But what was the point of trying to quit? What else could life offer him except loneliness and sadness?

He didn't notice the small woman on the side of the road until he had almost walked past her. "Here." She put out her hand in front of Naresh, holding a thin pamphlet. "Would you like a tract?"

Naresh stared at her oddly. His mind felt sluggish and slow. "A tract?"

"It tells about Jesus. He is the only way to eternal life."

Naresh took the tract. He didn't really know why, but something drew him to the words on the page. He moved to the side of the road and sat down, unfolding the tract. "For all have sinned and fall short of the glory of God," he read. Naresh narrowed his eyes, confused. He had been taught that good works gained one salvation. But...here, it said that everyone fell short of heaven? What did this mean? Naresh read on. "For the wages of sin is death, but the gift of God is eternal life in Christ Jesus our Lord." What was this gift? And who was Jesus? Naresh's mind swirled with questions. He thirsted for the answers like a parched man for water.

Someone sat down beside him. It was the little woman with the tracts. She smiled gently. "There is a fellowship nearby, if you would like to learn more."

Naresh nodded slowly, gazing at the tract.

"It was good to meet you." The woman extended her hand, and Naresh shook it. "My name is Sara."

Naresh decided to go to the fellowship. There was an eagerness stirring within him that he hadn't felt for years—it was hope of some kind. He knew that he could never be good enough to get to heaven. He had made too many wrong choices. But suddenly there was this message of grace, mercy, and forgiveness. It was radically different from everything he had grown up with, but it resonated with him somewhere deep inside. It felt real. It felt true.

That night at the Christian gathering Naresh first heard the entire Gospel preached, and he learned about Jesus's sacrifice and His resurrection. He saw the Christians praising God with pure, radiant joy shining on their faces. The air thrummed with life. Naresh attended the fellowship regularly for the next year. When he was seventeen years old, he put his trust in Jesus Christ and accepted Him as his Savior.

Because of his faith, Naresh's family was torn apart. They couldn't understand why Naresh had forsaken everything they had taught him to follow Jesus.

"But it is the truth," Naresh said gently. "Jesus is the Savior!" His mother gazed at him, tears filling her eyes. Then with a sob she turned away. Naresh longed to run and comfort her—to tell her that he was still her son and he still loved her.

His father stepped in front of him, and Naresh froze.

"You must leave our house," he said in a low voice.

Naresh stared at him. "Father...."

"Pack your belongings, and go!" His father whispered forcefully. His voice sounded hoarse and strained. Naresh stood for a moment, his hands trembling. At last he found the strength to turn and slowly walk to his room. As he left, Naresh saw tears beginning to stream down his father's cheeks.

Naresh began life on his own. He started training in God's Word, being mentored by a man named Robert, who worked with Big Life. Naresh also married and began a family. He found work as a watchman to support them, balancing his job with his studies. Naresh's faith grew stronger with each day. He missed his family, and sometimes life was very hard, but through it all he had Jesus. Each new day was a new reminder of His mercy. And at last Naresh had hope for the future—an eternal hope.

Naresh's mentor, Robert, introduced him to Pastor Benjamin. The two men talked with Naresh about Big Life Ministries, and their mission to spread the gospel throughout the land. Naresh felt a calling to join them in their work. Strengthened by the Holy Spirit, Naresh returned to his home village and began sharing the gospel there. As Jesus moved among the people, more and more opportunities arose for Naresh to visit villages and teach about Jesus. God is continuing to use Naresh—a young man who was once lost, confused, and hopeless but who is now alive in the power of Christ.

The Day of Salvation

Preeti's father was a successful business man of a high caste, and their family was well respected in the village. Her father was devoted to the Hindu god, Hanuman, whom he called upon to protect his house and his family from evil spirits. But his prayers for protection proved to be in vain.

Preeti's mother had died when she was a young girl, and for as long as she could remember, her brother had been bedridden with a strange illness. At the age of five he had stopped being able to walk. Slowly, his body failed. Now, at the age of twenty-four, he passed away. Preeti was only sixteen.

Preeti, her little sister named Sweety, and their father all mourned the loss. Now there were only the three of them.

Two months passed and Preeti became very worried. Something seemed to be wrong in the house. Preeti's sister and father were acting strangely—her sister withdrawn and quiet and her father unusually hot-tempered. He would fly into rages unexpectedly and without any reason. Her sister would only sit on the bed, staring at the wall and saying nothing, even when Preeti tried to speak with her. Sweety stopped going to school. Her father, who used to be so concerned over his household and his family, didn't even notice. Preeti didn't know what to do.

One day Preeti came home from school and found her father crouched in a chair. Something gleamed in his hand—a knife. Frightened, Preeti crept closer to see what he was doing. He was bending over his leg, where an accident had left him with a long scar just below his knee. As she watched, he dug the knife into his skin and reopened the wound, scarlet blood spilling down his leg.

"Father!" Preeti gasped, horrified. He jerked his head up, the knife pointing at her. She stumbled backwards.

"What are you doing?" he growled. The look in his eyes was maniacal, like an angry animal. Preeti shook all over, her eyes fixed on the bloody knife threatening her.

"Get out of here, now!" He stood up.

Preeti fled to the room she shared with her sister, afraid to look back. Inside, she slammed the door and leaned against it. Her heartbeat was racing, pounding painfully against her chest. Preeti turned to her sister, who was sitting on the edge of the bed.

Sweety had a pair of scissors in her hands and was trying to cut her arm. Preeti sobbed, running over and pulling the scissors away from her little sister. Sweety let her take them as her hands dropped limply into her lap. Her eyes were deep with sorrow. Preeti tossed the scissors onto the floor and climbed up beside her sister. "Sweety," she cried. "What is happening?" Preeti wrapped her arms around her sister, weeping. Sweety didn't move.

As the days progressed, her family's condition only grew worse. Sweety lay on her bed all day staring at the air. She hadn't spoken for weeks. Her father continued to cut at his leg, and Preeti was afraid to take the knife away. He would suddenly become angry and turn on Preeti and her sister threatening to kill them. During these times his eyes became distant, and he didn't recognize either of his daughters. Preeti feared for the lives of both herself and Sweety. But what could she do? She didn't want to ruin her father's reputation. She just had to pray desperately that her family would get better.

Then someone came to her and whispered a rumor. "It is witchcraft. Someone in the village gave your father food that was doctored with black magic." Preeti was terrified.

Her father stopped letting Preeti and Sweety leave the house. At night, he would burst into their room, clutching his knife, and scream at them in words that didn't make sense. Preeti became too scared to even speak to him, for she never knew when he would turn into a monster. She wept ceaselessly filled with horror and fear. She believed it was only a matter of time before he murdered both of them.

One night she awoke. She felt wet, as if someone had doused water on her. Then a pungent smell filled her nose, and she realized that it was gasoline. Her father slipped out of the room, leaving one end of it alight with flames. Preeti screamed and dragged her sister out of the room. They climbed through the bathroom window; Preeti was pulling her sister every step of the way, until they stumbled into the open air. Both were covered with dirt and gasoline. Sweety sat down on the ground, unresponsive, and Preeti collapsed beside her. Her house burned like a beacon below her, and she cried until her whole body ached and no more tears would come.

The damage to the house was minimal. But Preeti was broken. She decided to end her own life the next day. It was a peaceful, sunny morning. Her father and her sister sat, quietly gazing into the distance. Preeti felt almost happy, knowing she would soon leave this waking nightmare behind.

Then came a knock at the door. Preeti looked towards it, but did not move to answer the knock. A young man opened it and stuck his head inside. He smiled at her. "Forgive me. I heard of your troubles, and I have come to pray with you."

Preeti looked at him curiously. She did not know him, but there was no harm in a prayer. "Come in," she said.

The young man stepped inside, smiling at the smoke-blackened walls, at her father and his blood-stained leg, and at her sister. Then he looked at Preeti, and he said with full assurance: "Today is the day of salvation for this house."

The man, Aryan, told all three of them about Jesus. He shared from the book he carried with him, talking about Jesus's love and the salvation that He offers. Aryan prayed with each of them and pronounced the power of Jesus's blood over their house.

By the time he left, peace had come—true peace. Preeti could feel it in the air. She no longer desired to end her life; she felt now as if her life was only just beginning.

Five days later, Sweety turned towards her sister and smiled for the first time since their brother had died. Preeti threw her arms around Sweety and felt a thrill of joy as Sweety responded by snuggling into the embrace. Preeti's father became very quiet and reserved. He stopped cutting his leg.

Aryan took all of them to a church gathering in the village, and there Sweety and her father felt the healing of Jesus. Both of them began to cry. The whole family accepted Christ into their lives.

They were all baptized and began attending church with Aryan regularly. Preeti longed to learn more about Jesus. She eagerly studied the Bible and prayed constantly. Soon Preeti met Amit and discovered a passion to share Jesus' love with others. She now works to bring the gospel to Hindu and Muslim women in the Punjab.

The War Movies

Mufti had once been a Muslim soldier. He had fought in holy war against unbelievers. But now, years later, Mufti was a Christian. He worked in the background, secretly aiding his brothers and sisters in the faith and sharing the gospel with those who would listen. So far, his ministry had run smoothly, but Mufti could never be sure how long that would last.

Trouble began the day a man asked to borrow a room in Mufti's sister-in-law's house to hold Islamic classes for children. Mufti's sister-in-law, Yasmin, was happy to agree. She wanted the young people to learn the Quran, and she was glad to provide a service to the teacher, who was a relation of her husband.

The teacher's name was Zubar. One day, he asked if Mufti would come teach at his class.

"What do you want me to teach?" asked Mufti warily.

"About your years in the holy war," said Zubar.

Mufti refused. "No. These are children! They do not need to hear about war."

Zubar glared at him and strode angrily away.

Mufti was often at Yasmin's house, visiting with her and her husband, Hamid, but thankfully he didn't run into Zubar again. During his visits, Mufti talked with Yasmin and Hamid about Jesus. They had become more and more eager to listen each time he did so.

Today, however, they brought up a different topic. "It is Zubar," said Hamid gravely. "He is showing the children horrific videos of war."

Mufti looked sharply at Hamid. "How do you know this?"

Yasmin began crying. "Our own daughter is in his classes. She saw the movies and told us about the terrible images she was forced to see. All of the children are terrified."

Mufti rose to his feet, anger burning inside of him. "I will go talk to Zubar."

Mufti quickly walked out to Zubar's classroom, trying to control himself. He couldn't afford to make a disturbance, not with all the Christians who were relying on him. He just needed to talk with Zubar and get him to stop what he was doing.

Zubar opened the door when Mufti knocked. When he saw Mufti, an ugly look passed over his face. Mufti had to push his way into the room, where he saw a pile of DVDs lying on a table. With horror, he recognized the films as ones which the radicals showed to young men—soldiers—before they went to war.

"How dare you show these to children?" Mufti said to Zubar. "I know what these films are!"

Zubar slowly approached Mufti, an oily smile on his lips. "And I know what you are," he hissed. "I've been watching you. You preach the faith of the infidel god."

Mufti stared down into Zubar's face. "I believe in the one true God. And he would never teach anyone to kill." He left the room without another word, leaving Zubar to gaze after him with a look of hatred in his eyes.

Mufti continued to come to Yasmin and Hamid's house, even though he knew he had angered Zubar seriously. He sensed that his brother and his wife were very close to accepting Jesus. And truly, just a short while later, both Hamid and his wife came to salvation. Hamid immediately realized the full wrongness of what Zubar was teaching, and he ordered Zubar to stop the classes and leave his house.

Zubar was arrested for showing the war movies to underaged children, but the radicals got the charges dropped. Zubar was released, and soon Mufti and his family got word that Zubar was very angry and blamed Mufti for getting him in trouble.

Later, Mufti's friend, Amin, contacted him about an opportunity to take the gospel into the mountain villages. Mufti was eager to go. Mufti and his son decided to meet Hamid at his house where all three of them would head out to join Amin. That night, as the three Christians prepared for the journey, they heard fierce knocking on the front door. Before Mufti's son could open the door completely, eight men had burst into the house. One of them struck down Mufti's son with a club while two others guarded the house with guns. Mufti's son and Hamid were beaten, but the person the attackers really wanted was Mufti. They rushed on him with clubs. Mufti fought fiercely against them, but then Zubar came up behind and brought an ax down on the back of Mufti's head. Mufti collapsed on the ground. The attackers fell on him, beating him over and over with their clubs. Mufti lay on the ground, unmoving.

Finally Zubar and his men exited the house, leaving Mufti's body on the floor. Mufti's son and Hamid, bruised and bleeding from minor wounds, rushed over to Mufti. "He's still breathing!" Hamid exclaimed with a rush of joy. It was immediately followed by deep anxiety. Mufti needed medical attention and quickly.

They drove him to the hospital, but were turned away. There was no emergency care in their country, and before Mufti could be admitted they needed to file a report about the crime. With Mufti in the car, bleeding heavily from his head, they sped to the police station. But by the time they arrived, the radicals had visited and swayed the police in their favor. The officers refused to file a case. Panicked with fear, Hamid rushed to find a lawyer so that they could make a case against Zubar. Mufti's son stayed in the back of the car with his father, praying desperately over his unconscious body. Mufti had lost a lot of blood.

At last the police gave in. Hamid drove as fast as he could to the hospital, where Mufti, still unconscious, was finally allowed inside. He was in a very dangerous condition—he had suffered a severe wound to his head, as well as having one of his hands broken. The doctors quickly began work on him. They also provided treatment for Hamid and Mufti's son.

Frantically, Hamid tried to reach Amin, who was up in the mountains, expecting Mufti and the others to arrive. But Amin didn't answer.

Then, on the fourth day since Mufti had entered the hospital, Hamid received a call on Mufti's cellphone. Amin, worried about Mufti, had found a place where his phone would receive signal. Hamid was greatly relieved, even more so when Amin, a strong Christian leader, told his new brother in Christ that he would be at the hospital in two days. Hamid, Mufti's son, and the other Christians who had gathered all prayed ceaselessly for Jesus to save Mufti's life.

Then, a short time after Amin called, Mufti woke up. He was still weak, but everyone was filled with joy and praised God for sparing Mufti. Amin arrived on schedule two days later, and he too, after hearing the story, thanked God. Mufti spent the next two weeks in the hospital, steadily improving.

Mufti's healing was a source of great hope and rejoicing for all the believers. Spurred on by this reminder of God's power and presence, the Christians work even harder to reach Muslims with the good news of Jesus Christ.

The Alcoholic Fighter

Raja staggered backwards, tasting blood in his mouth. With a snarl of rage he hurled himself back on his opponent swinging his fist at the man's jaw. It collided with a bone-crunching thud and the man fell to his knees. Raja grunted in pain clutching his bleeding knuckles. He spat on the fallen man. "Get up. "

The man cowered against the ground. He had tears in his eyes, and he held his jaw gingerly. "Please..." he mumbled through his bleeding lips.

"Get up!" Raja shouted, kicking the man in his ribs.

The man crawled backwards, trembling now. "I'm done! I'm done, please, stop!"

Raja stood over him and curled his lip in disgust. "I'm done with you." He brought up his heel and kicked the man in the head. He fell back against the ground, his hands falling limply to his sides. He was dead or unconscious, probably the latter. Raja didn't care. He pulled the money out of the man's pocket and slipped it into his jacket. Then he walked away, leaving the body behind him.

A short while later Raja was at the tavern buying drinks with the stolen money. He sat alone at a table staring into the glass of alcohol. This was his life—fighting, drinking, and loneliness. He had driven everyone away. Now his only company was liquor. Raja drained his third glass and pocketed the rest of his money. As he stood up and walked to the door, two men entered the tavern. Raja shoved them roughly out of the way and strode through the doorway.

His house was empty and dark. Raja got a rag and slumped into a chair, wiping the blood from his face. Soon he let his arm drop to the side. What was the point? Did he think he could hide his misdeeds or clean his conscience with a wet cloth? He lived a sinful life every day. He had committed filthy deeds that not even he was proud of. Raja walked into the next room, where the idols were. Kneeling, he bowed his head and prayed. He did this everyday too—days of wickedness, nights of prayer. He prayed for peace, reconciliation, joy, everything that his life didn't have. Raja found no hope. But he continued to pray. Maybe there was some shred of faith left in him that still believed there was a God, someone greater than himself.

Raja looked at the idols, small statues of wood and stone. He didn't see sovereignty in them. The goddess Kali, who also received his prayers, had never revealed herself to Raja in anyway. When Raja got up from his knees, his heart was heavier than it had ever felt before. He had no purpose or fulfillment, just constant despair. The Hindu gods would not help him, or maybe they did not have the power.

But he knew somehow, without reason—but with absolute certainty, that there was a God somewhere. There had to be. However, where God could be found, Raja did not know.

The day was hot, dry and blazing. Raja leaned against the wall of his house, in the frugal shade. It had been many weeks since he had prayed to the idols. At first he had felt creeping unease at leaving the rituals he had followed since childhood. But nothing had changed, for better or worse. He watched the people walking by—very much aware that they were avoiding his eyes. Was his face still discolored by the ugly bruise spreading over his cheek? Raja took a sip from the bottle he held loosely in his hand.

"Excuse me," a friendly voice said.

Raja jerked his head around, startled. A young woman was standing close by, smiling at him. "I wondered if you'd like to hear about Jesus."

Raja couldn't say anything for a moment. He didn't understand why she had stopped to talk to him. He was an alcoholic, a fighter. Wasn't she afraid?

"I'm a follower of Christ," she continued. "He saved my life, and I want to tell everyone how they can be rescued too."

Raja shrugged. "Jesus?"

She nodded. "He is the Son of God. He died for us. We are all sinners and deserve death, but He died in our place and rose again. If we believe and ask Him to save us, we will have eternal life."

Raja turned away from her. "You speak nonsense." His voice trembled. "No one would love sinners." He stumbled into the house and closed the door before the tears could fall from his eyes.

Her eyes sadly followed him and then she went on her way.

Raja awoke the next morning with strange images in his mind. He had a dream of men, great men of faith—their names—they echoed like half-forgotten memories in his mind, vague and elusive. One had been John, he knew. Was it John? Already the dream was slipping away. But the next night it returned. And again the next night. There were three men who constantly appeared to him: Abraham, Moses, and John.

Raja now knew the dreams by heart, and their recurrence unnerved him. Who were the people? Their faces were unfamiliar, and their names meant nothing to him. However, every night they appeared, until Raja was driven desperate by confusion. He had to learn the meaning of this reoccurring dream.

Raja searched for someone who recognized the names of the men in his dreams. Each person he asked had no idea. At last he had found a man who knew.

"They are from the Bible," the man told him. "Men who served God."

Raja looked at the man in disbelief. "From the Bible...I've been having dreams about the followers of God?"

The man nodded. "It appears so."

But the answer struck him in a way entirely unexpected. He felt something touching his heart. The dreams had been a message, an awakening. They were from Jesus.

Suddenly Raja realized why his life was such a wreck—he was a sinner. Yet, Jesus loved him anyway. Jesus had died for him and He was the only One who could save him from death. Raja went home that night and prayed, not to the idols, but to Jesus. "Please," he prayed in a whisper. "I know I have done many wrong things. I am lost, broken, and worthless, and I need You to save me. I believe You died for me. I believe You love me. Please...save me!"

Something happened right there. Raja felt a great weight lift from his heart; all the guilt and shame and loneliness was washed away by immense, infinite love. Raja burst into tears, as he sobbed his thanks and praises to Jesus. He was a new creation.

Raja destroyed all his idols. He stopped drinking and, instead of fighting people, he shared his faith with them. Raja was ready to serve Jesus anywhere and in any way that He asked. For Jesus had loved him when he was yet a sinner and had called him into the light of His kingdom. Raja had nothing to give but his life, his love, and his complete surrender. He gladly gave everything.

He Wasn't Afraid

It was just a job, at first—not murder. It was just a way to earn money.

Noor Alam's employer, a gangster, had ordered Noor Alam to kill a man who refused to pay his debt. It wasn't the first time that Noor Alam had carried out the gangster's threats. But it would be the first time he had ever killed for him.

As the hour drew closer, a strange feeling gnawed at Noor Alam's stomach. Fear? Not fear of being caught; few of Noor Alam's many crimes had ever been traced to him, and the police were afraid of his employer. Fear of killing? Why should he be afraid? This man was a Hindu unbeliever. He deserved to die. And as a Muslim, it was Noor Alam's holy privilege to kill him. Noor Alam would earn double his usual wages for this job and have even more money to bring home to his wife and beloved son, Waqar.

Noor Alam took his gun and his bullets and went to the victim's house. When the home-owner opened the door to Noor Alam's knock, Noor Alam demanded the payment. For a moment the man looked at him, disbelieving, and then he laughed. "Does your master think a scrawny fool like you is going to scare me into paying him? Well you can tell him..." His scornful voice trailed off as Noor Alam pulled the gun from beneath his coat and leveled it at him. The man's smile froze in a twisted grimace; fear steeled his eyes. Noor Alam felt a wide smile spreading across his face as his finger moved to the trigger. A sense of complete, total control surged through his veins, making him dizzy. He was all-powerful, untouchable.

With one small movement, he pulled the trigger, and the man collapsed. Now Noor Alam laughed wildly. He held death itself in his hand.

The feeling of power was addicting, and Noor Alam wanted more. He craved control—something he had never known in his childhood. As a boy, he had been helpless, beaten and bullied. Now he knew the secret to power—making people fear you.

Noor Alam killed seven more people; he tortured and wounded many others. Everyone was terrified of him, and though he was imprisoned for short periods, he was always quickly released. There was nothing Noor Alam couldn't have. People would give him anything in exchange for their lives. Noor Alam vowed to never fear anyone or anything again.

But then his son fell sick. Noor Alam's prayers and the aid of the witch doctors did nothing for him. He rushed Waqar to a hospital. Waqar was admitted instantly, and Noor Alam sat beside his son's bed while the doctors ran hurried tests.

Noor Alam stared at Waqar's pale face. He was scared. What if he lost Waqar like he had lost his first three children? How could he bear it? He bent his head over the white sheets and cried, clutching at his chest as if to stop his heart from breaking. Waqar was too young...too precious...it couldn't happen. It *would not* happen.

Noor Alam felt his eyes burning again. *No!* He leapt to his feet, shaking with rage. Nothing would take Waqar from him. "You will live," Noor Alam said quietly, standing over his son. "Even if I have to kill every last person on this earth—you will live."

Noor Alam heard soft footsteps behind him, and he dashed the tears from his face.

A doctor came around to stand in front of Noor Alam. "He is bleeding inside," he said gently. "You must realize, this is very serious."

"My son will live," Noor Alam said coldly.

The doctor's face was tired, hopeless. "Sir, I am sorry—"

Noor Alam sprang forward, a knife in his hand. The doctor held his ground as Noor Alam pointed the weapon directly at his face. "Save my son, or I will kill you," Noor Alam hissed.

The doctor gazed steadily into Noor Alam's eyes, ignoring the knife. "I'm sorry," he repeated. "There is nothing I can do."

Noor Alam's hands began to shake. Where was the thrilling feeling of power, that mad joy he had come to rely on? This man, he wasn't afraid. The knife in Noor Alam's hand didn't frighten him. Noor Alam stared at the doctor in disbelief. He wasn't afraid of death.

Not like Noor Alam. He was terrified of death, and now it was claiming Waqar. Noor Alam slowly lowered the knife. "Nothing," he said, dazed. "You can do nothing?"

The doctor stepped forward, as if nothing had happened. "I cannot. But there is someone who can."

"The gods?" Noor Alam laughed bitterly. "I have already prayed to them."

"There is someone else we can pray to, who can heal your son. His name is Jesus. Would you like to pray to him now?"

Noor Alam had never heard of Jesus, but he nodded. The doctor and the murderer got down on their knees beside Waqar's bed, and the doctor prayed. His prayer was loving and compassionate, and he spoke to his God as if He was his closest friend. He asked for God to grant them Waqar's life. Noor Alam felt a presence unlike anything he had ever experienced stirring in his heart. He lowered his head, barely able to breathe. This was absolute, overwhelming power.

The doctor finished his prayer. "We must have faith now," he said. "Here," he went on, handing a small book to Noor Alam. "Read this. It will help you understand."

Noor Alam sat beside Waqar, devouring the words in the book. It spoke of Jesus, the Son of the one true God, who had come down to save the world from their sins. Jesus loved the world so much, He was willing to die so that they would have life. Noor Alam wept onto the pages, remembering the pain and sorrow he had caused so many and the lives he had taken. He knew that if he could see his heart, it would be black with sin.

He fell to his knees, again, and prayed. "Jesus. I believe that You have the power to save my son. Heal him, and I will follow You completely. I beg for You to forgive the terrible things I have done. Please."

Waqar was healed. Within a week, he had returned home, and Noor Alam began telling everyone about the power of Jesus. No one could believe it. How was Noor Alam, a merciless killer, now preaching about love and forgiveness and healing? Stunned by this miraculous transformation, many listened to Noor Alam and found salvation in Jesus. Noor Alam started working with Big Life Ministries as a pastor and church planter, bringing hundreds to Christ.

Some of the Muslims spoke out against Noor Alam, but few ever actually confronted him. This man had tortured and killed those who slighted him—they didn't dare tell him to stop witnessing! Yet one Muslim wasn't afraid. He was big and strong and twice the weight of Noor Alam. When he told Noor Alam to stop preaching, Noor Alam stared at him. His mind raced back to his childhood where he had been beaten so many times by other bullies. But now, he was filled with the power of the Holy Spirit, and for the first time in his life, he wasn't afraid.

Five
Bonus Stories!

Did
You
Know...

According to a U.S. State Department report, the last public Christian church building in Afghanistan was destroyed in March of 2010. It is estimated by Christian organizations that specialize in statistical information that the number of native Christians in Afghanistan in 2010 was only a few thousand at best.

Praise God that since 2010, the Lord has used the men and women who Big Life partners with in the country of Afghanistan to establish over 500 vibrant local churches.

These churches meet in homes as a strategic and biblical (Acts 20:20, 1 Corinthians 16:19, etc) way of avoiding the schemes of Satan and in order to easily multiply as the Spirit leads.

These 500+ churches represent nearly 3,000 faithful followers of Jesus Christ who are focused on being disciple-makers. A few of these men and woman are highlighted in this storybook.

Cowards

Musa first met Luqman in Pakistan. Luqman had brought his wife and four sons over from Afghanistan as refugees. Musa and Luqman became good friends. They liked to visit and talk together.

Luqman liked reading. So one day, Musa brought his friend a book.

"Here," Musa said, handing him the book. "I have been reading this, and it has changed my life."

Luqman looked at the cover, and he frowned. "The New Testament? No. This is an unholy, corrupted book! We must not read it."

"Please, Luqman." Musa gazed at him, his voice firm. "Read."

Luqman hesitated, holding the book uncomfortably. He glanced down at it, and then back up at Musa. "All right," he said at last.

Just as he had promised, Luqman began to read The New Testament. The words were unlike anything he had ever read—they were full of power.

Luqman met with Musa again, and as they talked, Musa began to smile. Musa could tell that Luqman was being affected by the message of the New Testament, in much the same way Musa had been.

I have so many questions," Luqman said softly, looking down at his hands. "Questions I never had before."

Musa laid a hand on his friend's arm. "Come with me. I know someone who can give us the answers we seek."

Musa introduced Luqman to Pastor Sheer Shah, a passionate preacher for Jesus Christ. It was Shah who had given Musa his first copy of the New Testament. When Musa and Luqman told him they had questions, he immediately sat down and listened. Pastor Shah was a highly educated, brilliant and knowledgeable man. He spoke with Musa and Luqman often, and their discussions were always deep and illuminating. They talked about the Quran and about The New Testament; Shah was able to answer all of Musa and Luqman's questions. They talked for months.

At last, Musa and Luqman accepted the truth. They, along with their friend Qazi, were saved by Jesus and baptized. Luqman was eager to serve his Lord, and he and Musa became very involved in Pastor Shah's ministry. Many people were coming to Christ. It was an amazing experience for Luqman.

Then the death threats began. Luqman refused to be troubled by them. He had known that the radicals would make trouble once they learned he was a Christian. Luqman was secure in his faith.

But the way the radicals chose to punish him was worse than anything Luqman could have imagined. Luqman's oldest son was kidnapped, and a short while later, his dead body was found lying on the side of the road.

Luqman's anger and sorrow consumed him. "Cowards!" He screamed through his tears. "Come and face me, instead of killing my children!"

The pain of his son's loss never left him. In time, he and his family moved back to Afghanistan, and Luqman joined the army as a soldier. He became a Major, and everyone under his command grew to respect him greatly. He cared about his men, really cared. They loved him for it.

One of Major Luqman's soldiers could see that something was different about his commander. He was amazed by Luqman's kindness and patience. Was he a Muslim? He was surely not one of those that followed the radicals or the Taliban. The soldier himself didn't believe in what the Taliban was teaching. Allah was a merciful God; he didn't ask for the slaughter of innocent people. However, he could not tell anyone about this. It was too dangerous. But then there was Major Luqman. Maybe he would understand. Maybe he would be able to answer some of his questions?

Luqman was sitting in his office when a nervous looking soldier stepped inside. "What is it?" Luqman asked gently, laying down his pen.

The soldier shifted, clearing his throat. "I-I wanted to ask you something."

"You may."

The soldier took a deep breath, and then blurted out, "Are you a Muslim?" He flushed a little, and went on, dropping his eyes. "I mean, you don't seem to be like one. You seem—different."

Luqman studied the soldier for a moment. Then he said calmly, "I am not a Muslim. But I do believe in one true God and one true Savior."

A look of immense relief swept over the soldier's face. "I am not a Muslim either," he said. "At least, not one like the Taliban. I believe in a merciful Allah. But what is this Savior?"

Luqman smiled, motioning for the soldier to sit. "Let me tell you."

Many others, just like this soldier, were brought to salvation by Luqman. He served the Lord ceaselessly, planting house churches, sharing Christ, and discipling believers. His ministry was beginning to grow and spreading quickly.

Then the radicals attacked again. Luqman's home went up in flames, and though Luqman and his family survived, nothing was left of their house. And his next oldest son disappeared—kidnapped. Luqman was gripped with horror, knowing what the Taliban would do next, and having no way to stop it. Luqman's second son was murdered.

Torn by grief and despair, Luqman pleaded desperately with God. "Please, Lord," he sobbed, "Give me the strength to forgive these cowards for what they have done." Every day afterwards, he prayed that the radicals would see the love of Jesus and be changed.

Luqman and his family were forced to constantly change their location. The fear of more attacks and deaths was always looming over their heads like a brooding storm cloud. But Luqman couldn't bring himself to leave the country. He feared what would happen to his team if they were abandoned by their leader.

"Luqman, please!" Musa pleaded with him. "You must leave, for your family's sake. Your brothers in Christ will carry on the work you've started. You must entrust the work to them now."

Finally, Luqman agreed, and he and his family moved to Europe. Before Luqman left, he gave his team enough money to purchase 300 gospels to give out among the people. After all, that was how it had all started for him—when someone had pushed the good news of Jesus Christ into his hands and said, "Read."

My Uncle is Here!

Buzkashi was a ferocious sport, played on horseback, with only one rule—to win, you had to drag the headless goat across your opponent's line. Many players were injured in the process, and it was well-known that buzkashi was a game that only the brave dared to take part in. Mirza Khan was the star of this particular game of buzkashi. He maneuvered his steed deftly, using the horse as a shield. Mirza was young, but he was athletic and played with a quickness of mind that matched those much older than he. In the final moments of the game, Mirza burst free from the tangled players and dashed across the line, the goat slung over his saddle. The onlookers erupted with cheers and applause. Mirza grinned in triumph, his eyes sparkling.

Amid the congratulations of the crowd, an older man came up and tapped Mirza on the shoulder. "Hello," he introduced himself. "I am a friend of your father's. You were only two the last time we met."

Mirza liked the man's kindly manner, and he shook his hand warmly. That day marked the rekindling of a great bond of friendship between the two of them. Mirza began calling his father's friend *Kaka*, which means uncle. His new uncle liked that very much.

War broke out a few years later filling the country with chaos. Mirza's uncle went to fight against the Soviet invaders, as it was considered honorable for an Afghani man to do. He hadn't seen Mirza Khan in some time. While Mirza's uncle was being trained in the army, he began to hear stories running through the camp. They were about a brave young commander, filled with courage and honor, and about his battles against the infidels. The soldiers reverently called him Babr, or tiger. Mirza's uncle was eager to meet the person who was the subject of all these tales, but the Babr was absent from camp at the time. At last he returned from the mission which had called him away. Mirza's uncle hurried out with the rest of the camp to meet this commander and his team. As Mirza's uncle drew close, he saw the man who had filled the whole army with such awe and respect. It was Mirza Khan!

When Mirza caught sight of his uncle, he ran to him and embraced him joyfully. "This is my kaka," Mirza exclaimed to the rest of the camp. "My kaka is here!"

Very shortly, Mirza had assigned his uncle to be part of his team. Mirza's uncle went on missions with Mirza and saw the way he fought against the enemy—often alone and out-numbered, throwing himself into the thickest part of the battle. By some miracle, he was never harmed, and he was never afraid.

"Be careful," pleaded Mirza's uncle.

Mirza's voice was intense as he replied, "I must fight. I must rid my homeland of these infidels who have trespassed on it."

Eventually, the Afghani armies fought the Soviets back. Mirza, his uncle, and all the other soldiers were ready to return home, their work finished. But another brutal war began, this time a civil war within Mirza's own country. The young leader was heartbroken. "How, Kaka?" he asked of his uncle. "How can I fight against my own countrymen?"

So Mirza and his uncle chose to leave for Pakistan. They stayed in a United Nations camp, where Mirza was married. In the camp, a preacher named Sheer Shah spoke powerful messages about the love of Jesus. Mirza's uncle listened intently and was soon saved. Because he loved his adopted nephew so much, Mirza's uncle began trying to witness to him. But Mirza was a fervent Muslim, and because he loved his uncle, he carefully avoided the subject. "Don't listen to them, Kaka!" he said. But Mirza's uncle knew he had found the truth and didn't stop sharing it with Mirza.

Back in Afghanistan, fiercely strict Islamic laws were being put in place by misguided zealots called the Taliban. The Taliban were unjust and brutal killing people who had done nothing wrong and treating the women cruelly. When Mirza heard of these things, he was confused and deeply saddened. "This is not what we fought for! What kind of Islam is this?" Mirza's uncle again shared the gospel with him, and this time Mirza didn't try to make him stop.

At last a new government was set up, and both Mirza and his uncle were offered jobs to work for the government. Mirza's natural leadership abilities and his passionate personality caused him to rise swiftly in his new career. And even more happily, the day came when Mirza and his wife accepted Jesus as their Savior. Mirza's uncle had never stopped witnessing to them.

Mirza's heart now belonged completely to Jesus. With the fiery energy that had always flowed through every part of his life, Mirza began to share the Good News. He wanted everyone to be saved.

The Taliban learned of his conversion and sent him threatening letters telling him to renounce his beliefs. Their schemes to scare him were hopeless for Mirza could not be shaken. He had never feared death, least of all now, when he knew that he would see his Savior the moment he passed away. Facing the persecution with a ready stance and a courageous smile, Mirza continued to witness.

It was a peaceful day as the sun radiated heat down on the earth. Mirza sat alone in his study surrounded by silence and the work he needed to complete.

Suddenly, an explosion ripped the house apart. When the smoke cleared, Mirza's study was demolished, and Mirza had gone to his Savior's arms.

The Taliban had planted the bomb on the front gate of Mirza's house. Mirza's wife and his eight children all survived, and Mirza's eldest son continued spreading the gospel just like his father.

Mirza had still been young, full of life and zeal for Christ. His uncle mourned deeply for him and for the loss of the many years Mirza could have had on earth, but he knew that one day he would see Mirza again. Mirza would come running to his uncle, just like the day he had arrived at the war camp, and say with his eyes laughing, "My kaka is here!"

The Explosion Next Door

Gull Bano grew up in a strict Muslim family high in social rank. When she was old enough, her marriage was arranged with an honorable man named Qazi. He was well-educated and had a good job. Gull Bano was happy living with him and soon they had begun a family.

But their peaceful life was violently shattered by the onset of war in Afghanistan. Gull Bano and her family fled to Pakistan, where they were able to find a home. Thus their new life began.

In Pakistan, her husband became good friends with a man named Musa. The two often had deep conversations at their house. One day Musa brought a new visitor with him—Sheer Shah. Gull Bano saw her husband listening intently to what these men had to say. Then she saw him reading some books that they had given him. With horror, Gull Bano realized that they were forbidden, Christian books. But when she faced Qazi about it, he simply asked her to sit with him and listen. He opened one of the Christian books, *The New Testament*, and began to read. Gull Bano could hear the passion in his voice.

He read something called "the sermon of the mountain." "Blessed are the pure in heart, for they shall see God…" Qazi read. Gull Bano's shock and fear seemed to melt away at these beautiful, tender words. Nothing she had ever been taught was able to compare to this message or make her feel the way she did now.

As time went on, Musa and Shah continued to come and speak with Qazi, and now Gull Bano listened too. Both men were highly educated scholars, and their teaching about Jesus began to speak to Gull Bano, as it had to Qazi. Soon, Qazi was saved and his wife shortly after him.

Back in their home country of Afghanistan, peace was beginning to settle. Qazi and Gull Bano were able to return to their home, where Qazi shared about his new life in Jesus.

Then came terrible news—Pastor Sheer Shah had been killed and Musa wounded by the radicals. Qazi and Gull Bano grieved deeply. Their fellow believers went into hiding—fearful for their lives.

Some time later, Musa met with Qazi again. They made a plan to work with Big Life Ministries in reaching Afghanis for Jesus. One part of this plan was to sneak 3000 New Testaments across the border to distribute among their countrymen. Qazi offered to do this. His occupation often sent him on business, and his official car was never checked at the border. The mission went smoothly, and soon Qazi and a group of believers were working to hand out the New Testaments.

When nearly half the books were gone, Gull Bano noticed Qazi becoming anxious and withdrawn. But when she asked him, he would only force a smile and tell her that everything was alright. At last Gull Bano went to one of Qazi's friends, Khalil, who looked after the house where the New Testaments were stored, and asked him what was troubling Qazi. Reluctantly, Khalil told her. "Qazi got letters from the Taliban," he said heavily. "They are threatening Qazi and the other believers if they will not give up their faith."

Of course, Qazi could not deny Jesus and do what the Taliban asked. Gull Bano's heart filled with love and pride for him, but still, she worried.

One day when the men were having a meeting in the New Testament house, a huge explosion shook the ground. Gull Bano and Khalil were in the house next door to the meeting. The windows around them shattered spraying glass over their heads.

With a cry, Khalil rushed from the house to see what had happened, leaving Gull Bano alone in the doorway. It was not proper for her, a woman, to go outside. Trembling, she gripped the door frame for support and prayed. "Please, please, my husband...."

Her skin chilled as she heard Khalil's shout of agony. The New Testament house had collapsed burying Qazi's body under the rubble along with his brothers in Christ.

One of the guests at Qazi's gathering had been a suicide bomber. As a result of the explosion, thirteen Christians were killed. The news of the tragedy spread, and the people who heard it were horrified. Everyone had greatly respected Qazi; they began to talk about Qazi's unwavering loyalty to his faith. Gradually, Jesus' gospel was shared among them, and many believed.

Gull Bano and her children left Afghanistan again, no longer safe. They mourned for Qazi and the others, but neither Gull Bano nor her children despaired. They knew that someday—a day not too far off—they would see Qazi again.

Two Brothers

Once there were two brothers, Shoukat and Imran. They were only two in a family of five boys and three girls, but what was unique about them was how different they were from each other. Imran was quiet and soft-spoken with a calm sense of strength about him. Shoukat, his older brother, was a short-tempered, arrogant bully, who liked nothing better than treating others poorly and hurling orders and insults.

When Imran and Shoukat were growing up together, Shoukat was always cruel and unfair to his younger brother. In their neighborhood, Shoukat cheated at games and bullied all the other kids. Imran was saddened knowing that his brother was hurting his friends deeply. In his quiet, firm way, Imran said to Shoukat, "Please stop this."

"Shut up, Imran," Shoukat spat at him.

Imran could not stop his brother, but he comforted the victims of his bullying and did his best to heal the wounds Shoukat had opened with his heartless words.

Then life turned ugly. Imran and Shoukat's parents both died from sickness within a short time of each other, and Shoukat, as the eldest, was left to take up the task of providing for the family. But Shoukat, irresponsible and still an angry boy, did not fulfill his duties. So even though Imran was one of the youngest in his family, he took it upon himself to find work so that his siblings could eat. Imran had grown up quickly into a kind, quiet young man with a heart well accustomed to bearing others' pain.

Shoukat grew as well. But he remained cruel with a temper that made him dangerous to those around him. While Imran was caring for his siblings, Shoukat went into training to be a soldier and left his family behind. The other siblings stuck together, for they understood and loved one another deeply. Imran was very thoughtful about their every need. He treated everyone around him in this way. He was compassionate and kind and always ready to listen and to lend a helping hand.

Shoukat remained away fighting until the war ended. Then he came home and tried to find a job. But no one would hire him because of his rude attitude and the way he thought he was better than everyone else. Shoukat, now married but without a job or money, had to live with his wife's parents.

Imran was still working hard, and his family had enough money to live in security and even comfort. Imran was also continuing to spend time with his good friend, Hafiz. They had played together as boys and had maintained a close relationship into adulthood. One day, Hafiz came to see Imran. He was very excited. "Imran, I must tell you something. I have become a Christian!"

Although he was a Muslim, Imran did not get angry or push Hafiz away. He could see that Hafiz was happy, and Imran didn't feel a need to take away that joy. But when Hafiz tried to witness to him, Imran gently stopped him. "Hafiz, Christians are good people, but they need to believe in Islam to escape judgment. I pray that they will."

However, Hafiz didn't stop speaking with Imran about Jesus. He loved his quiet, kind-hearted friend, and he wanted more than anything for him to be saved. Hafiz and Imran had long discussions about the Quran and the New Testament and Jesus's place in both. As Imran listened to Hafiz, he began longing to know this Jesus, who had loved mankind so much that he was willing to die in their place. At last, Imran gave his heart to Jesus. Both Hafiz and Imran wept with joy, and Hafiz baptized his friend.

Hafiz was working with Big Life to plant churches, and Imran soon joined him. Imran felt the love and grace of Jesus coursing through him like a flood, and he just had to share it. Imran was witnessing to everyone now, even—one day—to Shoukat's wife. But she refused to listen. She was very angry and went and told Shoukat.

Shoukat had become a dark, dangerous person. When he heard of his brother's conversion, he went to his mentor, a radical whose teachings he had been following, and told him what had happened.

The radical's judgment was unyielding. "Your brother has betrayed the Islamic faith. You are a soldier. It is your duty to kill him."

Shoukat went home and quietly told his wife to pack their belongings. He loaded his gun and went to find his brother. He went to his brother's workplace, but Imran had left. Shoukat went to find some of Imran's friends, but none of them had seen his brother. Shoukat's hand kept going to the gun, longing to pull the trigger. His brother must die. It would be done.

Finally, Shoukat went to Imran's house. His anger had been building, growing hotter and higher, a fire stoked into flame. Shoukat was consumed by only one thing. Imran must die. His brother must die.

Shoukat burst into the house whipping the gun from his pocket.

Imran turned to look up. Instead of rising to greet the visitor, his mouth dropped to the floor as he saw the gun. Shoukat stood in the doorway, his eyes glaring, his jaw clenched. Imran slowly got to his feet. "Brother...."

Shoukat straightened his arm, and Imran's body tensed, freezing of its own accord. A gun pointed at his chest. "Renounce your faith," Shoukat hissed between his teeth. His bloodless fingers were white on the gun's trigger.

Imran stayed perfectly still. "I cannot, Shoukat." His voice was steady. "Let me explain...." He took a step towards Shoukat.

"NO!" Shoukat roared, cocking the gun. "Stay where you are!" Imran stopped moving.

Shoukat's hands were trembling feverishly; the gleam in his eye was wild, crazed. "Renounce your faith or die!"

Imran felt overwhelming panic as he looked from the gun to his brother's enraged face... and then sudden, perfect peace. Imran swallowed, praying for courage. "No."

Shoukat pulled the trigger. Imran gasped with pain, clutching at his arm. Blood poured between his fingers, pain stabbed through his veins.

"No," Imran choked out.

Crack. Imran hit the floor on one knee, a bullet lodged in his leg. His blood pooled on the floor.

"RENOUNCE YOUR FAITH!" Shoukat screamed.

Imran looked up. His face was pale, but his eyes, as ever, were peaceful and kind. He gazed at his brother, and he felt a pang of deep sadness for him. Shoukat couldn't understand. "No," Imran whispered and smiled softly.

Three more bullets pounded into Imran's body, the final one finding his heart. Imran died with his gentle smile still on his lips.

Shoukat ran, leaving the horrified neighbors to find his brother's body. Imran was only thirty-two years old.

At Imran's funeral, the Christians who had come to mourn him were strengthened by the memory of Imran's steadfast spirit and his courage to stand up for what was right. His death inspired them to continue the Lord's work. Imran had died for his King, and they knew that his heavenly reward would be great.

Did
You
Know...

Bob Sjogren's original cartoon book is titled, *101 Differences Between Cats and Dogs*?

Originally designed for adults, this cartoon book quickly became loved by children and grand-children. It is still for sale and being used not only here, but also in China after being translated into Chinese.

These 101 cartoons are designed to make you think about God's glory in your life.

Find out more about the book at: UnveilinGLORY's bookstore: www.UnveilinGLORY.com/ bookstore

Baptizing Killers

Tapan's wife Sunanda was very sick. Tapan could do nothing to bring her relief. He prayed to the many Hindu gods, and he sought the help of doctors and even tried witchcraft. But nothing worked. It pained his heart terribly to watch his wife struggle knowing that he couldn't help her. So when a Christian church planter from a ministry called Big Life asked to pray over Sunanda, Tapan agreed. The Christian, named Bablu, prayed to Jesus to heal her.

Within a few days, Sunanda was recovering. It was a miracle! Tapan and Sunanda immediately recognized that this amazing power had come from Jesus. They asked Bablu to tell them more about Him. As Tapan and Sunanda listened to Bablu sharing the gospel, they understood the truth. Together they gave their lives to Jesus.

Both he and Sunanda were excited and eager to serve their Lord. They soon started a small church in their home, and Tapan told everyone he met about Jesus.

Tapan knew that there were many, many people throughout his country that needed this news. He asked Bablu to train him to be a church planter, so that he could bring Jesus' love to others, just as Bablu had brought it to him.

Tapan was often away from home now, ministering in other villages. During one trip, he received a short, urgent piece of news. "Your wife is sick."

Tapan's heart thudded hard against his chest. Memories of the fear, the helplessness came flooding back. Had Sunanda relapsed? Would Tapan be back in that position of worrying and waiting by her bedside, watching her suffer—and doing nothing?

Tapan caught the next train home. The countryside flashed past the windows, but Tapan saw none of it. He could only think of Sunanda. He had left her alone. *Why?* Now she was in trouble. He had to get back to her as quickly as he could. Tapan prayed that his son would stay by her side and comfort her. The carriage rattled and bounced along the tracks. Tapan pressed his feet against the floor of the train, feeling the engine humming beneath, and willed it to go faster.

Finally, after what seemed like ages, Tapan arrived back in his village. He rushed back to his house, fearing what he would find. *Sunanda...Sunanda...Sunanda*...the name pounded through his mind, beating against his temples like a second heartbeat. He was almost there...

Tapan rounded a corner, flying towards his house—

He jolted to a stop, stumbling forward on suddenly immobile feet. His house was gone. In its place lay a pile of rubble and wreckage. It had been completely torn apart. Tapan stepped slowly into the ruins, his shoes slipping on shards of broken masonry. The clatter sounded unnaturally loud in his ears. Everything else, even the air itself, was deathly still. He walked to where the center of his house would have been. He couldn't think clearly. Who had done this?

Tapan froze. Where was Sunanda? Where was his son?

"Sunanda!" He shouted, his cry echoing in the silence. "Sunanda, where are you? *Sunanda!*" His voice cracked with fear. He was trembling. Numbly, he staggered down from the pile of rubble and began to walk the grounds, searching for a sign of his family.

Then he saw something on the edge of the ruins—a still, long bundle. Tapan choked, panic almost blinding him. He ran across the yard, cutting his knees on stone as he tripped and staggered over the debris, hurtling to that indistinct shape on the ground.

"NO!" Tapan screamed. He threw himself down beside Sunanda's body, an icy horror running through him. It wasn't real, it wasn't real. Tapan clutched at his head, sobs shaking his shoulders. She was dead.

Sunanda had been murdered. Members of her and Tapan's own family had killed her for passing out tracts in the village. They had destroyed Tapan's home and taken his son, to raise him away from his Christian parents.

"It is the consequence of changing your religion," they told Tapan. "It is your fault that Sunanda is dead."

Tapan knew that they would come for him next. So he waited. He didn't feel shocked or even scared. Every part of him that felt or cared or loved was back beside Sunanda's still form, holding her in his arms, looking for any sign of life in her pale face. Sunanda was innocent, pure, and kind. They had barely started their ministry together. Why had God taken her away so soon? Tapan couldn't understand. But still he clung to Jesus. Jesus was the only thing Tapan had left. And Tapan knew that he couldn't forsake Jesus, because Jesus had promised never to forsake him.

No one ever attacked Tapan. For two years Tapan continued to preach about Jesus in the village, and no one bothered him. People began to say that his God was protecting him. And some people began to listen to what Tapan had to say.

Over those two years Tapan often sensed the empty space in his life where Sunanda had been. He always missed her, and he still carried the sorrow of her death with him. Tapan had been grief-stricken and heartbroken—all because of the ones who had killed Sunanda. But he wasn't angry anymore. Jesus said to forgive your enemies. "My enemies didn't deserve forgiveness," thought Tapan to himself, "but neither did I."

By forgiving, Tapan showed them the power of Jesus and his love. After a time, his relatives invited Tapan to live with them, so that he could be near his son. They even gave consent for Tapan to start a church in the village without fear of harm. Tapan moved into their house, doing chores in the morning and preaching in the afternoon. He taught others to share their faith just like Bablu had taught him. Tapan also started churches in other villages and trained people to lead them. He discipled dozens of Big Life church planters, who in turn started over 200 churches, where over 3,000 people worship weekly. And Tapan knew that God's work was far from finished. There would be much to do in India over the coming years.

As Tapan's ministry continued to grow, he was reminded of the first church he had ever started—he and Sunanda, leading a fellowship in their home. So many times he would long to simply see her smile. But Tapan remembered that someday he would see her again   and that brought him hope.

His relatives had seen that hope in Tapan. They knew that something real, something powerful had changed him. As a result, Tapan's mother was saved, along with twenty other members of his family—some of whom were his wife's killers. Tapan baptized them all, with a joyful smile on his face. He was so glad that he had followed Jesus's example and forgiven his family and hadn't harbored that anger inside him—for now he got to see them have their sins forgiven by Jesus and become his fellow believers in Christ.

A Big Life

(From the desk of John Heerema)

As a kid growing up in the Midwest in the 1960s, living a good life meant working hard, playing fair, going to church and counting your blessings. Those qualities were so ingrained in my family dynamic that I took for granted that the good life generally looked the same for everyone.

Flash forward four decades to the year 2000. It was a new century, a new millennium, a new high tech world. It wasn't the world my father grew up in. It wasn't even the world that I grew up in. Nevertheless, my idea of the good life remained steadfastly unchanged. Happily married, running a successful landscaping business and raising a beautiful daughter with a son on the way, surrounded by family and church friends, I remember counting my blessings and thinking "this is very, very good!"

But there was more—much, much more. A divine plot orchestrated by the living God.

Paul's words in Ephesians 3:20 say, "Now unto Him that is able to do exceeding abundantly above all that we ask or think, according to the power which works in us, unto Him be the glory in the church and in Christ Jesus unto all generations forever and ever. Amen."

Did that really apply to my wife and me? If the God that I had worshipped since I was a child had somehow shown me the extent of what was to come next, I'm not sure I would have believed Him. At the very least, I would have argued that surely He must have the wrong guy. God was getting ready to do things that were exceedingly and abundantly more than any of my family or friends could ask or think. And just like the disciples at the miraculous feeding of the multitudes, He was calling us out to be more than mere spectators—He was inviting us to get out of our seats, take the field, and get ready to participate in something very BIG.

In an era when the worldwide church is persecuted relentlessly, when Christians in the West are abandoning their faith in droves and record numbers of pastors are simply walking away from their pulpits, we are convinced that God is up to something big—very, very BIG. And that's why Big Life exists.

Since 2000, people of God have come together all over the world in the most unlikely of partnerships to participate in the greatest movement of God that recent generations have ever known. Today, hundreds of thousands of new Christians from every ethnic and religious background are worshipping the One True God, side-by-side, in Big Life house, village and city churches. New believers are growing stronger through life-on-life discipleship. New church fellowships are formed *daily* through evangelism, biblical discipleship and rapid, exponential multiplication. *At the current rate of church multiplication, it is mathematically possible that we could see the Gospel reach every tongue, tribe and nation within the generations that are alive today!* Now THAT is VERY big news!

Maybe you've wondered if you've missed the "exceedingly, abundantly more" that Paul talks about. Be assured, TODAY is just the beginning of what comes next. It's not too late to get out of your seat, take the field and participate like never before.

- Perhaps you've never been a part of a Christian church or fellowship.

- Perhaps you have, for whatever reason, left a church fellowship.

- Perhaps you are actively involved in your local church fellowship.

Regardless of what brought you to this page, this invitation is for you! You are invited to participate in what is possibly the greatest movement of God we will see in our lifetime.

Back in 2000, a woman handed a book to me in the hallway at church and instructed me to read it. The book was called *Unveiled at Last* (now titled *God's Bottom Line*) by Bob Sjogren. I read the book, in all honesty, because I expected that lady would be bugging me about it. What I hadn't expected was how that book would influence what came next. It has impacted hundreds of thousands of ordinary people all over the world who have simply said "yes" to the invitation to join God in His work. They are experiencing Ephesians 3:20 every day.

If someone handed you this book, it's probably in your best interest to read it. You never know. Maybe this is the beginning of your "above and beyond—Ephesians 3:20 experience." That would be very big indeed. Come and join us as we join God.

Sincerely,

John Heerema
   Executive Director
   Big Life Ministries

Contact us to learn more about how you can get involved in Big Life.

Info@BLM.Org BLM.ORG
P.O. Box 110431 Naples, Florida 34108
1-888-BIGLIFE

Did You Know...

UnveilinGLORY has multiple homeschool curricula for grades 7-12?

Each year is designed to build on the other and helps students realize that the glory of God is the central theme, not only for life on this earth, but for all of eternity!

As one 13-year-old wrote,

"I live in Fredericksburg VA and I'm 13 years old. I first heard about Cat and Dog Theology at the homeschool convention two years ago in Richmond. I had no other workshops to go to and my mom was waiting for my aunt to meet her so we looked in the schedule and saw your workshop. So we walked in and sat down (not expecting much, just another Bible study designed to get teens interested in the Bible) and after just a few minutes I realized this was no ordinary Bible study. I realize now it wasn't just an accident I came to your session, it was part of God's plan for my life. After the session we went to the curriculum hall right away and bought the set. I am so glad about what God is using you for. Your curriculum completely changed the way I think, view the Bible, and the way I live!"

To find out more,
turn the page or watch videos describing them at
www.CatandDogTheology.org

Homeschool
Materials: Grades 7-12

Year 1

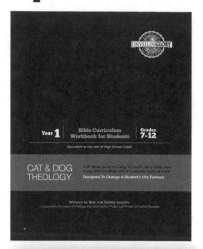

Life is not about us.
It is about living
for God's glory!

Year 2

Once we know His glory,
we want to take it
to the nations!

Year 3

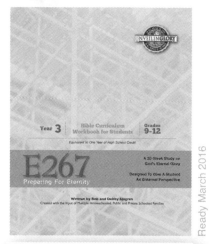

How we live our lives on
earth prepares us for
eternal glory!

Year 4

Understanding heaven gets us
excited as God puts His glory
on display—forever!

For Elementary Kids!!!